Professional Issues in Secondary Teaching

Professional Issues in Secondary Teaching

edited by

Carrie Mercier | Carey Philpott | Helen Scott

Los Angeles | London | New Delhi
Singapore | Washington DC

Los Angeles | London | New Delhi
Singapore | Washington DC

SAGE Publications Ltd
1 Oliver's Yard
55 City Road
London EC1Y 1SP

SAGE Publications Inc.
2455 Teller Road
Thousand Oaks, California 91320

SAGE Publications India Pvt Ltd
B 1/I 1 Mohan Cooperative Industrial Area
Mathura Road
New Delhi 110 044

SAGE Publications Asia-Pacific Pte Ltd
3 Church Street
#10-04 Samsung Hub
Singapore 049483

Editor: James Clark
Assistant editor: Monira Begum
Production editor: Thea Watson
Copyeditor: Rosemary Morlin
Proofreader: Avril Ehrlich
Indexer: Bill Farrington
Marketing manager: Catherine Slinn
Cover design: Lisa Harper
Typeset by: C&M Digitals (P) Ltd, Chennai, India
Printed in India at Replika Press Pvt Ltd

First published 2013

Library of Congress Control Number: 2012940853

British Library Cataloguing in Publication data

A catalogue record for this book is available from the British Library

ISBN 978-1-4462-0789-5
ISBN 978-1-4462-0790-1 (pbk)

CONTENTS

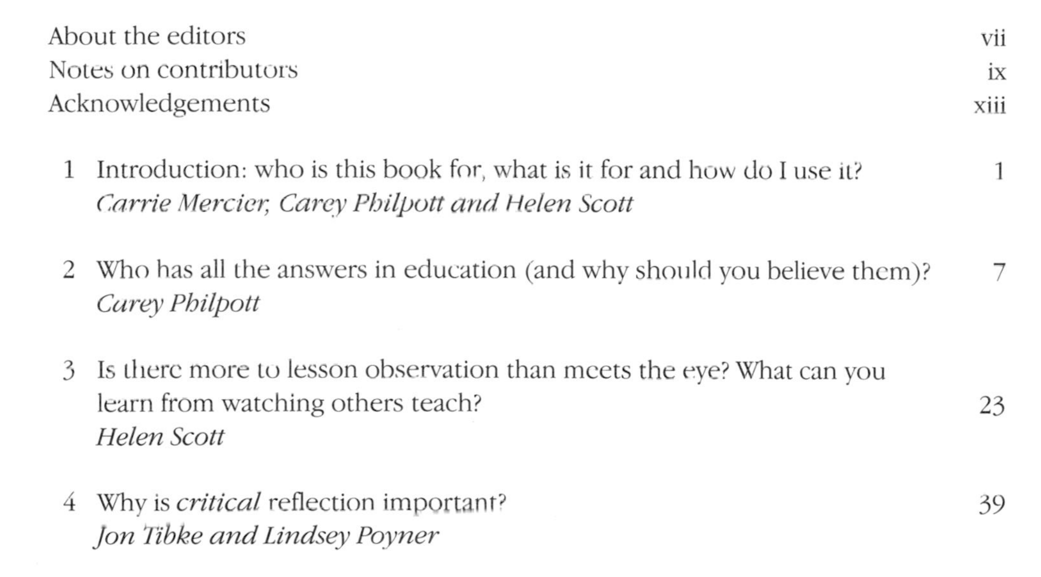

ABOUT THE EDITORS

Carrie Mercier

Carrie Mercier has worked in schools in Scotland, England and the USA and has published textbooks on skills in Religious Studies. She became involved in teaching both initial teacher education and CPD courses first at Westminster College and then at York St John. She went on to run the secondary PGCE in RE at St Martin's College Lancaster where she later became head of the Division of Philosophy and Religion. She is now programme leader for the Master's course in teaching and learning at the University of Cumbria. Her MPhil dissertation was on RE and racism and her current research interests include RE, ITE and teacher perspectives on curriculum development.

Carey Philpott

Carey Philpott has taught in both English and Scottish schools. In higher education in England, he has been a programme leader for secondary PGCE and secondary undergraduate QTS courses as well as a PGCE for the life-long learning sector. He currently works in the School of Education in the Faculty of Humanities and Social Sciences at the University of Strathclyde, Glasgow. His main research interests are the nature of professional learning and the role of narrative in making sense of experience.

Helen Scott

Helen has taught art and design in secondary, further and higher education. She currently works at Manchester Metropolitan University where she is Director of CPD and ITE Partnerships; her previous roles in higher education include head of School of Secondary and Post-Compulsory Initial Professional Studies, programme leader for the MA in education and course leader of the PGCE in secondary art and design at the University of Cumbria. Helen's research and expertise lie in the professional development of teachers and in the theory and practice of secondary art and design education. She is currently researching for a PhD in the use of critical studies in secondary art and design education.

NOTES ON CONTRIBUTORS

Camilla Cole

Camilla Cole has taught in a range of secondary schools in Merseyside, Birmingham and Australia. She moved into higher education in 2003 after being involved in teacher education in schools. Camilla currently leads the PGCE in Religious Education at Liverpool Hope University. She completed her MSc in education in 2005 with her dissertation on assessment in Religious Education. Her current research interests are leading to a doctorate in education and focus on professionalism in practice, particularly in the area of professional ethics and the teacher.

Tony Ewens

Tony Ewens has taught in a range of schools before moving into higher education where he became involved in RE and initial teacher education at St Martin's College, Lancaster. Tony went on to teach on a range of CPD and MA programmes for teachers at the University of Cumbria and was chair of Faculty Academic Standards Committee within the Faculty of Education. His areas of expertise and interest include values and leadership in education, church schools, school and community, curriculum and learning theory. He is now involved in writing textbooks on education and enjoying retirement.

Kathryn Fox

Kathryn Fox is the course leader for the PGCE in secondary Mathematics and the Subject Knowledge Enhancement Course at the University of Cumbria. She also works across a range of initial teacher education and CPD courses teaching mathematics and subject pedagogy with passion. Prior to this, she taught secondary mathematics in schools. She is a Fellow of the Higher Education Academy. Current research interests in education include the development of mathematics teacher identities, professional development in schools and student teachers' contributions to school improvement.

Gail Fuller

Gail Fuller completed her teacher training at St Wilfrid's CE High School in Blackburn with the Graduate Teacher Programme in 2001–2, beginning teaching after raising a family. She is now teaching Religious Studies at Ripley St Thomas CE High School in Lancaster where she is the professional mentor for newly qualified and recently qualified teachers. This work involves overseeing the induction programme for new staff and newly qualified teachers, mentoring recently qualified teachers in early professional development, as well as coaching for the MTL. Gail was ITT Mentor in Religious Education for a number of years before becoming Professional Mentor. She is currently finishing an MA in education with a focus on the beginning teacher and the NQT year.

Martyn Lawson

After a long career in the armed forces, Martyn Lawson became head of the ICT Department at an Independent Secondary School in North Yorkshire before moving into higher education. His first job at the University of Cumbria was subject leader for the secondary ICT PGCE programme. He is currently a programme leader for Master's-level provision and CPD in the faculty of education at the university where he also teaches on MA programmes. He has just completed his doctorate in education at Huddersfield University on assessing ICT in schools.

Lindsay Poyner

Lindsay Poyner is a Senior Lecturer in the Faculty of Education at the University of Cumbria. She has extensive teaching experience after teaching in schools in the West Midlands, Leicestershire and Greater Manchester and working as a School and Community Education Officer for the Museums and Art Gallery Service in Stockport. She has experience working in primary, middle and secondary education. More recently she developed an interest in ITE and now works in the field of Educational Studies, formerly being the Co-ordinator for Secondary Education Studies at the University of Cumbria. She has a National Professional Qualification for Headship (NPQH) and is a Fellow of the Higher Education Academy. Her wider interests include student teacher development and inclusion.

Carolyn Reade

Having worked in a development education centre Carolyn Reade went on to teach Religious Education and Geography in secondary schools in the North West of England. She joined St Martin's College's ELMAR (Electronic Media and Religion Project) where she became closely involved in pioneering the use of the web and new technologies to support learning in RE. Carolyn has maintained her interest in e-technologies as she has increasingly developed wide experience in initial teacher education. She is currently course leader for the undergraduate secondary RE and Education Studies courses and Senior Lecturer on the PGCE RE course at the University of Cumbria. In addition, she works on programmes for primary RE, graduate teachers and the 'QTS Direct' programme for existing teachers. Her MA focused on religious communities and her current research interests include approaches to religion and citizenship in education.

Joy Schmack

Joy Schmack began her career as a secondary RE and Drama teacher in Croydon. She then went on to be head of RE and Drama departments in three different schools before joining the Croydon Advisory Service as Primary and Secondary Adviser for RE and Citizenship and a Section 10 Ofsted Inspector. Joy was also later appointed as the borough's lead consultant for faith community dialogue and schools adviser for unaccompanied refugee children. She moved to Liverpool Hope University in 2001 and became Director of RE Services. Joy has run a wide range of CPD courses for primary and secondary teachers, governors and faith communities both nationally and internationally. She has been principal examiner for GCSE Hinduism and Buddhism and is currently Chief Examiner for GCSE World Religions short and long courses.

Patrick Smith

Patrick Smith has many years' experience of teaching in schools, further and higher education. He was an accredited team inspector for schools on behalf of Ofsted from 1997–2004 and is currently an additional inspector for higher education (initial teacher training). He is a Fellow of the Higher Education Academy. Patrick has provided numerous staff development courses and conferences for teachers specialising in Physical Education. His research interests include the leadership and management of change in education. In 2010, he was awarded the Vice Chancellor's Teaching Excellence Award for his outstanding contribution to teaching and learning in Physical Education. Patrick is currently Associate Dean (ITE and Quality) in the School for Education Futures at the University of Wolverhampton.

Jon Tibke

Jon Tibke has extensive experience in secondary schools including at a senior leadership level and is presently course leader for the PGCE secondary Music programme at the University of Cumbria. He has worked on several PGCE programmes, including two based on flexible models and is external examiner for a PGCE Music programme led by a university and LEA partnership. Jon is presently working as a teacher educator based in a school. This is the focus of recent research papers. He has recently presented a paper at the University of Oxford's 'What and how do teachers learn from experience?' research symposium, on how student teachers make sense of their experiences to construct professional learning. Jon's doctoral research is in the field of neuroeducation and the neuroscience of music, through which he seeks to create accurate, useable knowledge for music teachers.

Martin Watts

Martin Watts has more than 20 years' experience as a secondary school teacher and subject leader, most of which has been gained in the independent sector in South East Asia. More recently, Martin has enjoyed a period in UK higher education where he taught on postgraduate, Master's and doctoral programmes. His research in learning technologies has led to a further role as learning technologies leader in the overseas independent school sector once more. Martin has co-authored research on the application of online discussion forums to support the development of beginning teachers.

ACKNOWLEDGEMENTS

SAGE gratefully acknowledges the contributions of the following reviewers who read the proposal and draft chapters along the way:

Deb Heighes, Lecturer, University of Reading
Neil Herrington, Principal Lecturer, University of East London
Melanie Norman, Secondary PGCE Programme Leader, University of Brighton
Pete Sorensen, Lecturer, University of Nottingham
Stephen Wilkinson, Head of Secondary Education, Leeds Trinity University College

CHAPTER 1

INTRODUCTION: WHO IS THIS BOOK FOR, WHAT IS IT FOR AND HOW DO I USE IT?

Carrie Mercier, Carey Philpott and Helen Scott

By the end of this chapter you should be able to:

- understand the aims of the book and recognise the connection between these and some of your aims for your initial teacher education;
- identify some key issues for the secondary teacher and for secondary education today;
- begin to reflect on what perspectives you already bring to these professional issues and how you are going to prepare for meeting the challenges that these issues will present in the future.

The aim of this book is to help you through your initial teacher education (ITE) journey. It might help you to see your journey into teaching and your role as a teacher in a new light. Through the process of critical reflection on a range of issues related to becoming a teacher in secondary schools, you will encounter examples of how research and practice go hand in hand in teaching. The intention is that you perceive that being engaged in a process of enquiry is an essential part of becoming a professional in education and that the direction of travel that you follow in becoming a teacher will be important in terms of staying on track for your ongoing professional development.

The issues explored in this book are current but they all lead us back to some of the most central and enduring questions in education. Who has the answers in terms of what makes for good education? What kind of curriculum do we want for pupils? What is the role of the teacher? What is the nature of learning? What is the social function of schooling and how do we address the moral dimension at the heart of education? What is the purpose of research in education and how do we ensure it informs our practice? These are fundamental questions with which every generation of teachers needs to engage. The chapter headings are questions but we don't claim have all the answers. While we might present some orthodox answers, we also challenge these and ask you to reflect on different perspectives and come to your own conclusions.

The next two sections of this chapter give you an overview of how the whole book is organised and then how the individual chapters are organised.

How is the book organised?

The book is organised as a journey, or perhaps more accurately, two journeys. It is organised as a journey through time in relation to the processes of becoming a teacher. It is also organised as a journey through the different stages of thinking about teaching and learning that you might be asked to use during this process.

You are beginning a journey of developing the knowledge, skills and dispositions appropriate to being a successful teacher. Chapter 2 begins that journey by asking what the nature of those skills, dispositions and knowledge is, where you might find them and how you will go about developing them. This chapter explores the nature of professional learning and briefly surveys the recent history of official initiatives to provide teachers with professional knowledge. It then argues for a model of professional learning that is based on personal practical knowledge. This is knowledge that is gained by individual teachers through active enquiry into their own contexts. However, it is important that this enquiry is also informed by perspectives gained from the enquiry of others. The chapter concludes that teachers cannot expect to acquire professional learning through the unreconstructed transfer of other people's ideas. Nor can they learn effectively through personal inquiry that is not informed by the ideas of others. Effective professional learning requires dialectic between the two.

Observing will be an early part of your experience of learning to be a teacher and in Chapter 3, Helen Scott looks at how student teachers develop their ability to notice things. This chapter aims to help you consider what you can learn from watching others teach and how you can get the most from this activity. Whilst student teachers are often asked to observe others, especially at the beginning of their school placement, it is useful to go beyond the 'what to look for' aspects which are often emphasised and 'checked off' in a fairly superficial way. The starting point of this chapter is that there is much to be learnt from watching others work, but it is arguable how this activity can best be approached. The chapter describes and examines different kinds of approaches to undertaking lesson observation, and what might be gained from each one. It explores the notion that for student teachers the overall purpose of lesson observation is to go beyond superficial first impressions of others' work, to develop judgements which are based on an understanding and appreciation of the complex inter-relatedness of different relationships and actions in the classroom.

Closely connected to observing is the process of critically reflecting on what you have observed in order to decide what your observations mean. Beginning teachers are often asked to reflect critically on their school experience and in Chapter 4 Jon Tibke and Lindsay Poyner take a closer look at what is meant by this. This chapter aims to enable you to start to appreciate the benefit of learning to reflect in a purposeful and effective manner. Reflection does not simply happen through participating in teaching practice and writing assignments. Critical reflection, linked to sustained development during your initial practice and beyond, requires you to think more deeply about your actions and interactions with others and to consider what and how you learn from these experiences. As you develop your practice, the focus of your reflection will consider how your teaching impacts on the learning of pupils in your classes. This chapter will explore the reasons why it is important for you to reflect on your experiences during your first steps in teaching. It will *analyse* selected areas of research and *identify* some of the challenges that beginning teachers face in developing the skills of reflection. The authors offer *practical ideas* for you as a student teacher about how to manage the process of critical reflection and support you in *understanding* how reflective practice enhances the multi-faceted role of a teacher. They also draw on an individual trainee teachers' experiences and identify some potential starting points to show the *reflective process*.

As Scott and Tibke and Poyner argue, observation and reflection are not straight forward. We don't just passively register what there is to see. Noticing and interpreting through reflection are active and are influenced by who we are and the beliefs and knowledge that we bring to the situation. In Chapter 5 on professional identity, Martyn Lawson and Martin Watts explore questions related to the role of the secondary school teacher and how student teachers develop their identity as teachers. They draw on research in this field of enquiry. You will be encouraged to reflect critically on your own sense of identity within your subject and within the school. Lawson and Watts go on to explore the potential impact that the increasing integration of technology into classroom practice might have on your identity in the future. The chapter concludes with the view that your identity will continue to change and develop with new learning technologies and approaches to learning in schools.

As mentioned in the last paragraph, a particularly salient aspect of identity for you as a secondary school teacher might be your identity as a subject specialist. In Chapter 6 Kathryn Fox and Patrick Smith look at the importance of developing a philosophy for your subject. Your subject philosophy and the context of your practice continually evolve, and yet may be challenged by other professionals as you progress through your teaching career. Your subject philosophy will impact upon the opportunities that you offer your pupils. This chapter explores recent and relevant research that investigates these areas of study and gives practical examples through a number of curriculum areas. A key theme is the difficulty that you as a developing teacher may experience as you try to put your philosophy into practice. The chapter encourages you to meet those challenges.

Dividing the curriculum, and as a consequence teachers, into subjects is only one way of thinking about how schools need to be organised. In Chapter 7, Carrie Mercier looks briefly at different definitions of the curriculum and draws out some key issues that emerge from the story of how the curriculum has developed in secondary schools. She also explores two contrasting models of the curriculum and examines some of the theory behind them. The chapter includes the voices of teachers caught up in the process of curriculum change and raises questions about their different perspectives on the curriculum. In the course of the chapter, it should become clear to you that you need to reflect on your own role in the development of the curriculum and gain an understanding of the various curriculum models that are at work in your placement schools in order to be able to contribute to the curriculum development in your school in the future.

In Chapter 7, Mercier argues that thinking about the curriculum cannot be separated from thinking about teaching and learning methods. In Chapter 8, Tony Ewens examines theories of learning, especially those drawn from philosophy and psychology. This chapter aims to give you an overview of the key theories about the nature and processes of learning which you will find relevant to your classroom practice. The chapter will also examine the complex relationship between learning theory and subject teaching. The nature of knowledge, in any subject, is also complex, so you need a sophisticated approach when using theories of learning to enhance different elements of your teaching, for example planning and evaluating your work and considering how pupils develop mastery in your subject

How we conceptualise learning and the nature of learning that pupils engage in is closely connected to how we think about and use assessment. In Chapter 9,

Camilla Cole examines different perspectives on assessment including assessment for learning. Cole encourages you to take a fresh perspective on assessment – drawing on recent research and case studies, she asks you to reflect critically on your own experience of assessment and concludes that you may need to develop what you understand about assessment before you engage in assessing your pupils.

Chapters 8 and 9 focus on the qualities of pupils as learners and the nature of teaching, learning and assessment interactions with them. However, it is important not to overlook that not all pupils are the same. Responding to diversity has been a major challenge for trainee teachers. Research indicates that newly qualified teachers often feel that they are least prepared for this dimension of their role as teacher. In Chapter 10, Joy Schmack aims to challenge tokenistic approaches to diversity and identifies ways of embedding good practice in your teaching.

Considering diversity leads us to thinking about social, moral, spiritual and cultural education and the ways that this relates to positive outcomes for diverse communities. This is the focus of Chapter 11 by Carolyn Reade and Carrie Mercier. In this chapter, Reade and Mercier examine the way in which provision for the spiritual, moral, social and cultural development of pupils came to be a requirement for all schools. They look at how this agenda might be understood by teachers today and ask how it might translate into classroom practice. The spiritual, moral, social and cultural development of pupils has a significant place on the Ofsted agenda for the inspection of schools and this dimension of the curriculum is often seen as closely linked to the requirement that schools contribute to community cohesion. Reade and Mercier explore the idea that all teachers have a responsibility to ensure that there is a sense of shared values and common goals and that every pupil has a sense of belonging. They conclude by suggesting that this connects to the bigger picture and looks beyond the school gates to the contribution of the school to the development of wider society.

Chapter 12 explores an important staging post in your development as a teacher: the point at which you are preparing to move from the ITE phase of your development to the NQT year. In Chapter 12 on initial teacher education and induction processes in schools, Gail Fuller draws on a wealth of experience in working with beginner teachers in the school context. This chapter draws directly on concrete examples of reflecting on the induction experience, examining good practice and raising issues for the changing context in ITE. This chapter presents an opportunity for you to draw out key points to reflect on in anticipating your first few months in your first job, focusing attention on the relational and emotional aspects of teaching. It concludes that the newly qualified teacher will need to take on board the whole process of 'becoming' a teacher and all it entails which is more than just ticking the Teachers' Standards.

Chapter 13 on the value of Master's-level study might have relevance for you in this early post-qualifying period. Equally it might have relevance for you during your ITE course if Master's-level study is a feature of your course. In recent years, Master's-level study for teachers and student teachers was promoted and funded by the government for a number of reasons. It was promoted as a means of encouraging a particular kind of approach to the linking of theory and practice in initial teacher education, as a vehicle for experienced teachers' professional development, to enable individuals to improve their classroom practice and as a way of teachers implementing government education policies. Based on the experience of other European countries (for example, Finland), the view that creating a 'Master's-level profession' would raise the status of teachers in society and therefore attract higher qualified applicants was promoted, as well as the notion that this in turn would lead to improved educational outcomes for pupils. Most primary and secondary PCGE courses offer (or require) Master's-level modules to be taken by student teachers. This chapter examines definitions of Master's level and considers the particular benefits and challenges for student teachers.

In the final chapter, Chapter 14, themes and ideas that have recurred throughout the book will be drawn together. This chapter will also draw together the important lessons that recur throughout the book in relation to the importance of research and enquiry for classroom practice and for your career-long professional development.

How is each chapter organised?

Each chapter maintains a balance between specific details and examples from practice and wider critical perspectives informed by research. One of the main purposes of this book is to demonstrate the ways in which active engagement in, and with, research can challenge or alter our initial beliefs or assumptions about education. It may even cause us to question the understandings we have arrived at through practical experience. Although the chapters do not have a strictly identical structure you will find that all chapters contain 'case studies'. These are specific real examples that are intended to anchor or illuminate the more general points that they are making. Chapters will also have a number of 'points for reflection' that are intended as a stimulus either to further long-term exploration of the topic being discussed or as a mental preparation for the points that are going to be explored next in the chapter. Each chapter also ends with questions for review that invite you to reflect on what you may have learnt from the chapter as a whole. Finally, each chapter, in addition to a list of references that you can follow up, has recommended further reading.

CHAPTER 2

WHO HAS ALL THE ANSWERS IN EDUCATION (AND WHY SHOULD YOU BELIEVE THEM)?

Carey Philpott

By the end of this chapter you should be able to:

- discuss critically the nature of teachers' claims to understand education more than other groups;
- discuss critically how and where you develop professional knowledge most effectively;
- critically evaluate competing claims to be able to advance teachers' professional knowledge from researchers, politicians and CPD providers (among others).

This chapter considers the question of who it is who understands how effective teaching should be carried out; is it teachers, education lecturers in universities, educational 'theorists' or researchers, government ministers, commercial CPD companies or some other group entirely? Linked to the question of who understands how effective teaching and learning should be carried out is the question of what is the source of their knowledge or, put another way, why should we find their knowledge more credible than anyone else's? Considering this question will help you think about from whom you can learn most effectively and how you can learn most effectively.

Who knows how teaching should be done?

Point for reflection

- Where do you expect to find expert knowledge on how teaching should be done?

There is no shortage of people and groups of people who claim to understand how teaching and learning should be carried out. Very often these people will want to tell you what is wrong with much teaching and learning currently and what needs to be done to improve it. Among these people are lecturers on initial teacher education courses, education researchers in universities, politicians, school inspection bodies, think tanks, media personalities who make television programmes about their attempts to inspire and motivate disaffected pupils, the media in general, employers and employers' organisations, commercial continuing professional development (CPD) providers and people who write books like this one. Also, of course, we should include teachers. However, in recent decades teachers may have felt that their expertise, their claim to have the answers, has been marginalised.

The recent history of teacher expertise

Choosing the start of a historical process can feel slightly arbitrary but, arguably, a key moment in this perception of marginalisation was the introduction of the National Curriculum as a result of the 1988 Education Reform Act (HMSO, 1988). The National Curriculum meant that someone other than teachers in schools was deciding what should be taught and when it should be taught. This apparent marginalisation continued apace with the introduction of various government promoted strategies into schools such as the National Literacy Strategy in 1998 and the Key Stage 3 Strategy in

2000 (to name two). These strategies went beyond prescribing what should be taught and when it should be taught (although some of them did this in more detail than the National Curriculum document itself did) and also advocated particular strategies for teaching. So now decisions about what to teach, when to teach it *and how to teach it* were apparently being made by someone other than the teachers in classrooms and schools around the country. Taking these decisions away from teachers seemed to be the way that education was going to be improved. By the time that Assessment of Pupil Progress (APP) was introduced in 2004 the prescription had become very fine grained with guidance on what to teach broken down to specific years rather than the broader key stages of the National Curriculum and atomised into particular assessment outcomes within the original National Curriculum Attainment Targets. This detailed prescription in relation to what and when to teach was accompanied by numerous government-backed publications on how to teach and resources for increasingly frequent assessment of pupils' progress. Colleagues in schools often felt that hardly a week went by without more government guidance on how to teach, learn and assess arriving on their desks. Similarly, colleagues involved in initial teacher education courses sometimes felt that their job was now to familiarise beginning teachers with all this guidance and to develop their ability to 'deliver it' rather than develop beginning teachers' expertise in making decisions themselves about what to teach, when to teach it and how to teach it. This feeling was strengthened by the parallel historical development, starting in 1992 (DfE, 1992), of what eventually became the Standards for Qualified Teacher Status (QTS) (TDA, 2008) and then, most recently, the Teachers' Standards (DfE, 2011a) through which the nature of teachers' expertise was apparently prescribed by a government agency rather than by the teaching profession itself. Some people spoke about the de-professionalisation of teachers. Teachers were no longer considered to be sufficiently expert or knowledgeable, either individually or as a profession, to make decisions about the most effective ways of carrying out education or indeed about what skills, knowledge and values they needed to be effective teachers. To reiterate, the message seemed to be: if we want education to improve we need to take most of the important decisions away from teachers. Or put another way, the answer to the question 'who has all the answers in education?' would not be 'teachers'.

To be fair, it needs to be acknowledged that some of this guidance was based on research evidence on what was effective in education and, therefore, these are 'answers' that originated from within the education profession rather than outside it (although from education researchers rather than teachers). Also, some of it was based on spreading more widely practice that had been developed by teachers in some schools and which had been identified as good practice by school inspections. So, in this case, it could be argued that the 'answers' were coming from teachers. However, the experience of individual teachers and schools receiving this guidance was that it originated from somewhere other than themselves and that its authority came from its association with government agencies rather than with teachers. It also needs to be acknowledged that, with the exception of the National Curriculum itself (and the Standards for QTS), all of this guidance was only recommended and not compulsory. So, it can be argued that it only helpfully provided possible resources for teachers and that they were free to use their expertise to select what they judged to be valuable and to make their own decisions where they thought they had better ideas. So they could still be the source of the 'answers' themselves. However, in practice many of these recommendations were responded to as if they were compulsory and teachers and schools tended not to reject them or come up with their own alternatives. Why should this be?

In part this may have been because of the nature of the school inspection regime. Schools possibly felt that if inspectors believed that pupils' achievements were not as good as they could or should be, they would be further criticised for not using government-promoted strategies. A culture of compliance (Menter et al., 2006) created by the perception of a punitive inspection regime, which militated against experimentation and risk taking, was felt by many to exist in both schools and teacher education. A second reason could be a more general erosion of teachers' confidence in their own ability to make these decisions themselves or in their own authority to challenge these decisions. Perhaps teachers themselves didn't feel that they had the answers. This erosion can be attributed to many causes. One cause may be the very existence of all this guidance and its persuasive 'rhetoric of conclusions' (Clandinin and Connelly, 1995). Perhaps teachers became habituated to seeking the answers in the guidance and the idea that they might generate the answers themselves became less familiar to them. Or it might be that all the time and energy required to keep responding to new initiatives left little time or energy for developing or exploring alternative ideas.

Another reason for teachers' lack of confidence in their own ability to provide the answers could also originate in the 'discourse of derision' (Ball, 1990) to which teachers were subject for many years during education reforms in England and Wales. Schools and teachers en masse were repeatedly represented in the popular media as failing and reform was presented as something that must be done to teachers to tackle their inadequacy rather than as something that teachers might be at the forefront of leading. Although the most intense days of the discourse of derision are behind us, its longer-term effects on public perceptions of teachers (and perhaps teachers' perceptions of themselves) haven't gone away. It is still the case that media headlines regularly appear about the number of schools that are failing or 'only' satisfactory, the number of pupils who don't achieve government targets or the number of teachers who are inadequate. Television programmes are still made on the premise that there is something rotten in the state of education. The starting point for public discourse about education still often seems to be that things are not good enough. It is still axiomatic in some public discourse that education is inadequate and by implication (if not explicitly claimed) that schools and teachers are inadequate. This is not to argue that we should be complacent and assume teachers and schools cannot be improved. However, it is questionable whether we should start from the position that the system is fundamentally broken rather than fundamentally sound but capable of being improved. The significance of these reflections on the discourse of derision and its legacy for the question of 'who has all the answers' is that, again, the perception might be that teachers do not have the answers about education because they have already (within the terms of this particular debate) so signally failed to do an adequate job. Therefore, the answers need to be sought elsewhere.

This doubt about the educational expertise of the education 'establishment' (by which I mean at the very least teachers, teacher trainers and local authorities) can also be detected in other educational developments. At their inception, teacher training courses such as the Graduate Teacher Programme (GTP) and Teach First seemed to downplay the expert knowledge base that might be required to be a teacher and to suggest that all you need to know to be a teacher could be picked up as 'craft knowledge' on the job or that good academic subject knowledge was the most important thing for teaching rather than any specialist educational or 'teacher' knowledge. In other words, teacher knowledge was largely reduced to subject knowledge and teacher expertise was largely reduced to subject expertise. This may not be a case of suggesting that teachers don't have the answers to educational questions. In fact, the 'on the job' nature of these courses might suggest that teachers have more of the answers than teacher trainers or other academics do. However, it does tend to suggest that the knowledge teachers have and need to have (apart from subject knowledge) is not particularly specialist and doesn't take long to acquire.

Bringing it up to date

To bring this brief history more up to date, we need to consider more recent government publications: *The Importance of Teaching* (DfE, 2010a), *The Case for Change* (DfE, 2010b) and *Training our Next Generation of Outstanding Teachers* (DfE, 2011b). One thing that is immediately apparent from these documents is a careful rejection of the 'discourse of derision' in relation to teachers in favour of acknowledging 'that we have in our schools today the best generation of teachers we have ever had' (DfE, 2010b: 3). It also needs to be acknowledged that many of the proposals contained in these documents privilege the expertise of teachers over the expertise of other groups. For example, school autonomy is promoted through the creation of more academies and free schools. Centralised guidelines and prescription in relation to teaching are rejected in favour of allowing schools and teachers more flexibility and autonomy to decide the best methods of teaching. More control over teacher education is to be given to schools because they are seen as the most effective site of training. For this same reason, school-based routes are to be expanded. In recent decades, it has sometimes seemed as if teachers were seen as the problem in education. Now apparently they are being seen as the solution. So perhaps now we have arrived at a point in history in which the answer to the question 'who has all the answers in education' is 'teachers'.

This recognition of the professional expertise of teachers is very welcome. However, it may not be the whole story. The consequence of privileging the knowledge and expertise of teachers over other sources of knowledge and expertise in the particular way that it is done in these recent publications runs the risk of reducing teachers' professional knowledge and expertise to a kind of practical, applied craft knowledge and to ignore its intellectual and theoretical sophistication. The increased role for schools in teacher education and the increase of employment-based routes could be seen to imply that acquiring learning about education is no more than picking up practical strategies on the job. The creation of free schools could be interpreted as suggesting that people other than qualified teachers are as likely as teachers to understand how education can be carried out effectively. Teaching becomes reduced to a common-sense activity rather than one that requires a sophisticated professional understanding.

So where does this leave beginning teachers in terms of the most authoritative source of knowledge about teaching and the most effective way of developing that knowledge? In order to answer this question we need to ask another question first.

Point for reflection

- How theoretical and specialised is teachers' knowledge and how much of it is common sense or easily picked up as 'craft knowledge' on the job?

What type of knowledge is knowledge about teaching?

Exploring the question of who has all the answers in education can also cause us to ask the related question – what kind of knowledge is knowing how to teach? At first glance, this might seem like an abstruse kind of question. However, many teachers who have recently been working towards the Standards for QTS will be familiar with the idea that being able to teach can be broken down into three different types of accomplishment. In the language of the 2008 Standards for QTS these are 'attributes', 'knowledge and understanding', and 'skills'. So, in other words, part of what you need to acquire to be a good teacher (the attributes) is a set of values, dispositions, personality traits or beliefs (e.g. a belief that relationships with all pupils should be positive and supportive). Part of what you need to acquire is in the form of knowledge (e.g. knowing theories or principles of behaviour management) and part of it is in the form of things that you are able to do (e.g. being able to manage behaviour). While it is true that the 2011 Teachers' Standards are less obviously organised in this tripartite way, all of the 2011 standards can still be allocated to one of these groups. For example, attributes: 'showing tolerance of and respect for the rights of others' (DfE, 2011a: 9); understanding: 'have a secure understanding of how a range of factors can inhibit pupils' ability to learn, and how best to overcome these' (DfE, 2011a: 7); and skills: 'manage classes effectively using approaches which are appropriate to pupils' needs in order to involve and motivate them' (DfE, 2011a: 8). In fact, the tendency to understand the outcomes of education in these three ways is not confined to any particular document or policy but is widespread (Barnett et al., 2001).

So how might you acquire this knowledge?

Having accepted that not all of the accomplishments that a teacher needs are the same kind of thing we might then realise that not all these accomplishments are best acquired in the same kinds of way. Knowledge, in the sense that it is used here, may be effectively acquired by attending lectures or reading books. Skills are perhaps best acquired by ongoing practice in a 'real world' environment where we learn from the mistakes we make and try again. Attributes may be the most difficult to acquire as they are connected with the kinds of disposition, beliefs and values we have. Some of us may have a strong tendency to being positive and supportive with the most difficult pupils. Others may find that they are inclined to be more judgemental and punitive. It is not that they lack the knowledge or skills to be positive and supportive. It is more that they lack the inclination. It seems unlikely that you can acquire an attribute from attending lectures and reading books in the way that you can acquire knowledge or that you can develop it through practice in the same way that you can develop a skill. An attribute like this may be more about beliefs and convictions and these develop in different ways.

Having arrived at the conclusion that different types of teacher accomplishments are best acquired through different kinds of processes, we might now also raise a question about how transferrable these accomplishments are between people with differing degrees of current accomplishment. Transferrable, here, means how easily and effectively can they be packaged up in a form that allows them to be transferred from one person to another. It is arguably the case that knowledge is the easiest one of the three to transfer. Someone can write down a range of behaviour management strategies and pass them on to you via a handout, book chapter, article or lecture. As far as acquiring them as knowledge is concerned, you may not have to do much beyond remembering them in the form that they were given to you. You could then reproduce them in an essay and you may be assessed as having a good *knowledge* of behaviour management strategies. However, a word of caution is necessary here about this simplified presentation of knowledge. Although this type of rote learning of knowledge can be successful in many assessment situations, in other situations we need a more sophisticated view of the nature and acquisition of knowledge. Chapter 8 by Tony Ewens touches on this theme.

Skills are a different matter. You might say that skills are something that has to be learnt rather than something that can be taught. This means that you have to build skills for yourself by interacting with the environment in which they are acquired and used. I can't just hand my skills over to you via a handout or a lecture although I may be able to give you some assistance in building your own skills if I am around to help in the particular place where you are practising and learning. However, it will be likely that the nature of your skills will be personal to you and, to some extent, to the particular context in which you acquire them. It won't be possible for your skills to be a copy of mine in the way that your knowledge could be in the example given above.

Attributes are different again. This may be best illustrated by a case study. Case study 2.1 comes from observing a trainee PE teacher.

Case study 2.1 Different types learning in a PE lesson

The learning outcome for the lesson was that pupils would know how to serve in tennis. The trainee teacher described the process to pupils while demonstrating it physically. The pupils were then given some time to practise. By the end of the lesson it became apparent that all pupils had knowledge about serving a tennis ball in the way that knowledge has been described above. That is, they could all describe how it was supposed to be done in a way that reproduced how the teacher had described it. Therefore, some form of knowledge had been transferred. However, only a few of them had built their own skills of serving to the extent that they could actually serve successfully. The teacher was less successful here at developing a skill in others. What would the teacher need to do to increase the building of skills? The teacher circulated during the practice and attempted to assist pupils in building their own skills through feedback on what they were doing. With more of this help, she might have got all pupils to the stage where they had built their own skills as well remembering her articulation of the knowledge. However, how many pupils had the attribute of *wanting* to be able to serve in tennis? To how many did it matter? How many aspired to do it? It is difficult to be sure. What is clear, however, is that increasing the number of pupils to whom serving in tennis mattered, increasing the number for whom tennis was important, would be a different matter from either transferring knowledge or helping to build skills.

Points for reflection

- Can education change people's attributes?
- Do you expect teacher education will change yours? If so how?

Arguably, attitudes and values can't be transferred like knowledge can. Nor can they necessarily be built like skills can through assisted practice. Attitudes and values are developed through experience but it is a longer, more uncertain process than skills development and one that is even more personal and less amenable to being passed on from one person to another.

Who has all the answers in education revisited

Let's go back to the question of who has all the answers in education. In part, we have to answer this question by thinking about where answers come from in the light of the discussion in this section. If we stick to the simplified definition of knowledge above, it is possible that my knowledge could come from someone else. An expert could develop knowledge and pass it on to me through a book or lecture or training day. If, however, we think about skills and attributes, then these can't really come from anyone else but me interacting with my professional context. It isn't really possible for someone to develop skills and attributes for me and then pass them on to me. In this sense, only I have the answers. Or perhaps more correctly, only I can generate the answers; I can't just get them from someone else.

So far I have explored the question of what type of knowledge teacher knowledge is by thinking about the three categories that Teachers' Standards can be divided into. I chose these because they were likely to be familiar to many people reading this book. However, there are other ways of thinking about the type of knowledge teacher knowledge is. Jerome Bruner has suggested that knowledge can be divided into two types; paradigmatic and narrative (Bruner, 1986). Paradigmatic knowledge is the kind that deals with logical relationships between ideas. Pythagoras' theorem that the square on the hypotenuse is equal to the sum of the squares of the other two sides is a form of paradigmatic knowledge. However, when we are dealing with the social world, that is to say the world of people and their interactions, paradigmatic knowledge may not be the most appropriate form of knowledge. In the social world, we are dealing with knowledge about people's behaviours. People's behaviours are connected to a range of complex factors such as their sense of who they are, what they are trying to achieve, how they see their relationship with the people around them, what sense they make of their own past experiences and so on. Not only are these factors complex, but they can change over time too. When dealing with the social world, narrative knowledge may be a more suitable form for our knowledge.

Narrative knowledge

Narrative knowledge organises our understanding of how and why events unfold as they do in the social world. Narrative knowledge organises our understanding of what people are trying to achieve when they act as they do. It organises our understanding of how past events affect the current situation. It organises our sense of the effects that particular actions are likely to have in the future. When dealing with knowing about the social world, we need to recognise that no two social situations are exactly the same, although they may share features in common. We also need to recognise that even the same situation changes over time. There is a reciprocal relationship between the types of narrative knowledge that we have already developed as a result of past experiences and the way we make sense of new experiences that we have. When we have new experiences, we tend to make sense of them in terms of the kinds of stories (narratives) we already tell ourselves about how the world works. Sometimes, however, events cause us to revise the kinds of stories that we tell ourselves about how the world works so we go on to interpret new experiences through a new kind of story. In addition some of the new stories we acquire to organise our sense of the world we acquire through socialisation as we become members of new groups. For example, Carole Cain's (1991) research into American Alcoholics Anonymous showed how over time new members to the group acquired a new story by which to make sense of their past lives. This story was the one that was most prevalent in the AAA community and which new members acquired through interaction with existing members.

Teaching and learning is a fundamentally social activity and is intimately bound up with the types of issues referred to above such participants' sense of identity, their aspirations and the sense they make of their past experiences. Many writers on teachers and teacher knowledge (e.g. Carter, 1993; Clandinin and Connelly, 1995; Olson 1995) believe that the specialist professional knowledge that teachers have is primarily narrative in form. Teachers' knowledge is in the form of stories about the world of young people's lives, schools, classrooms and education and they use these to make sense of the experiences they have and to plan future actions. If the main form of teacher knowledge is narrative, then this has consequences for our question of who has the answers in education and why we should see their knowledge as more credible than other people's knowledge. It also has consequences for the question of how knowledge about teaching and learning is best acquired. Narrative knowledge by its very nature tends to be constructed by individuals in response to their own experiences in the specific contexts in which they work. It is not the kind of knowledge that can be easily codified and passed on from one person to another. Connelly and Clandinin make the distinction between what they call personal practical knowledge and 'theoretical knowledge claims uprooted from their origins and standing in abstract objective independence' (Connelly and Clandinin, 1995: 9) for which they borrow the term 'the rhetoric of conclusions'. They argue that the rhetoric of conclusions is typically seen as the most authoritative type of knowledge. This is the type of knowledge that results from, for example, large-scale research and which is then disseminated through publications, guidelines, training, etc. However, they argue that personal practical knowledge is more central to teachers' life and work and that it should not be regarded as an inferior form of knowledge. The rhetoric of conclusions is, in the view of Connelly and Clandinin, a form of knowledge that is unhelpfully abstract and detached from the specific social circumstances of individual teachers' lives and work and also from the specific circumstances in which it was generated. Personal practical knowledge, on the other hand, is intimately connected to the specific contexts in which teachers live and work and, therefore, has more validity and should be more highly valued.

If we accept this view, then the most powerful and useable knowledge for teachers is not in the form that can easily be generated by other people and then 'handed over' to teachers through courses or policy directives. How then can personal practical knowledge be developed if it cannot be formulated through research and/or policy created by others and then passed on to teachers? In the normal course of events personal practical knowledge is developed through ongoing day-to-day experience. Does this mean, then, that teacher knowledge is no more than common-sense craft knowledge of the kind that I criticised politicians for believing in earlier in this chapter? To answer this, we may need to briefly consider the nature of learning from experience.

Learning from experience

One of the most commonly cited models of learning from experience is Kolb's (1983) experiential learning cycle (shown in Figure 2.1).

In this model, experience becomes a source of knowledge through a process of, first, reflection on experience and then the organisation of that reflection into some kind of general understanding or model of the world. What it is important to recognise in this learning process is that the sense we might make of our experiences is not necessarily obvious or 'common sense'. You may well have been in situations in which you and someone else have apparently participated in the same experience but have come to quite different conclusions about the meaning of that experience; or, in other words, made quite different sense of it. As an Initial Teacher Education student, you may be aware of this during experiences in classrooms that you share with mentors

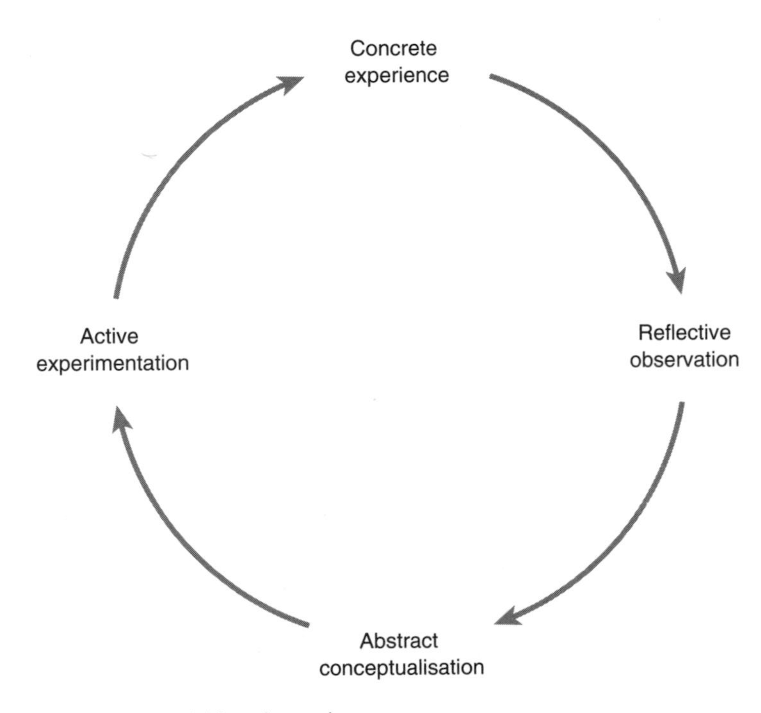

Figure 2.1 Kolb's experiential learning cycle

and/or university tutors. After the experience, when you are discussing what happened with your mentor or tutor you discover that you have each created different stories about what happened and why (see Philpott, 2011 for a detailed case study of this). This is because we reflect on and interpret our experiences according to the different stories about the world that we already have. Experienced teachers and university tutors will have developed different types of stories with which to make sense of the experiences they have. In the case of experienced teachers or university tutors, the narratives that they use to make sense of experience might come from their own earlier experiences or they might be informed by research findings and other forms of abstracted theoretical knowledge.

Two important things emerge from this model of teachers developing their professional knowledge. The first is that forms of relatively abstracted knowledge such as research evidence and educational theories are not irrelevant to teachers' personal practical knowledge. They are part of what informs and shapes it. However, they are not sufficient on their own and become useful through their interaction with personal practical experience. Another way of expressing this is to say that you cannot just expect to produce a general decontextualised set of prescriptions for teaching and learning and expect them to be directly and unproblematically applied to a diverse range of actual schools and classrooms. The second important thing is that personal practical knowledge may be doomed to 'reinvent the wheel' or to become trapped in a 'restrictive' (Evans et al., 2006; Philpott, 2006) learning cycle if the reflection and abstract conceptualisation parts of the cycle of learning from experience are not informed by perspectives, ideas and understanding gained from the knowledge of others such as might come from research and theorising. Or put another way, when reflecting on our experience, we have to consider and explore different ways that we might make sense of it by finding out about different possible frameworks for sense making. If we don't, we run the risk of getting trapped in 'groupthink' (Engestrom et al., 1995) or into the self-reinforcing closed world view that is one of the possible downsides of professional communities when they are not open to views beyond their own (Wenger et al., 2002).

Conclusion – so who does have all the answers and why should I believe them?

So what are the implications of this for our original question of who has all the answers in education and why we should believe them, and what are the implications for you as a beginning teacher? The preceding section argued that personal practical knowledge is the knowledge of teaching and learning that is most valuable for teachers. It also argued that personal practical knowledge is most valuable when it is informed by diverse perspectives arising from wider research and educational theorising. One conclusion that can be drawn from this is that understanding of teaching and learning is best generated by teachers when they engage in processes of informed enquiry. That is, when they intentionally set out to learn from their own experiences by reflecting on them and conceptualising with the help of research insights and theoretical perspectives from elsewhere. So, in this case, the answer to the first part of our question (who has all the answers in education?) is 'teachers who have actively engaged in a process of systematic and informed enquiry'. The answer to the second part (why should we believe them) is 'because they have developed the knowledge in ways that are deeply rooted in the specific social contexts in which they are working'. For the trainee teacher, this means that you should not expect to develop your professional expertise by listening to prescriptions from other people but by engaging in purposeful enquiry into, and reflection on, your own practice. However, this doesn't mean just coming to your own relatively unreflective and uninformed 'commonsense' conclusions. This enquiry and reflection will need to be informed by the ideas you gain from reading, lectures and other people. You cannot expect to learn to teach solely by picking up practical teaching tips from existing teachers. Nor can you expect to be able to take abstracted, decontextualised ideas from educational research, theories, lectures or books and hope to apply them unreconstructed to the particular circumstances in which you work. You need to recognise the dialogue that is necessary between these two sources of understanding if you are going to progress.

Reflective questions

1. Where do you think the current public discourse about education (e.g. media, politicians) suggests that understanding of good teaching can be found?
2. How will you make the best use of the dialogue between experience and other sources of knowledge (e.g. reading, lectures) that is necessary for you to learn to be a teacher?
3. How might your attributes need to change in order for you to be an effective teacher?

Recommended further reading

Brookfield, S. (1995) *Becoming a Critically Reflective Teacher*. San Francisco: Jossey-Bass.

This is an excellent book on the need to think critically about received wisdom and the need to build understandings which are localised and context specific.

Eraut, Michael (1994) *Developing Professional Knowledge and Competence*. London: Routledge.
Michael Eraut is a leading thinker in terms of exploring the types of knowledge and understanding there are in professional practice.

Rainbird, H., Fuller, A. and Munro, A. (2004) *Workplace Learning in Context*. London: Routledge.
A good general book to provide a wider theoretical and research context for thinking about how professionals learn.

References

Ball, S. (1990) *Politics and Policy Making in Education*. London: Routledge and Kegan Paul.

Barnett, R., Parry, G. and Coate, K. (2001) 'Conceptualising curriculum change', *Teaching in Higher Education*, 6 (4): 435–49.

Bruner, J. (1986) *Actual Minds, Possible Worlds*. Cambridge, MA: Harvard University Press.

Cain, Carole (1991) 'Personal stories: identity acquisition and self-understanding in alcoholics anonymous', *Ethos*, 19 (2): 210–53.

Carter, K. (1993) 'The place of story in the study of teaching and teacher education', *Educational Researcher*, 22 (1): 5–12, 18.

Clandinin, D.J. and Connelly, F.M. (1995) *Teachers' Professional Knowledge Landscapes*. New York: Teachers College Press.

Department for Education (1992) *The New Requirements for Initial Teacher Training* (Circular 9/92). London: Department for Education.

Department for Education (2010a) *The Importance of Teaching*. Norwich: The Stationery Office.

Department for Education (2010b) *The Case for Change*. Norwich: The Stationery Office.

Department for Education (2011a) *Teachers' Standards*. Norwich: The Stationery Office.

Department for Education (2011b) *Training our Next Generation of Outstanding Teachers*. Norwich: The Stationery Office.

Engestrom Y., Engestrom, R. and Karkkainen, M. (1995) 'Polycontextuality and boundary crossing in expert cognition: learning and problem solving in complex work activities', *Learning and Instruction*, 5, 319–36.

Evans, K., Hodkinson, P., Rainbird, H. and Unwin, L. (2006) *Improving Workplace Learning*. Abingdon: Routledge.

HMSO (1988) *Education Reform Act 1988*. London: HMSO.

Kolb, D.A. (1983) *Experiential Learning*. Upper Saddle River, NJ: Pearson Education.

Menter, I., Brisard, E. and Smith I. (2006) *Convergence or Divergence: Initial Teacher Education in Scotland and England*. Edinburgh: Dunedin Academic Press.

Olson, M.R. (1995) 'Conceptualizing narrative authority: implications for teacher education', *Teaching and Teacher Education*, 11 (2): 119–35.

Philpott, C. (2006) 'Transfer of learning between higher education institution and school based components of PGCE courses', *Journal of Vocational Education and Training*, 58 (3): 283–302.

Philpott, C. (2011) 'Narrative as a cultural tool for experiential learning in initial teacher education', *Storytelling, Self and Society*, 7 (1): 15–35.

Training and Development Agency for Schools (2008) *Professional Standards for Qualified Teacher Status and Requirements for Initial Teacher Training*. London: Training and Development Agency for Schools.

Wenger, E., McDermott, R. and Snyder, W. (2002) *Cultivating Communities of Practice: A Guide to Managing Knowledge*. Cambridge, MA: Harvard Business School.

CHAPTER 3

IS THERE MORE TO LESSON OBSERVATION THAN MEETS THE EYE? WHAT CAN YOU LEARN FROM WATCHING OTHERS TEACH?

Helen Scott

By the end of the chapter you should be able to:

- understand why observation of others can be a source of valuable professional development and understand what can (and can't) be learnt from watching your more experienced colleagues at work;
- consider models and methods for observing others from a range of perspectives, in the context of your own development as a teacher;
- learn from research approaches to observation and apply these to your observation of others.

This chapter aims to help you consider what you can learn from watching others teach and how you can get the most from this activity. Whilst student teachers are often asked to observe others, especially at the beginning of their school placement, it is useful to go beyond the 'what to look for' aspects which are often emphasised and can be 'checked off' in a fairly superficial way. The starting point of this chapter is that there is much to be learnt from watching others at work, but it is arguable how this activity can best be approached.

Whilst lesson observation is an incredibly common practice in schools, throughout teachers' careers, there is not a great deal of literature or research exploring how experienced teachers might best carry out the processes of watching their colleagues at work. Fortunately, there is quite a lot more research (some of which will be touched upon in this chapter) that has been undertaken related to the benefits, pitfalls and methods associated with student teachers observing others as part of their early development. You will no doubt receive guidance about observing teachers on your placement and be given a number of areas to focus on; for example, how the teacher speaks to pupils (their language, tone), how the lesson is structured (use of timings, pace, different activities), use of resources, assessing the pupils' learning and so on. The list will be long but probably useful in requiring you to look at things that you'll need to consider and undertake yourself once you begin to teach. However, is it possible to go much further with your own development through lesson observation than simply having your attention drawn to different things? Noticing the things you have pointed out to you 'in the moment' of a lesson will get you so far but there is more to observing others teach than simply noticing the presence of different activities and interactions; this is what I hope to explore in the chapter.

Why do we observe others teach?

As noted above, observation in initial teacher education tends to be used as an introduction and induction to becoming a teacher; you may find yourself watching a lot of lessons at the beginning of your course, then it may tail off once you are doing your own teaching. This is a mistake as you will continue to gain much from watching others (perhaps even more than at the beginning) once you are doing your own teaching. I will make an argument for you insisting upon continuing lesson observations throughout your placements and for the duration of your course. With the help of this chapter, you will be able to move away from *describing* the interactions and actions in a lesson to *elaborating* and *explaining* them (Santagata et al., 2007: 126). The underlying assumption of the observation process is that you can learn to be a teacher by watching a teacher. The question is what can you learn? Is learning to be a teacher merely a case of copying what someone more experienced than you does? What kind of knowledge can you gain or get access to by watching more experienced teachers? These are the kinds of things to be discussed in this chapter.

It is not unreasonable that the lesson is one of the sites that student teachers must feel comfortable in and with and therefore is the location of growing familiarity with the school and teaching itself; 'research findings have indicated that student teachers' confidence and wellbeing is linked to how quickly they adjust to the school's norms and conventions and interpret the significance of the micro-political culture' (Hayes, 2001: Hodkinson and Hodkinson, 1999 in Pinder, 2008: 2). The lessons that take place in different subjects within the school will certainly give you a very good introduction to the varied culture, practices and values in the school. Also 'the lesson as a unit of analysis reduces the complexity of teaching to a manageable size, while maintaining its character' (Santagata et al., 2007: 127). Observing people will help you to think about how all the different elements of a lesson may come together to create a particular kind of situation for a teacher and their pupils.

Case study 3.1 First impressions of observing others

A group of student teachers in the first few weeks of their first placement on their PGCE course were asked to observe several lessons in their subject and then to contribute to a discussion in a university session about what had struck them most. Here are some of their comments:

> 'I don't understand how the teacher got the pupils' attention – it was like magic – I couldn't see how she managed to get them so quiet and so engaged so quickly!'
>
> 'The teacher had a really annoying habit of repeating particular phrases when talking to the pupils and scratching their head a lot ... I bet these things really got on the kids' nerves.'
>
> 'There seemed to be loads of things that happened in the lesson which simply weren't commented upon – girls brushing their hair, a boy eating a bag of crisps, someone reading a magazine from cover to cover rather than looking for coloured images to use for their collage ... I can't imagine dealing with all of this stuff or why the teacher didn't do something.'
>
> 'The thing I noticed most was the noise – the chairs scraping on the tiled floor, pupils talking over each other, the teacher raising their voice, cupboard doors and drawers banged shut ... I had a massive headache by the end of the lesson.'

The student teachers quoted in case study 3.1 (all student teachers I have worked with over the last few years) have arguably all begun the process of adjustment to some of their schools (or particular subjects') norms through the things they noticed in observing other people teach. However, Santagata et al. (2007) in their work with student teachers, trying to enable them to develop better skills of lesson observation analysis, commented that 'when first exposed to examples of teaching, pre-service teachers tend to focus on irrelevant features, such as the way the person looks, the sound of their voice and the gestures they use (Fuller and Manning, 1973). Beyond attention to such superficial features, observing classrooms can become overwhelming' (Santagata et al., 2007: 124). I don't think that the things the student teachers quoted above focused on aspects of the lesson which are necessarily irrelevant, but some of the comments do suggest a kind of sensory overload, not uncommon when one experiences the classroom for the first time, no longer as a pupil, but as a teacher. You will probably recognise these kinds of comments from your peers and perhaps what you might say yourself, having observed other teachers' lessons, especially early on in your school experience. The comments can be interpreted in many different ways and say much about the individuals who made them, as well as the classroom environments they found themselves in. For example, the first comment implies that the student teacher picked up on the effects of actions made by the teacher, but could not understand (or see) how the effects had been achieved. The student who made the second comment has become fixated on a particular aspect they noticed – but they may be correct that once a pupil noticed the teachers' habits, they could become distracted, having a negative effect on the lesson. The third and fourth comments describe the overwhelming sensory overload of being present in the classroom noted in Santagata et al.'s (2007) comments above, which may have prevented the observer focusing on much else. Interestingly, the final student has described an experience not related to seeing. I would urge you as part of your observations of others to be excellent listeners as well as viewers; the aural and oral aspects of the lesson are strongly related to the actions and visible aspects of the teacher's and pupils' behaviours in a lesson. All the students' comments are very understandable and valid reactions to being in someone else's lesson, especially early on in a school placement. Is it possible to move on from these early first impressions to experience other people's work as something you feel you can learn from or put into practice yourself?

Points for reflection

- When in another teacher's lesson shut your eyes for a minute or so – write down what you can hear; what does this tell you about the lesson?
- Following taking notes in a lesson observation, review your writing to see what kinds of things in the lesson stood out for you.

Are there some things that you need to know about becoming a teacher that can only be known by watching others? Ainley et al. (2004) filmed experienced teachers' lessons and asked them to speak to researchers about how and why they had responded as they did, in their lessons. Some of the incidents were those where the researchers felt the teachers had demonstrated what they called 'attention-based knowledge'. Attention based knowledge is what enables experienced teachers to respond effectively to the events of the lesson, but can't be written in lesson plans as it is a response to something that happens in the moment (Ainley et al., 2004: 1–2). Ainley et al. go on to explain that

> a teacher's response to a situation ... is highly particular and not a response driven by a general rule that could have been articulated in advance of the teaching encounter ... attention is an active perceiving and involves selection on behalf of the subject. The knowledge which is gained by and from this attention informs subsequent actions. (Ainley et al., 2004: 2)

Some of the teachers could not remember what had made them act as they had; in other cases, teachers explained their actions or reactions to certain instances of pupil behaviour in terms of paying attention to the pupils' attention, for example if they felt the pupil had misunderstood something. Tuning in to these kinds of subtleties in a lesson could be incredibly helpful to you in responding to similar instances in your own lessons. Being aware of the concept of 'attention-based knowledge' and deliberately looking out for instances of this in the lessons you observe could be enlightening.

Pinder (2008) explored various issues relating to how student teachers she worked with in New Zealand learnt through observing others; 'the student teachers learnt through authentic experiences by making connections with previous learning; from observation and modelling; and through participating in trial and error and problem-solving activity' (Pinder, 2008: 9). Pinder quotes Russell's (1988) view that

> student teachers required knowledge or images of teaching before they could experiment, analyse, and evaluate and that meta-cognitive processes were integral to planning ... several spoke about images that were conjured up in their minds. Faranak [a student teacher in Pinder's research] explained how she made links in her mind when she saw teachers demonstrate the strategies that they had previously explained to her. (Pinder, 2008: 10)

Santagata et al. also noted that student teachers 'need concrete images of innovative and alternative teaching strategies' (2007: 125).

So does watching the lessons of others help to build links between theory and practice, and between your own practice and that of others? Many of the student teachers Pinder worked with used language associated with the visual and the word 'seeing' which meant different things to them. For example, in seeking out examples of how theory worked in practice in others' lessons, selecting particular strategies to deal with different issues, evaluating what worked well or less well in their view, and therefore making decisions about their own future actions in teaching, observation 'provided the security to trial ideas and helped to develop confidence ... observations were frequently used to make decisions about what they would use, modify or adjust before they would implement ideas themselves' (Pinder, 2008: 11). However, Santagata et al. found the idea of observation enabling links between theory and practice problematic for 'field experiences may expose student teachers to a narrow and unrepresentative sample of students. Preservice teachers may easily come to believe that only the strategies they observe are appropriate, regardless of the students they may eventually teach. Development of professional judgement adaptable to differing objectives and student groups may not be developed by limited field experiences' (Feiman–Nemser and Buchmann, 1985; Santagata et al., 2007: 124). They also note that student teachers' interpretations of others' lessons might be inadequate in terms of simply not realising they are seeing something good, bad, innovative, indifferent or something else entirely (Santagata et al., 2007: 124). It would seem that to get the most of observations, as a student teacher it is not enough for you to simply bear witness to the action in front of you, but to be able to interpret the complexity and nature of what you are seeing. Literature about approaches to research can help us to consider what we might need to think about when observing others. For example, Newby (2010) states

> There is a sense amongst some new researchers that observation is easy; all you have to do is walk around until something strikes you. The very great danger of this is that it is the most unusual things that are most striking and the most unusual things are not usually the most useful for understanding and explaining ordered situations and relationships. (Newby, 2010: 361)

Luttrell (2010), too, suggests the importance of a different approach; 'doing qualitative research involves a healthy scepticism about whether "to see is to know" and instead calls upon us to look at people (including ourselves as investigators), places, and events through multiple and critical lenses' (Luttrell, 2010: 1–2). If you substitute the term 'new researchers' for 'new teachers' and consider your observation of others as a kind of qualitative research Newby's and Luttrell's viewpoints may give you something to think about. Does seeing mean knowing? In a recent episode of 'Sherlock Holmes' (BBC, 2012), Holmes impresses a potential client by making detailed, descriptive comments and judgements about different aspects of the person's appearance and character. The perturbed young man exclaims 'but how do you all know all this?' Holmes replies 'I **don't** know, I just notice'.

How to approach lesson observation

So, it would seem important to be able to develop skills of evaluation and analysis to be able to interpret, and then perhaps put into practice as appropriate, what you experience and see when observing others. Noticing the nuances of the classroom situation and tuning in to the subtleties of what might look like an insignificant element or action by a pupil or teacher is important. We have discussed the importance of fixing images of teaching in action in your consciousness, as something concrete to compare your own teaching with. There are various views about how best to learn from watching others teach; 'what counts as effective guidance is still an open question' (Santagata et al., 2007: 124). It has been noted that you may well be given a list of areas/aspects to focus on, especially in early observation activities. But how can you approach the process to get the most from it? In this section, some different ideas for undertaking lesson observation will be considered.

Pinder (2008) found that students benefited from observing others but specifically from having a post-observation discussion with the teacher to explore some of the issues raised, and reflect on the lesson. This was not always easy to arrange but almost always valuable for the observer. If you are able to speak to those you have observed, it is likely that their perspective will give you a much greater appreciation of what went on in the lesson and enhance your understanding. Capel, Leask and Turner (2002: 65) suggest a stage before Pinder's; tell the teacher you are observing what you'd like to focus on *before* the lesson, not to make them change their lesson to fit your needs or interests necessarily, but to be able to be conscious of their actions (and decisions informing those actions) in the lesson, so that they can be recalled and explained afterwards. Taking this position of a focused approach to observation implies that you are really aware of the areas you need to develop in your own practice; if this is the case, you could go one step further and design your own observation tasks; this idea is promoted by Capel, Leask and Turner (2009). Leask et al. also suggest that you 'decide if you plan to be a systematic observer or collect evidence while you support the class teacher' (2002: 58). This is similar to ideas in literature about research and gathering data as an observer; for example, deciding if you are going to try to remain apart from the activity of the lesson, or join in; each of these is a valid way of approaching observation, but will have different effects or benefits. Sitting quietly in the same place in the classroom during the lesson may enable you to notice a greater range of activity; you are also more likely to have time there and then to reflect on what you are seeing. If you act in the observed lesson as a teaching assistant, you may miss certain interactions, and you will also have more of an effect on how the lesson progresses. But interacting with pupils in the lesson allows you to consider a different dimension (e.g., how pupils are feeling about the lesson) which you would not be able to access if you had decided to sit in the corner and take notes. Somekh and Jones (2005: 140) describe joining in a situation to be observed as 'participant observation' and state 'participant observers gain unique insights into the behaviour and activities of those they observe because they participate in their activities and, to some extent, are absorbed into the culture of the group' (Somekh and Jones, 2005: 140). It is important to note Somekh and Jones's warning that 'observers always have some kind of effect on those they are observing, who, at worst, may become tense and have a strong sense of performing, even of being inspected' (2005: 140). These kinds of negative effects could apply to teachers or pupils alike and can be avoided or at least minimised if you take a professional approach (e.g., being careful in your notes and spoken references to events in the lesson which didn't go well; even the best teachers are not perfect and even the most apparently confident may not relish being overly-scrutinised and/or criticised by a beginning teacher). Remember that pupils are also aware who you are and why you are there.

Points for reflection

- In your observation of an experienced colleague's lessons, try out the different role of 'participant observer' (supporting the teacher and the pupils) and 'systematic observer' (sitting quietly in the classroom); how do the different approaches help you to understand (and learn from) what is happening in the lesson?
- List some specific issues you would like to focus on in the lesson you will observe, which are related to your own areas for development, for example, time management, explaining concepts, behaviour management; during the lesson try to concentrate on examples of these issues.

As noted above, Santagata et al. (2007) used videos of lessons to enable student teachers to develop greater skills of analysis, arguing that videos could help students 'discriminate between ways in which learners comprehend subject matter, identify problematic features, assess student responses, and detect, diagnose and develop instructional responses to student errors' (Santagata et al., 2007: 125–6). Santagata et al. believed that student teachers watching films allowed for greater analysis than a 'live' lesson; their recordings of lessons could be watched more than once to consider different perspectives and paused to discuss particular points. The different perspectives students were asked to consider were:

1 parts of the lesson and learning goals (the main sections of the lesson and how each part related to the overall aims);
2 pupils' thinking and learning (focusing on pupils' behaviour and how they approached tasks given to them by the teacher);
3 alternative teaching strategies (what could be done differently and the possible effects of these suggestions) (adapted from Santagata et al., 2007: 128).

The student teachers watched the same filmed lesson three times, each time focusing on one of the above aspects; they

> improved their analyses of teaching by moving from simple descriptions of what they observed to analyses focused on the effects of teacher actions on student learning as observed in the video ...[the] video provided the opportunity to slow down the teaching process to reflect in ways not possible during live observations. (Santagata et al., 2007: 138)

Krull et al., (2010) proposed a model for student teachers to observe lessons which 'is based on the idea that the quality of lesson analysis skills depends mainly on teachers' perception of relevant instructional events and on their understanding of their events' (Krull et al., 2010: 197). In other words, to benefit from observing a teacher in a lesson, you must first know what a lesson is, and the conditions or 'critical events' most likely to result in pupils' learning. Krull et al. explore Gagné's and Driscoll's (1988) idea of the lesson as the sequence or unit of learner activities necessary for achieving the intended learning objectives '... teaching from this point of view means creating external conditions so that a pupil, in coping with them, acquires learning experiences' (Tyler, 1949). However, a teacher has to make 'a clear distinction between the analysis of the learner's task and the analysis of his [sic, the teacher's] task' (Krull et al., 2010: 198).

This is a fundamental point in not only preparing for your own teaching, but also in terms of an approach to watching others; when you observe a lesson, it will be useful to watch the pupils closely as well as the teacher, and of course the interplay between the two. Krull et al. discuss Gagne's nine 'phases' or 'events' most likely to happen within a lesson 'for supporting the internal processes of learning' (Krull et al., 2010: 199); these are

1 gaining attention;
2 informing the learner of the learning objective;
3 stimulating recall of prior learning;
4 presenting the material for learning;
5 providing learning guidance;

6 eliciting performance;
7 providing feedback;
8 assessing performance; and
9 enhancing retention and transfer. (Krull et al., 2010: 199)

It is important to note that the above may or may not happen in the order they are set down here, or may need to be repeated/revisited during a lesson. It will be interesting for you in your observation of others, to recognise these events or phases. Interestingly, Krull et al. trained a group of student teachers to use Gagné's list to observe their more experienced colleagues' lessons, and compared their resulting analyses with a group of similar students, who had not undergone training; the former group 'developed a higher sensitivity towards incidences of joint learning and teaching events' (Krull et al., 2010: 207). Krull et al. also recommended that although the nine areas provide a useful starting point, it would be appropriate for the elements of the model to be used as guidelines, or starting points for observing and analysing a lesson, rather than 'step-by-step recipes for lesson design' (Krull et al., 2010: 209).

Krull et al. also asked experienced teachers to use the framework to analyse their own lessons, which had been filmed; they found that the students trained in using Gagné's framework came up with similar levels of analysis, which proved useful to their development as teachers. Others have undertaken research in comparing how experienced and novice teachers approach the observation of their own and their colleagues' lessons. For example, Needels' (1991) work comparing experienced teachers with student teachers' analysis of observed lessons found that

> the experienced teachers ... elaborated more upon their assessment of the lesson. This elaboration is attributable to the greater knowledge about classroom teaching and learning that these teachers possess. In addition, the teachers displayed a deeper understanding of alternative teaching practices and temporal and logical sequences within the lesson. ...The specific topics they discussed showed a greater understanding of the complexity of teaching and the interconnection of elements of a lesson. (Needels, 1991: 278)

It will not be surprising to you that experienced teachers can 'see' more in a lesson than you, or understand the complexities of the different elements more thoroughly than a student teacher; but Needels makes the point that teacher education needs to

> place stronger emphasis on helping novice teachers to understand the complexities of teaching and the relationships between the elements of teaching ... consideration of the

interconnection of teaching strategies and content provides a richer understanding of classroom teaching. (1991: 278)

Points for reflection

- Use Krull's nine areas to structure your observation of another teacher's lesson and make notes in each section.
- Critically reflect on your notes and consider what they tell you about the lesson, but also about what you have focused on in terms of the different areas.
- Discuss your notes with the teacher you observed after the lesson; how does their view of the lesson compare to yours?

Case study 3.2 Noticing, interpreting and reflecting

'I watched how my mentor responded to a question by a pupil during the demonstration – it would have thrown me off course but the teacher just went with it – the whole direction of the lesson changed; this really made me consider those "in the here and now" decisions – there isn't really a right way to deal with these times when your realise what you decide will change the lesson, but it's important for me to at least recognise those moments for what they are.'

'In the lesson most of the pupils were very busy all the time and enjoying themselves but there was one boy who was doing very little and the teacher did not pick up on this at all – the boy was very quiet and didn't cause any trouble.'

'I didn't agree with how the teacher dealt with a pupil who kept on misbehaving – it wasn't effective at all – I would have taken a different approach.'

(Continued)

(Continued)

'My mentor who I observed gave a really difficult pupil "a look" and this sorted them out ... it was a small thing but made all the difference.'

The students' comments above show a difference from those made in case study 3.1; they were made by student teachers further into their PGCE course, who had gained more experience of observing others. The comments show differing degrees of noticing, interpreting and evaluating what they have seen of others' work. The students have commented on different elements within a lesson and one is left with the feeling that they have begun to learn different things from observation and they are beginning to see teaching not as a sequence of techniques and activities, but inter-connected events and interactions between teachers and pupils.

Conclusion

To conclude, I have suggested that there is much to be learnt from observing others, but you need to be prepared to go beyond simply watching and describing events if you are to really benefit from the experience in your own development. Some different models for drawing your attention to the different elements of a lesson have been suggested; it is also recommended that you video lessons and watch them again, from a variety of perspectives. The opportunity to have a post- or even pre-lesson observation discussion with the teacher you observe could also be incredibly useful in helping you to develop a greater understanding of the reasons your colleague acted as they did. These various approaches should enable you to evaluate and interpret the complexities of the different events in a lesson, in ways you can then test in your own practice. This process is unlikely to be straightforward, as all classrooms and groups of pupils are different; however, it gives you somewhere to begin to develop your own practices.

Reflective questions

1 Based on your understanding of the chapter, what do you think you can do in the future to get the most from observing others?

2 Reflecting on lesson observations you have undertaken so far, what have been the most useful things to you, in terms of helping you to progress?
3 What do you understand to be the key messages or themes from this chapter for you?
4 What advice would you give to students beginning their PGCE course about how best to approach lesson observation?

Recommended further reading 

Newby, P. (2010) *Research Methods for Education.* Harlow: Pearson Education.
This is very thorough guide to many different aspects of research; the section on observation in Chapter 8 (pages 360–83) provides lots of starting points for how to do lesson observation, and discusses important issues in observation, such as bias, different kinds of roles observers take and provides some interesting historical perspectives on how observation has developed as a research practice.

Wragg, E.C. (2011) *An Introduction to Lesson Observation* (Classic Edition). Abingdon: Routledge.
This is a recent edition of a book considered *the* classic text on lesson observation written in a very accessible and clear style; it includes many excellent suggestions for approaching observation, with case studies and photographs, in different contexts.

References

Ainley, J., Luntley, M. and Jones, I. 'What teachers know'. Paper presented at the British Educational Research Association Annual Conference, University of Manchester 16–18 September 2004. Available online at http://www.leeds.ac.uk/educol/documents/00003870.htm (accessed 11 November 2011).

Capel, S., Leask, M. and Turner, T. (2002) *Learning to Teach in the Secondary School A Companion to School Experience*, 3rd edn (5th edn 2009). London: RoutledgeFalmer.

Capel, S., Leask, M. and Turner, T. (2009) *Learning to Teach in the Secondary School A Companion to School Experience*, 5th edn. Abingdon: Routledge.
This is an excellent guide to many different aspects of initial teacher education; the different sections related to lesson observation are very useful and consider many different aspects of the process and suggest all kinds of foci which go beyond the 'tick list' approach.

Feiman-Nemser, S. and Buchmann, M. (1985) 'Pitfalls of experience in teacher preparation', *Teachers College Record*, 87(1), 53–65 in Santagata, R., Zannoni, C. and Stigler, J.W. (2007) 'The role of lesson analysis in pre-service teacher education: an empirical investigation of teacher learning from a virtual video-based field experience', *Journal of Math Teacher Education*, 10, 123–40.

Fuller, F.F. and Manning, B.A. (1973) 'Self-confrontation reviewed: a conceptualization for video playback in teacher education', *Review of Educational Research*, 43 (4): 469–528.

Gagné, R.M. and Driscoll, M.P. (1988) *Essentials of Learning for Instruction*, 2nd edn. Englewood Cliffs, NJ: Prentice Hall in Krull, E., Oras, K. and Pikksaar, E. (2010) 'Promoting student teachers' lesson analysis and observation skills by using Gagné's model of an instructional unit', *Journal of Education for Teaching*, 36 (2):197–210.

Hayes, D. (2001) 'The impact of mentoring and tutoring student primary teacher's achievements: a case study', *Mentoring* and *Tutoring*, 9 (1): 6–21.

Hodkinson, H. and Hodkinson, P. (1999) 'Teaching to learn, learning to teach? School-based non-teaching activity in an initial teacher education and training partnership scheme', *Teaching and Teacher Education*, 15 (3): 273–85.

Krull, E., Oras, K. and Pikksaar, E. (2010) 'Promoting student teachers' lesson analysis and observation skills by using Gagné's model of an instructional unit', *Journal of Education for Teaching*, 36 (2):197–210.

Luttrell, W. (ed.) (2010) *Qualitative Educational Research Readings in Reflexive Methodology and Transformative Practice*. Abingdon: Routledge.

Needels, M.C. (1991) 'Comparison of student, first year, and experienced teachers' interpretations of a first grade lesson teaching and teacher education', 7 (3): 269–78.

Newby, P. (2010) *Research Methods for Education*. Harlow: Pearson Education.

Pinder, H. (2008) 'Navigating the practicum: student teacher perspectives on their learning'. Paper presented at the British Educational Research Association Annual Conference, Heriot-Watt University, Edinburgh, 3–6 September 2008. Paper accessed via Education Online 10 November 2011URL:http://www.leeds.ac.uk/educol/documents/174930.pdf

Russell, T. (1988) 'From pre-service teacher education to first year of teaching: a study of theory and practice', in J. Calderhead (ed.), *Teachers' Professional Knowledge* (pp. 13–34). London: The Falmer Press, in Pinder, H. (2008) *Navigating the Practicum: Student Teacher Perspectives on their Learning*. Paper presented at the British Educational Research Association Annual Conference, Heriot-Watt University, Edinburgh, 3–6 September 2008. Paper accessed via Education Online 10 November 2011.

Santagata, R., Zannoni, C. and Stigler, J.W. (2007) 'The role of lesson analysis in pre-service teacher education: an empirical investigation of teacher learning from a virtual video-based field experience', *Journal of Math Teacher Education*, 10, 123–40.

Somekh, B. and Jones, L. (2005) *Research Methods in the Social Sciences*. London: Sage.

Tyler, R.W. (1949) 'Basic principles of curriculum and instruction', Chicago: University of Chicago Press, in Krull, E., Oras, K. and Pikksaar, E. (2010) 'Promoting student teachers' lesson analysis and observation skills by using Gagné's model of an instructional unit', *Journal of Education for Teaching*, 36 (2): 197–210.

CHAPTER 4

WHY IS *CRITICAL* REFLECTION IMPORTANT?

Jon Tibke and Lindsay Poyner

By the end of this chapter you should be able to:

- understand the concept of learning from reflection as a professional activity;
- examine key theories and models that underpin reflective practice;
- explore how you might respond to a variety of situations upon which you reflect;
- consider evidence from recent trainee teachers of their perceptions and experience of reflective practice.

By studying this chapter, we hope that you will start to appreciate the benefit of learning to reflect in a purposeful and effective manner. Reflection does not simply happen through participating in teaching practice and writing assignments. Critical reflection, linked to sustained development during your initial practice and beyond, requires you to think more deeply about your actions and interactions with others and to consider what and how you learn from these experiences. As you develop your practice, the focus of your reflection will enable you to consider how your teaching impacts on the learning of your pupils. This chapter will explore the reasons why it is important for you to reflect on your experiences during your first steps in teaching. It will *analyse* selected areas of research and *identify* some of the challenges that beginning teachers face in developing the skills of reflection. We will offer *practical ideas* for you as a student teacher about how to manage the process of critical reflection and support you in *understanding* how reflective practice enhances the multi-faceted role of a teacher. We will also draw on an individual trainee teacher's experiences and identify some potential starting points to demonstrate the *reflective process*.

Learning from reflection, reflective practitioner, and reflective practice: what does all this mean?

Reflection is a word with which you will already be familiar and it is linked to *learning about something or learning from something*. For example you revisit in your mind something that has already happened and plan ahead, taking account of your evaluation of past events, in order to anticipate what might happen in the future. Sometimes reflection may also help you to identify future learning needs and provides an opportunity to try out ideas developing from thinking about *something*.

In the context of *your* professional development, the importance of a clear and shared understanding of the concept of *critical* reflection and the way it relates to the development of your classroom practice and professional role is of paramount importance. As a beginning teacher, you are likely to be encouraged to become a 'reflective practitioner', as this is seen as an essential attribute of effective, well qualified teachers who are able to evaluate their work and plan their own development. However, at this stage we will begin by focusing on how you can start to learn from reflection about your practice and that of others.

Case studies will be used in order to simplify and unpick reflection; as we explore the various stages of the process, you will start to become aware that reflection can happen at any time in response to a range of stimuli and does not follow a pre-set sequence. Learning through reflection requires you to revisit many of your beliefs, assumptions and actions and is therefore a challenging, reflexive and often untidy process. As Boud and Walker (1998) point out, models and cycles can help us understand the concept of reflection but should not be looked on as an 'operational process'. Moon (2008) raises a further consideration in pointing out that the cycles and phases of models are often over-simplified, under represent the haphazard nature of the reflective process and suggested steps or stages are unlikely to match exactly the specific nature of individuals' experiences. However, models of reflection can support us in finding somewhere to begin the process.

Dewey (1990) suggested that reflection is a form of problem-solving and proposed three attributes that are important to the process of reflective thinking:

- **open-mindedness** – being aware that there is a dilemma and being open to thinking about it in different ways;
- **responsibility** – wanting to respond to the dilemma in a different way and being willing to act, being responsible for your own learning;
- **wholeheartedness** – accepting that actions have both intended and unintended consequences and a realization that dilemmas are often ill structured and can have different outcomes depending on the situation.

When used in the context of your earliest placement experiences and observations, reflection may simply involve thinking, discussion, dialogue or description of something that has caught your attention or interest. So, at a simple level, reflection is part of your *cognitive processing*, that is noticing and thinking, and needs your active engagement; however, it is not a passive process and requires intentional action. In order for you to enhance your professional development, you need to do something more than just thinking, pondering or meditating about an issue. Critical reflection requires you to also consider your beliefs, attitudes and assumptions whilst organising and reorganising your knowledge and understanding (Alger, 2006). This can sometimes be an uncomfortable and challenging process.

Case study 4.1 The reflections of Laura

In the following case study you have an opportunity to explore the reflections of Laura, a student teacher on her first school placement, and your own initial reactions and further thoughts. To start with, we will consider a classroom management issue in relation to effective lesson starts. In the early stages, Laura had been provided with a framework in her placement journal to guide her initial steps in **critical reflection**: (Ward and McCotter, 2004). Laura was observing her subject mentor's lesson.

(Continued)

(Continued)

Dilemma: how should I start a lesson and deal with a late pupil?

Step 1: make a record of your experiences

> 'In my first week of placement I observed my subject mentor starting a lesson. A pupil entered the room 5 minutes late and *was ignored by the teacher who continued with the lesson as if there had been no interruption!*'

I made a note of this in my lesson observation notes.

Step 2: initial analysis

> 'Following the lesson observation, I did some reading about behaviour management (school policy and a text book) and talked to some fellow students. I was quite shocked when the teacher ignored the pupil, when I was at school teachers were quite strict and would not tolerate this lateness, let alone ignore it!'

In the scenario above Laura is engaged in the **process of reflection**. This has led to the development of a **theory** about how best to deal with late pupils at the start of a lesson. Note also that **feelings and beliefs based on prior, personal experience** are also involved in Laura's reflective process.

Step 3: develop a plan of action

> 'From what I have learnt so far and after discussing this with fellow students, I decided that the teacher was wrong. In addition the school policy about behaviour code states that pupils should not arrive late to lessons and the staff handbook states that all late arrivals must be recorded. After further consideration I have decided that when I take the class I will have zero tolerance for pupils coming in late to my lessons.'

Points for reflection

- If you had observed something similar what would your response be?
- Reflect on Laura's scenario by considering the following prompts:
  - What is your analysis? Draw on your own experiences.
  - What would you think?
  - What would you feel?

- What would you decide to do?
- Why?
- To what extent do you think that Laura displays Dewey's three attributes of reflective thinking? Consider how Laura displays these three attributes in more detail:
  - **open-mindedness** – being aware that there is a dilemma;
  - **responsibility** – wanting to respond to the dilemma in a different way and being willing to act;
  - **wholeheartedness** – aware that actions have both intended and unintended consequences.

In considering Dewey's three attributes that foster the reflective thinking process, Laura has clearly decided to take **responsibility** for dealing with a late pupil. She is **wholehearted** in the way she intends to apply her plan. However it could be argued here that Laura's prior experiences have influenced her perceptions and future planning. She has yet to develop a more **open-minded** consideration of her options, so in order for Laura to start to be 'critically reflective', she needs to consider the implications for her practice right from the start. Ideas gathered from observations of practice are part of the reflective process (Pollard and Collins, 2005).

Table 4.1 summarises her reflection on this issue so far.

Table 4.1 Scaffolding to promote reflection at the start of placement

Dilemma 1: How to start a lesson promptly and deal with a late pupil.		
Step 1:	Observation. What gets your attention? What are you aware of? What is your perception?	A pupil comes into class late when the teacher is explaining the lesson. *The teacher ignores the late pupil.*
Step 2:	Initial analysis. What do you think? Why do you think this? What do you feel?	I felt shocked that the pupil was rudely interrupting the lesson and the teacher did nothing. When I was a pupil, teachers were stricter.
Step 3:	What is the plan of action? Why has this decision been made? What is the likely result of this action?	The school behaviour code says that punctuality is important and there will be consequences for bad behaviour. I will challenge late pupils to my lessons and give them a detention. This will set an example so pupils will know not to mess me about.
	What feelings are involved?	Anxiety in case pupils 'try it on', worried about them challenging my authority.
Step 4:	Re-consider the event: what other perspectives could have been considered?	The subject mentor: The pupil: The class:

Points for reflection

- How might this Laura develop her practice in step 4?
- Suggest alternatives by considering the dilemma from different perspectives:
  - perspective of the subject mentor;
  - perspective of the late pupil;
  - perspective of the rest of the class.
- What might be both the intended and unintended consequences of their actions?

Developing critical reflection

The cognitive skill of 'critical reflection' is the start of your development as a reflective practitioner; reflection on your practice goes further than just a simple evaluation. Deeper consideration of alternative approaches will enable you to examine a range of considerations and perspectives in order to enhance both your understanding of the circumstances and the actions you subsequently choose to take. In a professional context, this will include a consideration of the theories that underpin your practice.

Laura has reflected on one of her learning experiences; however at the moment she has only considered the dilemma from her own perspective. Her reflection is limited to how she will respond to the late pupil and her reason for choosing this plan of action. In developing her plan, she draws on her own experiences as a secondary school pupil and her own values, attitudes and beliefs as a beginning teacher.

Further reflection will enhance the quality and depth of Laura's learning and will help her to re-examine her prior experiences alongside theories introduced on her course. By considering the situation from the perspective of others, she can develop an awareness of the possible implications of her decision to have '*zero tolerance for lateness*'. Rather than thinking that an action is '*right or wrong*' she will start to consider '*What could have been done differently? Is there an alternative?*'

Unforeseen situations trigger the need to explore alternative ways of acting in a situation and in teaching and working with children and young people you will have to deal with complex and ill-defined dilemmas. Reflection is helping Laura to understand the complexity of a seemingly simple dilemma and as she gains in experience this will help her to develop the capacity to make judgements even when situations are less familiar (Brookfield, 1987).

Often there will not be one straightforward solution to a dilemma and if Laura had talked things through with her subject mentor too, she may have gained an insight into the reason why her mentor chose to act in the way he or she did. Dialogue and the sharing of ideas, actions and thoughts have shaped your thinking from your earliest years and you did not do this in isolation from others; your understanding of the world around you has been developed through interacting with and through other significant people (social constructivism). The same is true with your school experience in which you have the opportunity to develop both your practice and to explore the theories that underpin this. As Dysthe states, 'the learner builds knowledge through discussions with peers, teachers and tutors' (2002: 343).

Your course is likely to emphasise that you need to start to become more aware of the reasons for professional action and to make links to theories of learning introduced as part of your course. Your professional studies are part of your development in becoming 'open-minded' and 'responsible' as well as becoming more aware of the reasons behind your perceptions. One way to do this is to question, compare perspectives and consider new ideas and information – 'wholeheartedness'.

As a reflective student teacher, we hope that you will seek to understand how you learn and by doing so you will start to develop a deeper understanding of how children and young people learn (Moon, 2008).

Case study 4.1 continued Laura's reflections at the end of week 3

As noted above, Laura had observed her mentor early on in her placement and was shocked by the teacher ignoring a pupil who arrived late and the absence of any apology from the pupil. Here are Laura's later thoughts and reflections after talking to another student in the staffroom later in the day, and in subsequent weeks:

> 'In the staffroom later I told the other students, they were shocked too as the pupil had shown complete disrespect for the teacher. The school policy says we should follow C1, C2 etc.; and my reading says that you should make sure that you are consistent. I have decided that when I take the class I will have zero tolerance for pupils coming in late into class and will ask them why they are late and give the an immediate C1.

(Continued)

(Continued)

Week 3: now is my chance to teach a lesson I am feeling excited and a bit nervous but have planned everything carefully – my mentor will be observing

Evaluation following my first lesson with Year 9 which was observed by my subject mentor:

I have been in this school now for 3 weeks and I have the mentor's Year 9 class to teach, my mentor was sitting at the back and observing my lesson. All was going well at the start of the lesson and the pupils were sitting in silence as I was talking about the work.

Then pupil X came in late and so I asked them why they were late, told them to sit at the front where I could keep an eye on them and gave them a break time detention to make up the missing time. X then said, 'It's not fair'! I can't really remember what happened next but the pupil kept on arguing with me and before I knew it the whole class started to misbehave, I couldn't get them to listen to me. Then my mentor had to calm things down before I could get on with the lesson.

The whole thing turned into a bit of a disaster. That pupil (X) is quite rude and badly behaved and so are the rest of the class. The mentor undermined me in front of the class, I am really feeling quite angry about this all and very unhappy because I had spent hours preparing this lesson and it went badly wrong and I really wanted to create a good impression and get a positive observation.

Two days later: I was thinking about that lesson again because I have my weekly meeting with my mentor. I have noted some points that I need to discuss further with them.

I was re-reading my evaluation of the lesson, now I have calmed down a bit I have a slightly different perspective*; I don't think that my mentor was trying to undermine me at all – they have a responsibility to the class and to me and could see that things were going downhill when I was not aware of what the whole class was doing*. I was so determined to make the pupil do what I wanted – I had my attention on X and not on the class*. I now realise that behaviour management is a bit more than just sticking to the policy and that I was the one who asked the pupil to explain and then I didn't give them a chance*. Both the pupil and I lost our tempers – how can I expect the pupil to keep calm in that situation? I wouldn't like to be treated like this and would have probably reacted in the same way if I had been a pupil (in fact that was my immediate reaction to the mentor stepping in to calm the class down – emotional again!)*

* These are the points that I need to work on and develop and will discuss with my mentor. Perhaps ignoring the pupil lets both the teacher and the pupil remain in control in some way. Behaviour management is a bit more than just following the rules; it is not just about bossing people about because I am the teacher and then expecting them to do what I say.'

The diagram below is developed from Kolb's learning cycle and incorporates ideas developed in this chapter. Some students engage in reflection (to the right of the diagram); however their focus is concentrated on themselves. This is the likely situation at the start of the first practice. As knowledge and understanding of the complexity of a teacher's role develops, reflection encompasses more of the elements shown on the left of the diagram. Truly reflective practitioners (we would argue) never stop learning and continue to reflect on ways in which they can develop their practice.

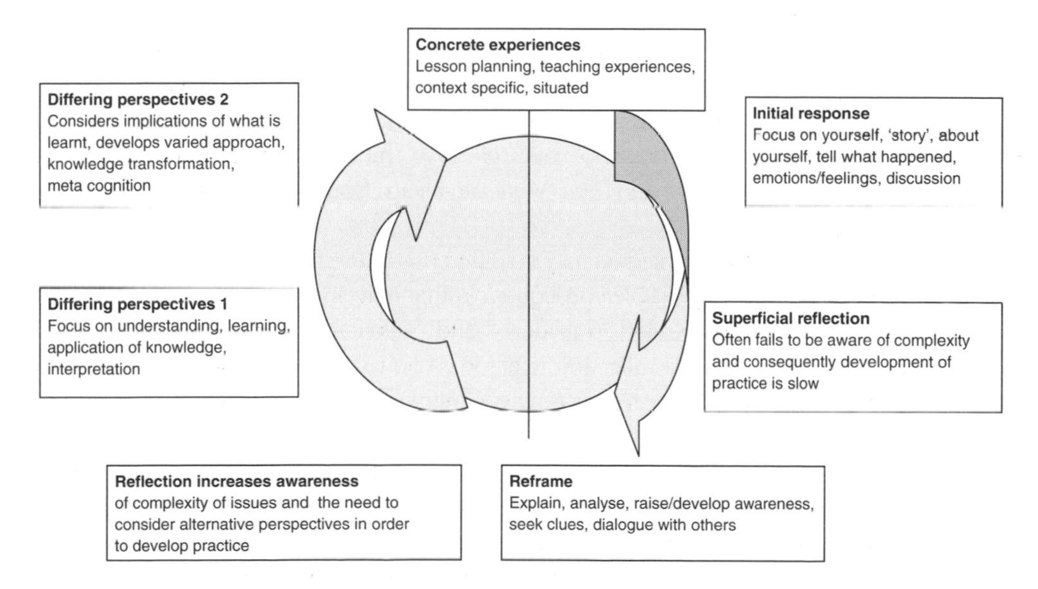

Figure 4.1 Reflection for beginning teachers, adapted from Kolb's learning cycle (Kolb, 1984)

In Laura's account note the significance of dialogue. This may be with fellow students, school colleagues and tutors; dialogue offers a range of perspectives and the chance to 're-frame' the dilemma. Moore and Ash (2002) point out that this dialogue also occurs with family and friends. This can be helpful, but perhaps needs caution, as you are bound by expectations of confidentiality and professional standards. Your university tutor or other professional can provide important support and coaching as you 're-frame' the event; in addition, they can provide critique in their feedback to challenge your assumptions further. Thus reflection is not solely introspective and your engagement in discourse with others moves your reflection away from introspection to that of a deliberative effort to improve future actions.

This is what Laura thought in week 4 of her school experience reflections: '"learning from reflection" is building on previous experiences in a positive way to further your development; it means analysing your performance to better understand what worked and what could be done to improve things'.

Ward and McCotter (2004) describe the development of reflective thinking and use the terms 'focus, enquiry and change' to describe the kind of reflection that beginning teachers develop as they evaluate, understand and improve their teaching, focusing on its relationship to pupil learning. An important turning point occurs when a beginning teachers moves away from a narrow analysis of their own performance and behaviour to a wider consideration of the effect of their actions on pupils' learning.

Critical reflection therefore starts as a deliberate process: taking time within the course of your work to focus on your performance: the initial stage will comprise routine reflective thinking. Often you may do this as part of a lesson evaluation. Then as you develop your practice we would encourage you to start to review the thinking that led to particular actions because this will develop your reflective thinking further; for example, by considering 'What happened?' and then 'What can I learn from this?' as part of your reflective dialogue.

Finally in order to inform what you may do differently in the future you need to consider a range of options and the possible consequences that may arise (the stage of transformative reflection). Ideas are recalled, considered and evaluated in order to govern future actions and behaviour. Critical reflection may force you to face uncomfortable questions, and so it may prompt you to restructure your strategy or your ways of framing and re-framing the 'problem'.

A further dimension occurs when you consider how your emotions may have guided your decision making and actions (Gibbs, 1988). Beginning teachers often find reflection difficult in the early stages and it takes time to develop; when you go into schools for the first time as an educator you will be encouraged to make sense of experiences and to reflect on or reason why things happen. It could be argued that the **process** of reflection for you is fostered using observation-based reflective practice and is as important as the gaining of new insights (Schön, 1987; Kolb, 1984). Thus reflection that aids your development should enable you to consider what you have learnt from the experience and how this relates to theories that you have been taught or researched.

There are several models of reflection that you may come across in your reading of the literature. For example: Kolb's learning cycle provides a model for reflection where 'concrete' experience is often used as a starting point although reflection can begin at any point in the cycle. Moon (2008) considers the changes adults make to their 'meaning schemes', made up of values, attitudes and emotional responses and that new perspectives are developed when the meaning schemes are changed to accommodate alternative perspectives. Gibbs (1988) and Johns and Graham (1996) add to this by linking the influence of feelings and emotions in their respective reflective models. As a beginning teacher, your attention is drawn to the fact that feelings, prior experiences and many unchallenged assumptions influence your responses and expectations and that by developing awareness through critical reflection you can start to consider why things happen in certain ways. Thus it is the individual **process** of learning through reflection prompted by both curiosity and questioning, together with an eagerness for information and an ability to draw on initiative and imaginative vision, that underpins the thinking on reflection in education. Atkins and Murphy (1994) make direct reference to personal views and feelings that may influence your reactions and thoughts, suggesting that the reflective practitioner should 'analyse feelings and knowledge relevant to the situation' and 'to imagine and explore alternatives'. Gail Fuller's chapter in this book also explores the importance of acknowledging the emotional dimension in developing your own identity as a teacher.

As already noted, in the early stages you are likely to be guided by your own personal experiences of being a pupil together with theories taught on your course. These guide your decision-making and reflection as you make the transition from student teacher (being taught) to classroom teacher (learning to be a teacher). Laura is actively engaged in learning from the past and the present; her perceptions of new events are affected by this in order for further learning to take place and she is deliberately trying to make sense of her experiences (Boud, 2001). You need to be aware that emotions play a factor in our learning; this may lead to a focus on negative events as Laura did. It is important to examine successful phases of learning in order to identify what factors underpin effectiveness and how these might be replicated in other circumstances. It is neither healthy nor professionally effective, to dwell exclusively on difficulties and errors, important though it undoubtedly is to analyse such experiences in the context of your first classroom experiences.

Brookfield (1987) reminds us that positive experiences and 'joyful incidents', provide opportunities for 'sudden insight or self-awareness' and that these events are 'fulfilling' and illuminating. Laura thought that reflection gave her a means to improve her practice by evaluating what she had achieved so far and building upon this. She also thought that by considering her practice, in terms of what went well and what could have been better, she could adapt future practice in the classroom and beyond.

Developing practice through critical reflection

Laura is now half way through her first placement and is starting to consider a range of different strategies and ideas. Open-mindedness to new and different ways will help you start to get an insight into the complexities of teaching and that there is no one 'best' solution or approach. This is the first step to becoming a critically reflective practitioner, developing awareness of both your own practice and thinking as it is at the present time and of ways in which you can develop them further. Laura has now moved beyond a simple description of events with one explanation for an action or behaviour and is able to consider others' perspectives and offer alternative approaches. Reflection developed in this way means that you are less likely to become complacent and more likely to look for alternative ways to be more effective. One way in which you may develop your critically reflective skills is by developing empathy – being able to see a situation from another's point of view.

Once again it may be helpful to continue to reflect on the original dilemma faced by Laura.

Laura started to acknowledge that there are a range of responses to a given situation and that she may need to adapt her approach for specific pupils and/or classes or at differing times of day. She began to imagine the negative and positive effects of taking certain decisions, for example, if she decided to keep latecomers in at break time, she might gain credibility with the pupils as their teacher for carrying out school policies, but she would be giving up a lot of her own valuable time. Reflection can take place in anticipation of events. Teachers can be proactive and consider a range of options in order to prepare for what might happen.

Points for reflection

You have planned a ten-minute starter activity using the interactive whiteboard; however the computer system was down and you have to make up an alternative and think on your feet. Your mentor was observing you.

- What would your reflections on this situation be?
- Consider how you would deal with a situation like this in the future and the reasons for your chosen approaches.

We consider that it is important for you as a beginning teacher to consciously reflect on the ways in which you can develop your present understanding, and consider the possible consequences of alternative ways of doing this by 'reframing the event'. Note that the focus is the link between your behaviour and actions and the impact they may have on the response of other people. One way that you might explore the development of your own practice is by engaging in activities and reading mindfully, what Brookfield (1987: 22) defines as, 'a readiness to test the validity of claims made by others for any presumed givens, final solutions, and ultimate truths against one's own experience of the world', in order to develop knowledge and professional understanding. You may wish to consider the ethical, moral and political contexts of educational, social and emotional issues and questions related to equity, access and social justice.

Finally, as you develop your practice through critical reflection, you will start to become more aware of the impact of your teaching on the learning of the pupils. Here is an example of the initial reflection from Alex who has almost completed his first teaching placement.

> Learning from reflection means the contemplation of a learning experience and subsequent changes in practice ... Initially I had a challenge preparing lessons to accommodate the needs of pupils in one of my Year 10 classes. There were many SEN pupils that required a lot of differentiation preparation. Through reflection and discussion with the learning assistants and my mentor, I was able to develop a number of teaching and learning strategies to include the pupils more effectively. For example: one particular pupil gained more from a visual style of recording information rather than writing.

Case study 4.2

Steve is now two weeks into his final placement and is teaching a Year 9 class His target is to focus on the learning of individuals in the class. He

(Continued)

(Continued)

supports what he considers a lively, engaging approach to learning, with much discussion and practical activity. The class have not been taught in this manner before.

Leigh, a Year 9 pupil, has caused a number of difficulties in the first few lessons with Steve. Initially, Steve has taken a patient approach to some silly behaviour and low-level disruption for which Leigh appears to be the focal point.

Having followed the first steps of the school's consequences system, Steve eventually keeps Leigh in for a lunchtime detention, as there has been no improvement. During the detention, Leigh tells Steve about some lessons that 'went down well' last year. Steve is unsure whether this is some sort of advice or implied criticism of his lessons.

Following the detention, Leigh makes promises of improved behaviour and concentration and these seem genuine, but in the next lesson there is no improvement and Steve takes a much more stern and demanding approach. Leigh becomes upset and insists that, 'I really did mean to try to make improvements.'

On reflection after the lesson Steve thinks: 'it was not until I thought about what had happened that I understood that I had been manipulated by the pupil'.

Points for reflection

Consider the case study above.

- What factors do you think influenced the actions of a) Leigh and b) Steve?
- What impact might Steve's personal feelings and beliefs have had on working towards a resolution of this issue?
- What additional information might Steve seek and from what sources?
- How might Steve re-focus the issues so that this becomes an issue related to promoting learning rather than behaviour management?

Conclusion

We believe reflection is a form of learning encouraged in many teacher development courses as a way to connect the theory and practice elements. Critical reflection is a form of cognitive engagement and provides opportunities for deeper processing about an event or dilemma which can then provide insight and alternative perspectives. Reflection provides a means to consider and reconsider your own values, attitudes and beliefs and depends on you developing an awareness of the constructed nature of knowledge and understanding.

Reflection also provides opportunities to learn from experiences and identify personal learning points. Critical reflection gives you the awareness to recognise the link between your emotional state, motivation and rational thought. Reflection provides a 'thinking space' in which you can recognise that your own behaviour has an impact on the behaviour of others (both intended and unintended).

Reflective questions

1. Consider Dewey's three attributes of open-mindedness, responsibility and wholeheartedness. How do you usually respond to unforeseen situations?
2. Provide examples using Dewey's three attributes. Why do you react in this way?
3. Considering your previous experiences what might be the barriers to reflection in your developing practice?
4. How have your ideas about your practice changed as your course has progressed? What will be your next steps and why?

Recommended further reading

Boud, D. (2001) 'Using journal writing to enhance reflective practice', *New Directions for Adult and Continuing Education*, 90: 9–17.

A useful article considering the value and process of writing as a form of reflection.

Pollard, A. (2008) *Reflective Teaching: Effective and Evidence-informed Professional Practice*, 3rd edn. London: Continuum.

A well-established introduction on reflection in teaching and learning that provides a good balance between theory and practical examples.

Yeomans, J. and Arnold, C. (2006) *Teaching, Learning and Psychology*. London: David Fulton Publishers.

A readable and non-technical introduction with practical insights into how to use an understanding of psychology to enhance teaching and learning.

References

Alger, C. (2006) '"What went well, what didn't go so well": growth of reflection in pre-service teachers', *Reflective Practice*, 7 (3): 287–301.

Atkins, S. and Murphy, K. (1994) 'Reflective practice', *Nursing Standard*, 8 (39): 49–56.

Boud, D. (2001) 'Using journal writing to enhance reflective practice', *New Directions for Adult and Continuing Education*, 90: 9–17.

Boud, D. and Walker, D. (1998) 'Promoting reflection in professional courses: The challenge of context', *Studies In Higher Education*, 23 (2): 191–206. Education Research Complete, EBSCOhost (viewed 16 July 2012).

Brookfield, S. (1987) *Developing Critical Thinkers: Challenging Adults to Explore Alternative Ways of Thinking and Acting*. San Francisco: Jossey-Bass.

Dewey, J. (1990) *The School and Society* and *the Child and the Curriculum* (with new introduction by P. W. Jackson). Chicago: The University of Chicago Press (original publication 1956).

Dysthe, O. (2002) 'The learning potential of a web-mediated discussion in a university course', *Studies in Higher Education*, 27 (3): 339–52.

Gibbs, G. (1998) *Learning by Doing: A Guide to Teaching and Learning Methods.* Oxford: Further Education Unit, Oxford Brookes University.

Johns, C. and Graham, J. (1996) 'Using a reflective model of nursing and guided reflection', *Nursing Standard*, 11 (2): 34–8.

Kolb, D. (1984) *Experiential Learning: Experience as the Source of Learning and Development.* Englewood Cliffs, NJ: Prentice-Hall.

Moon, J. (2008) *Reflection in Learning and Professional Practice*. Abingdon: RoutledgeFalmer.

Moore, A. and Ash, A. (2002) 'Reflective practice in beginning teachers: helps, hindrances and the role of the critical other'. Paper presented at the Annual Conference of BERA, Exeter, 12–14 September, 2002.

Pollard, A. and Collins, J. (2005) *Reflective Teaching: Evidence-Informed Professional Practice*. London : Continuum, University of Cumbria Library Catalogue, EBSCOhost (viewed 16 July 2012).

Schön, D. (1987) *Educating the Reflective Practitioner: Toward a New Design for Teaching and Learning in the Professionals.* San Francisco: Jossey-Bass.

Ward, J. and McCotter, S. (2004) 'Reflection as a visible outcome for preservice Teachers', *Teaching and Teacher Education*, 20 (3): 243–57.

CHAPTER 5

WHAT IS MY PROFESSIONAL IDENTITY?

Martyn Lawson and Martin Watts

By the end of the chapter you should be able to:

- consider your beliefs about teaching; generally what a teacher does and what 'teaching' actually is and then specifically about what you do when you are teaching;
- reflect critically on the factors that might influence your professional identity and how it may, or may not, change over time due to your experience, context or circumstances;
- consider how personal, local and national factors may influence a teacher's identity throughout their career;
- reflect critically on the impact that technology might have on your professional identity as a teacher.

In this chapter we begin by exploring different ways in which a teacher's identity evolves in the course of their experience in the school classroom. We then go on to look at the way in which classroom technology is having an impact on the role and identity of the teacher. Throughout the chapter, we will illustrate our ideas with examples from case studies and interviews with teachers. We have been able to draw on interviews with teaching colleagues working both in the UK and overseas in order to gain a wider perspective and to anticipate how the education system you are entering may change over the course of your career. The international context is provided by a small-scale study conducted in an International School in South-East Asia which provides an opportunity to speculate on future changes as a result of increased technological integration in schools.

Points for reflection

Before we get into the chapter, reflect on these questions:

- What is school for?
- What is education for?
- How are teaching and learning different?
- What types of activities do teachers do?
- What types of activities do learners do?

Hopefully your thinking in response to these questions will provide some stimulus as you follow the rest of the text in this chapter.

The beginner teacher's identity

In 2004, Twiselton published the findings of research she had undertaken with students on initial teacher training courses. She identified a model reflecting three different identities of student teachers. Twiselton suggested that such teachers could be divided into 'task managers', 'curriculum deliverers', or 'concept builders'. There is, of course, a hierarchy implicit in this. A 'task manager' is seen as a teacher who is primarily concerned with basic control over a class and keeping the children occupied by giving them things to do which may or may not develop their learning. A curriculum deliverer is more concerned with getting through the curriculum whether or not the children absorb the learning that is within the curriculum. At the top of the hierarchy is the 'concept developer' whose main focus is on ensuring that children understand and learn appropriately for their age and subject requirements and expectations. Of course, this is a simplified view of teacher identity and, within the model, there is nothing to say that a teacher may not assume different roles at any given time, or indeed exhibit elements of all three roles at once! Also, although the model is presented as hierarchical, thus implicitly, the highest level of the model would appear to be more worthy than the lower ones, this structure can be misleading in terms of over-simplifying the issues. For example in the case study below, the teacher had no option but to concentrate on keeping order in the classroom.

Case study 5.1

This case study is taken from a small-scale unpublished research project by M. Lawson and M. Watts, (2010).

'I'd been teaching for about seven years when I found myself working in a school in a very deprived area of a large Northern town. The school was located on an estate with very high unemployment, many social problems including crime, drugs and prostitution and where many of the children had parents in jail or on remand. The school was at the very bottom of the league tables for SATs results that year. Yet, school was one constant in these children's lives. Whilst everything else around them was perhaps in turmoil, school provided an atmosphere of care and some element of discipline in their otherwise troubled existence. I was asked to take on a Year 6 class by the head teacher. With this class, all I could do was keep order. I didn't teach for a whole term, I just attempted to keep the children safe, quiet and under some kind of control. I kept them busy with "things" to do and the curriculum basically went out of the window. Nothing in my teaching (or life) experience had prepared me for this and it was a source of real concern to me that I wasn't able to teach them any of the curriculum, yet I know I taught them many things related to social skills, concern for others, taking turns and general courtesy. Ofsted would have labelled my teaching unsatisfactory, but I know that these children really got something out of the time we had together.'

Of course, this case study represents an extreme situation, but it illustrates how, for this teacher, task management was about as much as she could achieve with this class. Interviews with other teachers also confirmed how the 'task manager' aspect of teaching can be the dominant personal concern. An interview with an early-career physics teacher entering his third year of teaching revealed that he had similar experiences in his first teaching role. 'Our expectations of the students had to be moderated by the experiences and background of the pupils. I was sometimes happy when we could just engage in meaningful discussion about physics.' This teacher had recently moved on to his second school in which he found pupils had higher expectations of their own learning. Interestingly he found, at this early stage of his career that lesson planning was very important to his role as a teacher and as task manager. It was only later in his third year of teaching that he found he was beginning to feel more confident about reducing a burdensome planning regime and about digressing from lesson plans as learning opportunities dictate.

Different identities?

During our professional lives as teachers we may find that we will need to adopt different identities to respond to different situations. For example, you may sometimes feel under pressure to deliver the curriculum at all costs even at the cost of the quality of learning that is taking place. In our interviews with early and middle career teachers, a recurring theme emerged in which teachers perceived, and commented upon the tension between providing what they considered to be good learning experiences and the need for curriculum coverage in order to prepare pupils for summative assessment. This perception appears to 'hold-back' or delay progression towards the development of a professional identity that Twiselton (2004) describes as a 'concept builder'. The demands of the external assessments that are a part of the education system may be perceived as a restraint on the opportunity for teaching colleagues to engage in activity that goes beyond curriculum delivery.

Points for reflection

- Do you see a tension between the different teacher identities in Twiselton's model?
- Is there one identity that you might assume more readily than either of the others?

- Is there something about your context or school which means that one identity assumes more importance?
- Are you comfortable with the identity you are developing?
- Does it align with your beliefs about teaching?

In a seminal book in the field of psychology published in 1957, Leon Festinger introduced the concept of cognitive dissonance. Cognitive dissonance is based on the idea that we do not feel comfortable when there is conflict between our beliefs or attitudes and our behaviour. When people find themselves in this state of dissonance, either they have to change the belief or attitude they have, or they have to adjust their behaviour, or it might be that they have to change both of these things and so reduce the cognitive dissonance. Research suggests that it is more often attitude or belief that changes, rather than the behaviour. For example, Aronson and Carlsmith (1963) carried out an experiment with two groups of children in which they were prevented from playing with a particular toy. With one group, the threat of moderate punishment was employed if they played with the toy. With the other group, severe punishment was threatened. After the experiment when the threats of punishment were removed, it was found that the group that had been threatened with moderate punishment no longer wanted to play with the toy. In other words, this group had changed both their attitude and their behaviour. However, the group that had been threatened with severe punishment was more likely to play with the toy. In other words their attitude remained the same and, once the threat was removed, their behaviour stayed constant as well. The implication is that moderate and relatively benign influences which are frequent and ubiquitous can cause us to modify our behaviour, our beliefs and our attitudes, whereas severe threats may cause us to modify our behaviour, but have less influence on our long term attitudes. In the light of this research on cognitive dissonance, it is interesting to look at the tensions that may exist in the developing professional identity of the teacher.

Case study 5.2

This case study of a newly qualified secondary teacher is from a small-scale research project by M. Lawson and M. Watts, 2010. Before I started teaching I had a very

(Continued)

(Continued)

idealised view of what teaching was all about. I anticipated a classroom where I could provide my students with a broad educational experience that they would be eager and willing to 'lap up'; a place where everyone was learning all the time and every one was being challenged to develop. Of course, my first encounters with classes in school quickly dispersed this view. I tried hard to create the type of learning environment that I had in my mind, but the students found my ideas difficult to deal with and the school had a very different view of what effective classroom practice should look like. With support from the colleagues around me I developed a much more pragmatic and realistic view of what teaching is about. I realise now how naïve I was when I started and how essential it is not to be too ambitious about what you think you can achieve.

In this example, we can see aspects of cognitive dissonance reduction in action. Over time, this teacher's attitudes and beliefs about teaching changed as he became acclimatised into the school setting. He has managed to reduce any dissonance that he experienced at the start of his career and he has accepted the school norm by changing his attitudes and beliefs to be in alignment with his behaviour.

Reflective question

- If you were to find yourself in the same position in your NQT year, how would you seek to reduce cognitive dissonance and resolve the tension between the two conflicting aspects of your professional role and identity?

Tensions in teacher identity

In their article on the Personal and Professional Selves of Teachers: Stable and Unstable Identities, Day et al. (2006) recognised the changing nature of teacher identity over time and established from a basis of research and literature some of the factors that influence these changes in professional identity. Day et al. cite the research of Beijaard (1995) and focus on the identification of the positive influences on a teacher's professional identity. Central to these influences is the move from a teacher-centred approach to a pupil-centred approach to learning in schools. In other words, where subject knowledge and content dominates the curriculum, then the teacher's professional identity is to do with being a 'subject specialist' or expert. Whereas in contexts where the learning is pupil-centred the professional identity of the teacher as 'teacher' is important. In the next example we hear from a teacher of sociology in a secondary school reflecting on the fact that her identity as a sociologist developed during her study for her first degree, but her professional identity was now more closely aligned to considering herself to be first and foremost a teacher, as she explained 'I'm no longer actively involved in the practices, the research, (nor am I) engaging with relevant current affairs that I was as a sociologist.' The evidence suggests that not all teachers develop a strong professional identity from previous study or experiences, but when they do, they may experience interesting tensions between their old identity as a subject specialist and their new identity as teacher. (Chapter 6 further considers subject specialism.)

This is captured in the case study of a mid-career teacher who had a very clear view of his identity as a historian, but who was now working as a teacher. This teacher was adamant that the two identities, historian and teacher could be complementary but he admitted that sometimes the 'teacher' identity comes to the fore, such as when behaviour and class management were necessary. This teacher believed there was a complementary nature to the teacher/historian identity divide. As a 'teacher' he could best set the learning environment for the other personality, the 'historian', to develop the skills and concepts necessary for the learner to better understand the discipline. However, he admitted that 'tensions can exist.' This tension emerges particularly when contextual influence such as the school-driven requirement for assessment data meant that the 'teacher' becomes the dominant identity. He acknowledged that these swings in identity were temporary as some syllabus requirements were slightly more manageable and so the 'historian identity can come forward as skills and concepts associated with being an historian are covered.' Syllabus time constraints brought the teacher identity back to the forefront allowing him to ensure the class was able 'cover the course.' Later he observes, 'the historian has a chance to re-emerge as the syllabus coverage becomes less emphasised in relation to the skills and concepts of being an historian.' This case illustrates an interesting 'Jekyll and Hyde' duality where teachers actively swap between identities depending upon context and demand. In their work on 'The Changing Concepts of Teaching and Learning', Stoll and Fink (1996) challenge teachers to move away from a 'delivery' model of education and encourage them to move towards an emphasis on constructing environments that are about how to facilitate the pupils' learning. This connects with the tensions related to the professional identity of teachers and suggests that it depends on whether we are talking about 'schooling' or 'learning' and how perhaps traditionally teaching has concentrated on the former rather than the latter. Stoll and Fink (1996) draw attention to the fact that in some schools, the emphasis on the things pupils need to learn in order to become effective, mature citizens replaced a more traditional approach which focused on what teachers were supposed to cover or deliver. With this shift in emphasis, the accountability falls on the teacher to, 'address the learning of each pupil' (1996: 122). If we accept this as the appropriate model of education then we might also accept the learning outcomes model in which student 'being' (tolerance, caring, responsibility) transcends but is supported by student 'doing' (critical thinking, problem solving) which in turn transcends and is supported by student 'knowing' (subject disciplines) (1996: 123). However, Stoll and Fink (1996) also point out that it is easier to assess student knowing than to assess student doing or student being. This assessment conundrum brings us back to what teachers often identify as a tension between wanting to engage in activities which promote higher-order learning to support 'doing' and 'being' but feeling constrained by the more easily assessed 'knowing' domain and these constraints may lead to tensions in teacher identity. Looking at the conversations with teachers, the evidence often illustrates this tension. In this next extract from a conversation with a teacher in a secondary school, this tension is highlighted particularly clearly.

Case study 5.3

This case study of a mid-career chemistry teacher is taken from an unpublished, small- scale research project by M. Lawson and M. Watts (2010). Although project work and the development of 'soft' skills through challenge-based learning are fine, these skills are rarely assessed. Exam results are used to measure the effectiveness of a school and the performance of a teacher, and this has led to teachers being encouraged to have improved examination results as a professional target and used as a measure of professional success ... and ... public exams test knowledge which can best be taught directly (delivered) because (that approach) ensures coverage and enables tracking of (a learner's) understanding of exam focused content.

We can see tensions emerging here in the professional identity of the teacher. If we return to Twiselton's model we can recognise the tension between this teacher's aspirations towards becoming the 'concept builder' versus the externally mediated pressure to adopt the role of 'content deliverer'. Several of the respondents we spoke to, especially those at an early or mid-career stage, revealed that they considered development of subject discourse or concept building within learners to be an aspiration but conceded that the demands of external examinations and the need to 'cover the course' were often paramount.

Classroom technology and the impact on teacher identity

We have identified some of the factors that may influence the teacher's sense of professional identity and we have looked at the tensions that may emerge as that professional identity develops in different contexts. In this second part of the chapter, we will focus on how changes to teacher identity may arise as a result of the increasing integration of technology into teaching and learning. To do this, we will refer to the results of a small-scale survey carried out in a British school located overseas because we consider that what is happening in this school reflects a growing trend among schools both home and abroad, to integrate technology into the teaching and learning process. We will argue that the integration of technology will entail the teacher shedding certain deeply held beliefs regarding teaching and learning and may necessitate the building of an amended identity for the teacher and perhaps for the profession as a whole. To begin with, even at a basic level, the integration of technology into a teacher's practice requires an expanded skill set and even that basic skill set appears to be expanding. For example, the use of interactive whiteboards, virtual learning platforms, electronic messaging and communication of student work by computer is already requiring teachers to enhance their previous skill set and their classroom practice. But some of these activities do not necessarily reflect a fundamental change in the teacher-led approach we might associate with traditional structures in teaching and learning. More recent technologically based changes in social networking are enabling us to re-appraise the transmission and sharing of ideas and information. It could be argued that the integration of technology into the work of the teaching profession will result in quite significant changes to structures, approaches, skills and beliefs associated with teaching. This may result in an increasing pressure for change in terms of teacher role and identity. Where there is broad acceptance of the need for technology integration then identity will change naturally as a result but, where this belief is not shared we may see tensions emerge.

Points for reflection

- What evidence of technology integration has emerged from your recent visits to schools?
- Has the situation changed since you were at school as a pupil in the classroom?
- How do you think this impacts on the role and identity of the teacher in the secondary school?

The way that technology impinges upon the role of the teacher has been investigated in a number of contexts, for example Johannesen and Eide (2000) observed that technology was becoming increasingly powerful and reliable and, at the same time, easier to use. You could argue that this trend is still continuing and, as with most things associated with technology, this is a trend which will accelerate. The increasing integration of technology into the curriculum fits well with a move towards more student-centred approaches to learning. This integration of technology into a learner-led environment may well result in the teacher's role becoming much more about creating the environment and opportunity for learning and reflection than on the transmission of subject knowledge. You might want to argue that this is the environment a teacher will find in their schools more and more. Long-serving teachers will have witnessed the need to adapt their practice to accommodate this changing context of learning. In their study, McGhee and Kozma (2001) observed that new technologies enabled information to be presented in a variety of different ways and that project-based activities through which teacher and pupils construct knowledge together mean that learning then becomes more about the creation of knowledge rather than the acquisition of facts. In this new classroom it is argued, students are engaged in solving complex, authentic problems that cross disciplinary boundaries. (You may want to look at Chapter 7 on the curriculum in relation to this.) The suggestion is that the school classroom has moved from a place where knowledge is imparted to a place where knowledge is created through active participation by the learner. This fits well with the move towards the learner-centred approach we have referred to earlier in the chapter.

In the light of greater technological integration in schools, McGhee and Kozma (2001) identified a new set of teacher roles which are emerging. These roles are: instructional designer; trainer; collaborator; team coordinator; advisor; and monitoring and assessment specialist. We can unpack these roles in turn – first the 'instructional designer' role has emerged from the increasing opportunity for teachers to use and adapt online or 'soft' resources to construct learning opportunities. We might describe these as learning objects which support learning usually via a learning platform interface or online interface. You could view this as a 'mash-up' of resources rather in the way recording artists mash-up records to produce a fresh new product. The 'trainer' role describes the process whereby a teacher uses his or her own experiences of learning new technologies and passes this experience on to the learner. In this respect, teacher and pupil often become co-learners. The 'collaborator' role describes a variety of activities teachers undertake to work with their colleagues to improve their instruction. These activities include informal sharing with colleagues, team teaching, and learning activities conducted in conjunction with other colleagues. This altered notion of the 'collaborator' role may have emerged as a result of the networked environments often characterised by a technology-rich environment. The 'team-coordinator role' is not completely new because learners have often been grouped to learn in the past. But the changing view of the learner as a knowledge creator, in combination with the technology to better support collaborative construction of knowledge, places more sophisticated demands upon the teacher when adopting the team-coordinator role. The move towards more 'blended' learning, where traditional face-to-face classroom teaching blends with online or technology-based learning, is also putting pressure on the teacher to explore the mechanisms by which technology can mediate collaborative and team learning. The increasing application of technology-mediated collaborative activities within and outside the classroom has certainly resulted in the need for new skills and knowledge when performing the team-coordinator role. McGhee and Kozma (2001) also contend that the increasing focus on 'assessment for learning' (see the chapter on assessment to understand what is intended by this term) has required a different pedagogical approach to setting targets and planning a personalised learning experience for pupils and necessitates the role of 'monitoring and assessment specialist'.

Points for reflection

- Do you see any of these different teacher roles emerging in your school experience or within your own professional practice?

(Continued)

(Continued)

- In what ways do you feel that your role in setting up online learning is different from the face-to-face teaching?
- Does this impact on your sense of identity as a teacher?

The changing role of the teacher in the classroom with integrated technology

During our interviews with teachers, the respondents readily recognised elements of the different roles that McGhee and Kozma have identified. For example, in one interview, a mid-career teacher acknowledged that he was increasingly adopting the role of 'instructional designer' as he was engaged in the construction of online resources for use in a virtual learning platform. He used text, audio and video alongside links to relevant research sources and audio podcasts. This expanding role as 'instructional designer' is even more evident in teachers who have progressed to the stage of creating the raw material, such as the videos and podcasts, for their pupils and colleagues to use. We are increasingly recognising this role as a necessary development in terms of the professional identity of the teacher and we find that teachers are having to develop the skills for such tasks as instructional design to construct interactive activities, support materials and lessons.

Ertmer and Ottenbreit-Leftwich (2010) argue that technology knowledge and skills should be considered as indispensable to a teacher's toolkit. They go as far as suggesting that effective teaching cannot occur unless relevant technology tools or resources are employed in some way. The authors highlight that technology can support traditional teaching approaches, but technology also provides educators with new and arguably better instructional strategies which necessitate a new approach to teaching and learning. Strict adherence to previously held beliefs about their identity and role in the classroom can prevent teachers and learners from experiencing these new and potentially powerful approaches to learning. But, this is the issue with technology. It is a disruptive influence on traditional approaches which makes some traditional approaches obsolete, or at best, inefficient. It could be argued that some teachers are in the process of going through deep changes to their core beliefs and identity as a result of technological change, which is making their professional lives seem increasingly difficult. As Ertmer and Ottenbreit-Leftwich (2010: 258) observe, 'beliefs, attitudes, or pedagogical ideologies' may need to change in order for some teachers to adopt technology more effectively into their classrooms. They suggest that some teachers will be hesitant to adopt curricular innovation, especially technological innovations which are occurring on an almost constant basis. Teacher belief systems are observable measures of how likely teachers are to adopt new technologies into their practice and it should be acknowledged that teachers hold belief systems in which they may or may not accept that technology brings benefits to teaching and learning. They also argue that these beliefs act as a filter in terms of how teachers process new information which they receive through professional development opportunities. Often their previous belief systems influence how they might change their future approach and Ertmer and Ottenbreit-Leftwich maintain that the culture of the teaching profession to which many teachers are exposed is one in which technology is not viewed as a necessary aspect of good teaching and learning. This in turn might mean that the role of instructional designer is not regarded as a part of the teacher's role or identity.

This links with the notions of 'cognitive dissonance' discussed much earlier in the chapter. Within a school culture where technology is seen as a valuable asset to teaching and learning, new teachers who are immersed in that culture will more readily begin to accept the importance of technology into their own belief systems and so adapt their view of the professional identity of the teacher to suit the context and the role. But, even for technically proficient teachers, immersion into a culture in which technology is *not* seen to be valuable might mean that they are deterred from using some of the very technologies they value highly in their personal lives.

Points for reflection

It might be interesting for you to consider your own experiences here.

- How does the culture of your present context or training environment view the value of technology in teaching and learning?
- Is this culture at odds with your own belief system?

One problem with the introduction of technology into cultures or practices that follow a traditionally held belief system is that it 'consistently destabilises the established routines of classroom life including the norms of time and space' (Somekh, 2008: 452). The so-called 'disruptive' nature of technology can be a challenge to the teacher's role and identity in the classroom. Teachers must see firsthand that technology can have a very positive contribution to both teachers and learners alike. It may be that it requires an organisational culture change and a change to the individual belief system of a teacher if the technology is to radically shift away from traditionally held views of teaching and learning.

As a beginner teacher going into schools, you might hold the view that technology will greatly enhance education and that technology can be a great agent for change and improved learning in the classroom. Some might argue that those of us who share this view are naïve in that it is not enough to expect technology itself to be a change agent, but rather the teachers must take on this role by adapting their deeply held beliefs in their practice and by moving away from some of the traditional approaches to teaching and learning. This role as 'change agent' can be an exciting and challenging one and teaching and learning are at a pivotal point in which our previously held notions of education may well be 'flipped' into something which looks fundamentally different from the model which has persisted in many schools until now. The place of technology has been integrated into our traditional notions of schooling but practitioners are witnessing or feeling the tensions. Maybe these tensions are due to the fact that the traditional role of 'schooling' is at odds with 'learning' and perhaps the whole idea of 'schooling' needs to change. However, technology is allowing us to pose some interesting questions about our traditional notion of how the classroom operates and how it is still relevant in the developed world's increasingly personalised environment. We believe that the identity and role of the teacher will need to adapt to become one of 'change agent' if we are to see the potential for technology to transform the approach to learning.

We began this chapter by posing a series of questions about teaching and teacher identity which would help you begin to think about your own beliefs and your identity as a teacher. We have offered you different models for reflecting on the nature of the role and identity of the teacher which we think will be useful in helping you to reflect on your own development and the way in which you will approach your role in the classroom. We have used some case study examples to illustrate how context and environment will impinge upon your changing notion of your professional identity. We have reflected on some findings from research which may help to explain why these changes occur. In the last part of the chapter, we speculated that developments in technology will contribute to an increase in the pace and magnitude of the change in terms of the role and identity of teachers.

Conclusion

If we accept our initial premise that a teacher's identity is central to his or her belief system then rapid change in technology may necessitate a teacher to modify currently held beliefs to accommodate the change. From this perspective, it is probable that a changing identity will be inevitable throughout a teacher's career (see Chapter 12 for another perspective on how the teacher's identity changes). It is for the individual to decide how best to manage these different identities. We have discussed a range of influences on teacher beliefs and found that these beliefs may be modified in one way or another, often over time and sometimes without the teacher realising the change that is occurring. However, for a teacher to be a change agent, it will necessitate actively acknowledging a belief system and putting into practice an approach to teaching and learning which reflects those beliefs.

Reflective questions

1. To what extent are the three tiers of Twiselton's model of teacher identity mutually exclusive – could you argue that the same teacher might adopt any one of these roles or identities on different occasions or in different contexts?
2. What is the evidence to suggest that the integration of new technologies in the classroom environment is changing the nature of teaching and learning? Does the integration of new technologies impact on the role and identity of the teacher? To what extent do you think this is the case in your curriculum area?

Recommended further reading

Dymoke, S. (2012) *Reflective Teaching and Learning in the Secondary School*, 2nd edn. London: Sage.
There is a good section in Chapter 1 relating to identity and self-reflection.

Forde, C. McMahon, M., McPhee, A.D. and Patrick, F. (2006) *Professional Development, Reflection and Enquiry*. London: Sage.
Chapters 3, 5, and 6 of this book consider professional identity from different perspectives.

Wenger, E. (1998) *Communities of Practice*. Cambridge: Cambridge University Press.
This is a classic text with much to say about identity and professional practice within communities.

References

Aronson, E. and Carlsmith, J.M. (1963) 'Effects of severity of threat in the devaluation of forbidden behaviour', *Journal of Abnormal and Social Psychology*, 66: 584–8.

Beijaard, D. (1995) 'Teachers' prior experiences and actual perceptions of personal identity', *Teachers and Teaching: Theory and Practice*, 1 (2): 281–94.

Day, C., Kington, A., Stobart, G., Sammons, P. (2006) 'The personal and professional selves of teachers: stable and unstable identities', *British Educational Research Journal*, 32 (4): 601–16.

Ertmer, P. and Ottenbreit-Leftwich, A. (2010) 'New teacher and student roles in the technology-supported classroom', *Journal of Research on Technology in Education*, 42 (3): 255–84.

Festinger, L. (1957) *A Theory of Cognitive Dissonance*. Evanston, IL: Row Peterson.

Johannesen, T. and Eide, E.M. (2000). 'The role of the teacher in the age of technology: will the role change with use of information- and communication-technology in education?' *European Journal of Open, Distance and E-Learning*. Available online at http://www.eurodl.org/?p=archives&year=2000&article=81 (last accessed 7 June 2011).

McGhee, R. and Kozma, R. (2001) 'New teacher and student roles in the technology-supported classroom'. Paper presented at the Annual Meeting of the American Educational Research Association, April 2001, in Seattle, WA. Available online at http://edtechcases.info/papers/teacherstudentroles.pdf (last accessed 7 June 2011).

Somekh, B. (2008) 'Factors affecting teacher's pedagogical adaption of ICT', in J. Voogt and G. Knezek (eds), *International Handbook of Information Technology in Primary and Secondary Education*. New York: Springer, pp. 449–60.

Stoll, L. and Fink, D. (1996) *Changing Our Schools: Linking School Effectiveness and School Improvement*. Buckingham: Open University Press.

Twiselton, S. (2004) 'The role of teacher identities in learning to teach primary Literacy', *Educational Review*, 56 (2): 157–64.

CHAPTER 6

WHAT IS THE ROLE OF THE SUBJECT SPECIALIST IN SECONDARY EDUCATION?

Kathryn Fox and Patrick Smith

By the end of this chapter you should be able to:

- understand what it means to develop a philosophy for your subject and how may this impact upon students' learning and access to the curriculum;
- understand what it means to be a subject specialist;
- understand which opportunities for learning may be presented through thematic approaches and how teachers might effectively link learning across the curriculum?

This chapter enables you to explore the importance of developing a philosophy for your subject. Your subject philosophy and the context of your practice continually evolve, and yet may be challenged by other professionals as you progress through your teaching career. Your subject philosophy will impact upon the opportunities that you offer your students. This chapter explores recent and relevant research that investigates these areas of study and gives practical examples through a number of curriculum areas. A key theme is the difficulty that developing teachers may experience as they try to put their philosophies into practice. This chapter explores the role of the secondary teacher as a subject specialist.

In considering what it means to be a subject specialist, you will be offered a model for reflecting on your subject knowledge. This chapter also explores learning through thematic approaches and links across the secondary school curriculum.

What does it mean to develop a philosophy for your subject?

Teachers are responsible for the learning of the students in their care. The extent to which this responsibility is fulfilled is often judged in a number of ways. For example, teachers may be judged on their ability to manage pupil behaviour, their learning and the appropriate setting of differentiated learning tasks; one could argue that such an analysis of teacher effectiveness is only based on what is seen. However, there are many underlying factors that may have enabled the teacher to command such mastery of the classroom which are not so easily observed. These may include the teacher's values, beliefs and attitudes which they impart to their learners.

As Shulman (1987) noted, teachers communicate their own values, ideas and attitudes in their interactions with their students. How teachers define themselves (Lasky, 2005) to themselves and to others is something that evolves over time. Such an evolution is shaped by significant others with whom teachers interact, either in their training, continuing professional development or in a variety of professional and sometimes non-professional settings. It is also very difficult to ignore the impact government policy may have on teachers' values, beliefs and attitudes, for example, through reforms to the curriculum and the required knowledge base for their subject.

The values, beliefs and attitudes that underpin your personal philosophy for the teaching of your subject may well represent an amalgam of various ideologies (Green, 2002). If we wish to understand why teachers value their subject we need to appreciate the myriad social and political influences that have shaped our thinking and our practice. Green (2002) describes the development of our philosophies through a process of 'socio-genesis'. In essence this means a process which results from your own family values, beliefs and attitudes or the network of social relationships that help to shape your philosophy.

A number of authors (e.g. Ellis, 2007; Green, 2002) have discussed the interconnectedness of teachers' beliefs about education in general; for example, the aims of the curriculum, its breadth and balance and which subjects should take precedence over others. However, Van Driel et al. (2007) argue that very little is known about teachers' subject specific beliefs; for example, why importance is attributed to the teaching of particular or periods in history, the choice of specific authors in the teaching of literature, the selection of certain artists or artistic movements and the exclusion of others in art and design, or a preference to expose young people to what may be regarded as an alternative or innovative curriculum offer.

Van Driel et al. (2007) point out that studies of teachers' beliefs have focused in the main on more generic aspects such as the curriculum or teaching and learning. Few have identified clear connections between teachers' beliefs about their own subject or the teaching of specific topics, or indeed between teachers' subject specific and general belief systems. However, they cite Green (2002) who puts a counter argument suggesting that people 'tend to order their beliefs into clusters', which are not necessarily consistent with other beliefs that they hold. For example, a mathematics teacher may hold a fundamental belief around the importance of not labelling children as failures if they fail to achieve in mathematics. And yet the same teacher may well support a strategy of ability grouping or setting in mathematics in order for them to achieve best outcomes for their students, despite evidence that this practice can reinforce educational inequalities (Boaler and Wiliam, 2001). Likewise, the physical education specialists may hold conflicting beliefs around the value of competitive team games on the one hand and the need for students to experience alternative game activities that develop cooperative skills on the other. Similarly, the same teacher can espouse the value of educating their students for life-long physical activity, so they continue to participate fully in physical activity after schooling. And yet teachers may deliver the same activities year after year, aware of the fact that those same students will not continue to pursue those activities later on in their lives.

According to Pajares (1992), there is evidence that aspects of classroom practice are linked to teachers' educational beliefs and values. However, a strong counter argument to Pajares' (1992) findings is one that particularly resonates with trainees and beginning teachers. Teacher-training establishments have at times been described as undermining government policy and preferred practice. However, these same establishments would rather they were recognised for their creativity, inventiveness and ability to provide alternative ways for students to learn successfully. As you enter the profession, as a recently qualified teacher, there may be a tension between your outlook and your context, meaning that you may feel stifled by the response 'this is how we do it here'. This inhibiting culture may mean that you are unable to put your pedagogical beliefs and ideas fully into practice.

Many innovations that you as a beginning teacher may bring to your new school may be seen as impractical by your more experienced colleagues who may identify barriers. These could be physical barriers for example, such as lack of resources or time. New ideas may upset routines and create feelings of insecurity and uncertainty and may not fit with experienced teachers' beliefs, or indeed the whole school culture and ethos. As a result, you may have to make compromises in translating your beliefs into practice. You will need to develop an understanding of the culture and context in which you find yourself. As a beginning teacher, you could discuss with your mentor how your ideas can assimilate into the school and ensure you are aware of the school's current practices, agendas and direction.

It is more than likely that innovations in teaching and learning will come from government-driven initiatives. The very nature of the innovation may be counter to the teacher's existing beliefs. One such example is the discussion on curriculum and assessment reform, whereby students may no longer be reassessed in public examinations to achieve a higher grade. If at first you do not succeed, you cannot try again. Such reforms may well sit uncomfortably with a teacher's deep-rooted beliefs and values around self-esteem, fairness and equality of opportunity. The Advisory Committee on Mathematics Education (ACME) claims that early and repeated entry at GCSE for the purposes of 'banking' desirable (often C) grades has negative implications both for the development of student understanding and in terms of their entitlement to be taught a full programme of study through compulsory schooling (ACME, 2011).

Findlay (2010) explores the influences on the development of the professional identities of secondary English teachers, their understanding of their subject and how it should be taught. Findlay also explores the philosophies or 'models' of English expressed by teachers and how this has changed over time. She investigates the actualisation of the subject in the classroom and how that relates to teachers' espoused beliefs. Despite their varied professional experiences, Findley found a number of common emergent patterns in terms of the respondents' beliefs about their subject:

- A belief that English is set apart from other subjects because it is more focused on the personal development of the child.
- Grammar teaching is a legitimate aspect of the subject but teachers do not enjoy teaching it and regard it as a chore.
- ICT is acknowledged as an asset to teaching English because it helps to foster independent learning and students' sense of ownership and engagement with literary texts.

- The future of the subject is perceived to be driven by assessment. Teachers regard the demise of Key Stage 3 testing as positive and hope for more autonomy and creativity in their teaching, but regard the prescribed curriculum as overloaded. (Findlay, 2010: 4)

Points for reflection

Pupil-teacher relationships are key to successful teaching and learning.

- What are the particular aspects of your subject that may foster positive relationships with pupils in your view?
- What is it that makes your subject special?
- How does your subject pedagogy enhance pupil/teacher relationships?
- Reflect further on these questions and discuss with your peers and more experienced colleagues to compare your different views.

All subject specialists can (and do) argue that their subject is special and can enhance pupil-teacher relationships like no other. Common positions taken are that the 'creative' subjects (e.g.: drama, music, art, physical education) develop pupils' passion for learning, their independence, social skills, self-esteem and self-confidence. However, if you are a teacher of mathematics, physics or chemistry, there is no reason why your subject cannot contribute in a similar way if you allow your pedagogy to do so.

You will continue to develop your own teacher identity and amend your beliefs and practice throughout your career. The early development of your teacher identity will be characterised through your training and the significant others involved. For most of us, it is likely that our teaching practice will be perceived as more influential than our university-based learning (Green, 2002). What tends to make a significant difference to our practice, particularly in our early years of teaching, are not necessarily our values, beliefs and attitudes but the circumstances we find ourselves in, such as the nature of the particular school or department in which we are based.

Lasky (2005) tells us that 'individual capacity' is what we bring with us to the school setting. Our individual capacity could be, for example, our level of personal commitment, willingness to fit in, ability to work collaboratively with colleagues and our resilience. However, as a beginning teacher we are often very vulnerable individuals. As a new arrival in a secondary school with experienced colleagues you may have little control over what you teach and perhaps how you teach. You may, as Lasky puts it, be 'forced to act in ways that are inconsistent with (your) core beliefs and values' (2005: 901). As a student teacher, you may be unwilling to open yourself up emotionally to challenge the circumstances you find yourself in and you may wish to avoid confrontation with more experienced colleagues. Such a stance may inhibit your professional development and have a negative impact on your teaching and your pupils' learning.

Siskin (1994) suggests it is daily routines in secondary school departments that espouse a shared sense of culture and community. It will be your sense of 'agency' or your perceived ability to shape and change current practices in your department that will determine whether or not you become an 'agent'. In secondary schools, Hargreaves (1994) recognised that norms are developed in schools and within their departments; established norms may come into conflict with your own professional values, beliefs and attitudes.

Green's research (2002) analysed everyday philosophies of secondary physical education teachers and concluded that newly qualified teachers found themselves more or less 'at the mercy' of their head teachers, head of department or more experienced colleagues. However, several new teachers recognised that even head teachers operate within a constraining remit, either from the governing body or the current government. The internal and external 'markets' (local, regional and national league tables) and concerns surrounding the perceived prestige of the school in the context of the 'market' was particularly evident in Green's research.

Whilst your values, beliefs and attitudes towards teaching and learning in your subject may be formed very early on in your professional life, there is little doubt that over time these will evolve and change throughout your career. Ultimately your personal philosophies may be compromised and re-examined and tensions may continue to exist between your values and beliefs in terms of your teaching and your pupils' learning.

Points for reflection

- Consider the values attitudes and beliefs that you hold in relation to the teaching of your subject.
- What impact may these have on pupils' progress and levels of engagement in their learning?

What does it mean to be a *subject specialist?*

Lawson's and Watts's chapter asks you to consider teacher identity as well as the way your context may affect the way you enact that identity. Here we focus our attention on your identity as a subject specialist. Planning for learning is a feature of a teacher's role; from long-term planning to individual lesson planning a sense of the structure and connections of the subject matter enable us to plan in a way that develops learners' understanding and enables progression. Additionally with a secure understanding of your subject you will be able to respond more effectively to the direction of pupils' learning within your lessons.

Traditionally, assumptions were made that advanced knowledge of subject matter was a vital part of a teacher's knowledge base. Schulman's (1986) seminal work considered the way in which knowledge of subject matter transferred into knowledge for teaching. This classification of teacher knowledge separates the knowledge that teachers draw upon in order to teach into pedagogic, subject matter and curriculum knowledge. More recently Wright et al. (2007) refer to the need to transform subject knowledge into the context of the secondary classroom, describing a form of teacher knowledge that is developed from reforming your subject knowledge base to represent ideas for children in the classroom.

Banks et al. (2005) develop this further with a situated perspective, arguing that Schulman's classification of teacher knowledge places subject knowledge as a fixed body of knowledge in the mind of the teacher. They instead present a model of teacher knowledge developing from interaction within and between school knowledge, subject knowledge and pedagogic knowledge. They argue that teacher professional knowledge emerges from enquiring into the interface between these classifications.

In this section we examine subject knowledge for teaching and ask the reader to consider the development of appropriate subject knowledge as linked to three overarching themes:

- the development of depth of knowledge about subject structures and key concepts;
- the development of breadth of knowledge about subject themes and processes;
- The development of a broad perspective of the place of the subject within the school curriculum and beyond.

If you are about to embark on an initial teacher education (ITE) course you will already have some subject knowledge to draw upon. This may be linked to prior learning in the subject, academic qualifications and workplace experience. An ITE course will require you to develop subject knowledge appropriate for teaching and those teaching subjects other than those for which they are qualified will be expected to develop their subject knowledge. Courses designed to support subject knowledge development prior to a PGCE have also been available for a number of years, for example, two-year PGCE and subject knowledge enhancement courses (there have been a number of government initiatives in Mathematics, Science and Modern Foreign Languages to support non-specialists). As a beginning teacher, you will constantly go through a process of refining and adding to your subject knowledge. There will always be 'more' subject matter to learn! Here we suggest a framework for reflecting upon how your existing subject knowledge is assimilated into subject knowledge for teaching.

Subject structures and key ideas

Subject areas are often structured with deep connections between areas of learning. As a teacher, an understanding of the rich links and structures of your subject will be a necessary resource for supporting conceptual development in your students. Sometimes these deep connections are developed as a result of studying subject matter from a variety of perspectives.

An example of this may be found in mathematics by considering a particular type of challenge that secondary students usually encounter; multiplying a two and a three digit number together (e.g. 16×538 if you want to try the activity). Trainees on a mathematics course were asked to carry out the calculation prior to a session; feedback suggests that this is a straightforward task for those trainees. The trainees were then asked to find and explain *three further methods* for carrying out the calculation. This comment reflects common feelings of frustration: 'I was initially annoyed by this task. I had found an answer ... as required! I don't need to do this again and I don't need another way to do this. Can't we just move on?' We have seen earlier in the chapter that unacknowledged assumptions about the nature of the subject impact upon our practice; consider the balance between process and product (i.e. the method and the answer) here. Further reflection on the task presented a realisation that 'This provides an insight in to the subject tool kit required by a teacher. No longer is it possible to rely on the one method that until now has suited my own learning and apply this whenever needed.' In order to prepare for working with pupils, it is necessary to appreciate a variety of methods and understand each one's potential for learning. For example, in the above calculation a child who is familiar with doubling could use this to multiply 538 by 2 giving 1,076. Doubling

1,076 will provide the answer to 538 × 4; doubling this answer will give the answer to 538 × 8 and finally doubling again will give the answer to 538 × 16. Why would a teacher select this method over a 'standard method'? Standard recipe methods represent a finished product, a contraction of a process; a teacher of mathematics needs to provide children with experience of multiplying in a variety of contexts in order for them to develop a secure understanding of the notion of multiplication itself. In this approach to 538 ×16 'multiplication as repeated addition' underpins our doubling and adding, and the approach may also support children who do not yet have other secure methods to draw upon.

It is necessary for the mathematics teacher to draw on a range of representations and to be aware of the mathematical implications of each of these. Schulman's conception of pedagogical content knowledge considers representations as vital for teachers of *all* subjects. He goes on to point out that:

> Since there are no single most powerful forms of representation, the teacher must have at hand a veritable armamentarium of alternative forms of representation, some of which derive from research, whereas others originate in the wisdom of practice. (Schulman, 1986: 9)

Wisdom of practice may arise from the process of teaching; we suggest that the trainees described above deriving multiple approaches to solving equations, being taken from their comfort zone of their tried and tested favourite approaches, have the potential to learn valuable lessons enabling them to develop such a toolkit.

Having an appreciation of these connections as a teacher also supports the development of your understanding of progression in your subject and your ability to respond to learners by applying your subject knowledge with flexibility; you will be able to select from a variety of explanations, representations and approaches to a topic area. The National Curriculum (2007) may provide a framework for understanding requirements for progression but school curricula are developed over time and you will work within different statutory frameworks. An understanding of the nature of progression and the connections within a subject area within current school frameworks will equip you as a teacher to engage critically with government or school requirements. In other words, a strong sense of the nature of knowledge within a school discipline provides you with a supporting framework for interpreting the requirements of the profession. Day and Gu's (2010) study of teachers found that in-depth subject content and pedagogical knowledge are linked to children's achievements, taking a view that this is a career-long endeavour. As we said earlier, here will always be 'more' subject matter to learn!

Subject themes and processes

To develop as a subject specialist, it is also necessary to develop a broad knowledge of the key themes and processes of your subject and the ways that these are expressed both in the school curriculum and in the world beyond. This may involve identifying and solving 'problems' within a subject, developing understanding of specific themes and attending to your ability to function competently and confidently in your subject.

Consider how subject thinking may be manifest in contexts other than the school curriculum. Boaler (2009), for example, identifies that differences between ways of thinking in school, real life and professional mathematics may explain some of the issues relating to pupils' disengagement.

Subjects across and beyond the curriculum

The above classifications of 'structures and key ideas' along with 'themes and processes' need to be situated within the curriculum in order for you to fully develop your subject knowledge for teaching. You will need to reflect critically upon the nature of your subject and consider its place in the school curriculum. Finally you will need to consider the relevance and application of the subject beyond school.

Points for reflection

- Consider why you like your subject.
- What is it about your subject that draws you in and what is it about your subject that you would champion as a teacher?

Here are responses to the reflection questions from trainees on teacher education courses. Compare their response to yours. What are the similarities and differences?

> *'This subject challenges us to think more diversely about given problems broadening our viewpoints. A logical step by step approach enhances underpinning knowledge that can in turn be transferred to any given subject. This lays the foundations to develop skills needed to excel in a wider context. For me the biggest draw to the subject is the application in the real world.'*

> *'I like this subject because there are multiple ways of finding solutions to problems and it is a really good feeling when you solve a problem ... there are solutions that can be found, it is not just a matter of opinion.'*

Case study 6.1 Is mathematics always right or wrong?

The above trainees were asked why they like their subject. Prior to ITE, 'typical' responses to this for mathematics applicants often include responses along the lines of 'I love my subject as answers are always right or wrong'. This view will be grounded in prior conceptions and experiences. Given that applicants to mathematics ITE programmes will have had a mainly successful experience of studying mathematics, this view about answers (with its implicit positivist ontological stance) has not been a barrier for them to successful learning. Consider however, how this may be a barrier for some learners. A child who has applied a standard recipe approach to 538 × 8, who has forgotten to place a required zero, is incorrect. They may, however, have drawn on a correct process by deciding to multiply 500 × 8 and 30 × 8 and 8 × 8 and add up the answers demonstrating clear understanding of mathematical place value. A classroom that values this problem solving and connectionist approach has the potential to build confidence and competence in comparison to a negative and demoralising classroom where 538 × 8 = 4088 is simply incorrect. It *is* incorrect but it is not *simply* incorrect!

A view often expressed amongst Religious Education ITE applicants is 'My subject does not have correct answers'. This may be a positive feature for these successful learners but where this clashes with pupils' wishes for answers, what is seen as a positive feature may have a de-motivating or negative effect. Assumptions about the nature of subject learning need to be critically examined in order to caution against the risk of reinforcing perceptions of subjects as impenetrable, leading to pupils viewing them as not suited to their ways of thinking.

Point for reflection

- Return to your ideas about reasons why you like your subject and critically reflect upon the unintended barriers to learning that these distinctive features may present to pupils.

We claim that subject-specific pedagogy is not a separate entity, but is rather a product of the deep subject knowledge described above. Consequently, secondary subject specialists have a great deal to offer each other both within and across the curriculum.

What opportunities for learning may be presented through thematic approaches and how do teachers effectively link learning across the curriculum?

The former Qualifications and Curriculum Authority (QCA) Chair of Curriculum, Mick Waters, attempted to address the perceived curriculum crisis in secondary schools. The QCA designed the 'big picture' (2008) which invited teachers to think more radically about how they deliver the Key Stage 3 curriculum. In fact, Waters was simply suggesting to teachers to think more freely about how they teach in order to engage their students more fully in their learning. Waters wanted to enable teachers to develop 'successful', 'confident' and 'responsible' learners, and yet this ideal was later much maligned by educationalists and the Coalition government in 2010.

The QCA model encouraged teachers to 'delve deeper' and 'linger longer' on matters that straddle subjects, for example sustainable development in geography and the links to science, mathematics and technology. To simply 'get through' the subject matter year on year was not enough and the intention was to encourage a much more connected learning experience for pupils.

The Universities Council for the Education of Teachers (Kirk and Broadhead, 2007) gave a very good summary of the purpose and nature of subjects.

> There are those who look upon subject teaching as the transmission of slabs of content for no worthier purpose than examination success, and the subject teacher, operating within a highly restrictive pedagogical range, as having no loftier ambition than to crowd students' heads with facts. Of course such characteristics represent an absurd caricature of subject teaching. Properly conceived, however, they differentiate and coalesce over time, subjects constitute the available ways we have of explaining and interpreting the world of subjective experience, of analysing the social environment and of making sense the natural world. (Kirk and Broadhead, 2007: para. 39)

Kirk and Broadhead (2007) acknowledged that subject knowledge does not necessarily have to be transmitted through subject specific teaching and that for early years and primary teachers, an integrated approach is often the preferred model of delivery. But why is the same approach rarely adopted in secondary schools? Is it because the depth of knowledge and understanding required within and across the secondary curriculum is too much to ask of teachers? Or is it that as subject specialists, secondary teachers are very aware of their lack of understanding outside their subject area or their 'conscious incompetence' (Howell, 1982)?

Putwain et al. (2008) found that a thematic approach to teaching humanities in Key Stage 3 had particular benefits for pupils' learning, behaviour and pupil-teacher relationships. They acknowledge the criticism that exists around delivering a subject-based curriculum that is fragmented and simply housed in departments with little connection to real world matters. How the curriculum is integrated and to what degree is another aspect to be considered. At the one end of the spectrum, the curriculum could be delivered as a totally non-integrated model whereby the subjects are all taught in total isolation to one another; at the other end of the spectrum the learners become responsible for the integration process and use a network of resources including subject experts to make appropriate connections. Secondary schools tend to operate mainly within the subject delivery model with some integrated elements or tools that support students' learning, for example 'learning to learn', study skills, general studies, 'humanities week' and so forth.

One should also consider where secondary students come from. Primary school curriculum models are usually much more balanced in terms of an integrated approach to teaching and learning and subject-based learning. Mathematics is normally taught as an isolated subject (Boyle and Bragg, 2008) throughout primary school, whereas subjects such as history and geography are often combined in a humanities-type model. Consequently, many secondary schools have adapted a more integrated approach to curriculum delivery in Year 7 and a number have openly advertised teaching vacancies for experienced primary school practitioners so they may deliver an integrated curriculum in Key Stage 3.

Savage (2011) explores alternative ways in which the secondary school curriculum may be reconstructed so that it builds on individual subject cultures. Such cultures should include a clear understanding of how pupils learn and of the many different pedagogical approaches available that can facilitate learning.

We are unlikely to escape the fact that assessment of pupils' performance in subject-based public examinations will be with us for a long time. However, the use of thematic units of work that thread learning through the subjects could enhance pupils' performance. Putwain et al. (2008) found that the integrated curriculum can facilitate learning of new material, particularly where this lacks structure in a subject-based curriculum.

To create a more coherent approach to teaching and learning in the secondary school, teachers need to develop a greater understanding of what is taught by their colleagues. Otherwise the curriculum is simply taught in isolation. The very best trainee teachers have a good understanding of what their pupils are learning in other subject areas. For example, mathematical connections may be made with Year 7s who are studying histograms whilst pupils can populate graphs with data recorded on heart-rate monitors during their physical education lessons. Many such links are possible if a deeper understanding develops between teachers delivering the curriculum. This may be further strengthened through the sharing and developing of pedagogic practice.

Points for reflection

Consider a key idea or concept within your subject.

- What are the potential connections between what you teach in your subject and what your colleagues teach in theirs?
- How may a thematic approach to teaching and learning enhance pupils' learning?

Conclusion

In summary, we have discussed the connections between beliefs, values and classroom practice. We have looked in depth at one of the facets of the role of the teacher, that of a subject specialist and have looked at the challenges and opportunities presented by this aspect of your role. Finally, we have examined opportunities for learning through thematic approaches and ways to effectively link learning across the curriculum. As a secondary teacher you will have the opportunity to develop meaning for and with your pupils, subject learning in school playing a part in this learning contextualised within the developing and dynamic wider role of the twenty-first century teacher.

Reflective questions

1 Why do you think that it is important to develop your values and beliefs about your subject?

2 What benefits could there be in sharing subject based philosophies with colleagues?
3 How could a thematic approach to teaching and learning of particular themes or concepts enhance students' learning?

Recommended further reading

Boaler, J. (2009) *The Elephant in the Classroom: Helping Children Learn and Love Mathematics.* London: Souvenir Press.

This research-underpinned book examines the way that different mathematical experiences may impact upon children's learning.

Ellis, V. (2009) *Subject Knowledge and Teacher Education: The Development of Beginning Teachers' Thinking*. London: Continuum.

This book explores teacher knowledge and suggests, in considering teacher development, we pay careful attention to the context of schools and subject communities.

Savage, J. (2011) *Cross Curricular Teaching in the Secondary School.* Abingdon: Routledge.

This, and other books in the series, considers that a disciplinary approach is needed in order to embed models of cross curricular teaching and learning within the pedagogy of practitioners.

References

Advisory Committee on Mathematics Education (2011) 'Position paper on early and multiple entry to GCSE mathematics'.

Banks, F., Leach, J. and Moon, B. (2005) 'Extract from new understandings of teachers' pedagogic knowledge', *Curriculum Journal*, 16 (3): 331–40.

Boaler, J. (2009) *The Elephant in the Classroom: Helping Children Learn and Love Mathematics*. London: Souvenir Press.

Boaler, J. and Wiliam, D. (2001) 'We've still got to learn students' perspectives on ability grouping and mathematical achievement', in P. Gates (ed.), *Issues in Mathematics Teaching*. RoutledgeFalmer.

Boyle, B. and Bragg, J. (2008) 'Making primary connections: the cross curriculum story', *The Curriculum Journal*, 19 (1): 5–21.

Day, C. and Gu, Q. (2010) 'The new lives of teachers', 1st edn. Available online at http://www.dawsonera.com/depp/reader/protected/external/AbstractView/S9780203847909 (last accessed 27 April 2012).

Ellis, V. (2007) 'Taking subject knowledge seriously; from professional knowledge recipes to complex conceptualisations of teacher development', *The Curriculum Journal*, 18 (4): 447–62.

Findlay, K. (2010) 'The professional identity and practice of secondary school English teachers in the UK', 0261. Available online at www.beraconference.co.uk/2010/downloads/.../pdf/BERA2010_0261.pdf

Green, K. (2002) 'Physical education teachers in their configurations: a sociological analysis of everyday "philosophies"', *Sport Education and Society*, 7 (1): 65–83.

Hargreaves, A. (1994) *Changing Teachers, Changing Times: Teachers' Work and Culture in the Postmodern Age.* Toronto: OISE Press.

Howell, W.S. (1982) *The Empathic Communicator.* Minneapolis, MN: University of Minnesota, Wadsworth Publishing Company.

Kirk, G. and Broadhead, P. (2007) *Every Child Matters & Teacher Education: A UCET Position Paper*. Occasional Paper no 17, London.

Lasky, S. (2005) 'A sociocultural approach to understanding teacher identity, agency and professional vulnerability in a context of secondary school reform'. *Teaching and Teacher Education*, 21 (8): 899–916.

National Curriculum for England (2007) *The National Curriculum for England: (Key Stages 1-4).* Department for Education and Employment. London: The Stationary Office.

Pajares, M.F. (1992) 'Teachers' beliefs and education research: cleaning up a messy construct', *Review of Educational Research*, 62 (3): 307–32.

Putwain, D.,Whitely, H. and Caddick, L. (2008) 'Evaluation of a thematic approach to the delivery of the humanities curriculum in Key Stage 3'. BERA Annual Conference, 3–6 September.

QCA (2008) 'A big picture of the curriculum'. Available online at http://www.all nsc.org.uk/files/Big_Picture_2008.pdf (last accessed 5 December 2012).

Savage, J. (2011) *Cross Curricular Teaching in the Secondary School*. London: Routledge.

Shulman, L.S. (1986) 'Those who understand: knowledge growth in teaching', *Educational Researcher*, 15 (2): 4–14.

Shulman, L.S. (1987) 'Knowledge and teaching: foundations of the new reform', *Harvard Educational Review*, 57 (1): 1–22.

Siskin, L.S (1994) *Realms of Knowledge: Academic Departments in Secondary Schools*. London: Falmer Press.

Sotto, E. (1994) *When Teaching Becomes Learning*. London: Cassell

Van Driel, J.H., Bulte, A.M.W. and Verloop, N. (2007) 'The relationship between teachers' general beliefs about teaching and learning and their domain specific curricular beliefs', *Learning and Instruction*, 17, 156–71.

Wright, C., Ellis V. and Peverett, M. (2007) 'Planning for learning', in V. Ellis (ed.) *Learning and Teaching in Secondary Schools*. Exeter: Learning Matters: 45–62.

CHAPTER 7

WHAT DO I NEED TO KNOW ABOUT THE CURRICULUM?

Carrie Mercier

By the end of this chapter you should be able to:

- develop a critical understanding of the development of the secondary school curriculum;
- analyse two different approaches to the curriculum and evaluate the arguments for these contrasting models;
- consider a range of teacher perspectives on curriculum issues;
- reflect critically on the teacher's role in curriculum development in the secondary school.

In this chapter you will be encouraged to engage with different perspectives on the nature and development of the school curriculum. You may have thought that, unlike your primary counterpart, you would not have to consider the whole school curriculum, as on entering the secondary sector you usually have a specialist subject focus. However, it is important for all teachers to understand how their area of activity fits into the broader picture. When you go in to school, you will recognise many of the subjects from your own schooling and you might believe that these different areas of the curriculum have been set in stone for all time. On the other hand, you might see some subjects that are different from those that you knew as a pupil and you might want to ask who decided that these are the subjects on the school curriculum and why these were chosen. In this chapter, we will be reflecting on such questions and issues. We will also ask how the curriculum has changed and developed and whether there are different ways to put together the school curriculum.

As teachers, we may find ourselves challenged by learners asking 'I am not religious so why do I have to do RE?' or 'I don't want to go to France so why do I have to learn French?' Such questions keep us on our toes and prompt us to ensure that our area of the curriculum is engaging and relevant to the pupils we teach. While the pupils might demand of us a curriculum that is interesting and meaningful to them, often it is not the teachers but others making the decisions about what learners need from their schooling. The evidence from research indicates that all teachers need to reflect on the nature of the curriculum and develop the knowledge, understanding and skills that will enable them to contribute constructively in curriculum development and change in their schools (Clark, 2005; Flores, 2005; Richards and Shea, 2006). It is important to stay informed about the big picture when it comes to the school curriculum so that we are not in danger of being misled (Kelly, 2009) by others whose interest is political rather than educational.

Points for reflection

- Do you think that pupils should have a say in what their curriculum includes?
- Do you think we should ask their parents?
- Should the politicians decide what the school curriculum is, or the subject academics, or the exam boards or should we ask the employers?
- Do you think teachers are best placed to judge what the curriculum should be for their pupils?

What is the curriculum?

The word curriculum goes back to the Latin term for the race course. It has come to refer to a course of study. In the context of education in schools, the curriculum is usually understood in terms of 'what is taught'. In other words, it often refers to the subjects on the timetable or the content of the lessons. But the definition of the curriculum is not always quite that straightforward. First, we might ask how we separate *what* is taught from *how* it is taught. The English teacher who wants her pupils to learn to debate effectively needs to think about *how* the pupils will learn the skills as well as *what* she is going to teach. In other words, the so-called curriculum is bound to include aspects of pedagogy (learning and teaching strategies) as well as subject content. It might be helpful to understand the curriculum in terms of 'what is learnt' rather than 'what is taught'. This allows us to take account of the whole curriculum – after all, what is learnt in school goes beyond the sum of the individual timetabled subjects. A consideration of the whole curriculum would have to take account of the learning achieved in after-school clubs, Red Nose day activities and the school musical as well as the regular subject lessons. There is also what has been called the 'hidden curriculum' (Illich, 1973) to take into account. This idea of the hidden curriculum is a reminder that there are things learnt in school that are not identified on the timetable, for example the values that might be acquired in the way teachers talk to pupils or the habits and behaviours that are drummed into pupils through the routines of the school day. In fact, it could be argued that these things that are learnt in school are as much a part of the curriculum as the taught lessons. If you want to reflect on a broader definition of the curriculum, you might like to read what Kelly (2009) has to say in his discussion. However, for the purposes of this chapter we will limit ourselves to the definition of the curriculum as 'the learning experiences that are planned within the school' (Pring, 1989).

How did the curriculum come to be the way it is now?

The development of the secondary school curriculum has not been a straightforward journey and it would be a great 'mistake to regard the history of education as steady uninterrupted progress from the earliest beginnings to the present system' (Gordon and Lawton, 1978: 61). For much of the period during which schooling developed in the UK, it was the curriculum in primary schools that was intended to provide the basic education for all in terms of reading, writing and arithmetic. Indeed, for a long time it was thought that secondary education for everyone might give the working classes 'ideas above their station' (Gordon and Lawton, 1978: 52) and so there was very little on offer beyond primary school for the majority of young people. However, by the end of the Second World War, the 1944 Education Act 'heralded a new era' in secondary education in England and Wales (Carr, 2007) and every young person was to receive some form of secondary schooling. Local education authorities set about serving the needs (as they saw them) of different sections of society. For example, grammar schools were to offer a curriculum designed for those going on to further study and technical or modern schools were to provide a more practical curriculum to prepare pupils for the world of work. The 1944 Act did not define curriculum subjects for these secondary schools. The guidelines in the Preamble were very broad, indicating that public education should contribute 'towards the spiritual, moral, mental and physical development of the community' (DES, 1944). In fact, the only requirement in terms of the content of the curriculum was the provision for religious instruction. In the 1960s, despite the move to comprehensive schools, there was no central government guidance on what should constitute the curriculum in these schools. During this time, teachers enjoyed considerable freedom in terms of developing the curriculum for their pupils. Indeed, this period has sometimes been regarded as a 'golden age' (Kelly, 2009:191) in education.

In 1964 the Schools Council for the Curriculum and Examinations was set up in England to develop support materials for the different areas of the curriculum. This was by and large teacher–led and it was up to the individual school to decide its own curriculum. As a result, there remained a considerable degree of diversity in terms of the secondary curriculum in schools. In the 1970s, in Scotland, the Munn Report (SED, 1977) set out a curriculum for secondary schools that was organised around two concerns, on the one hand, skills for the workplace and on the other, access to traditional subject disciplines or 'modes of experience'. Meanwhile in England the guidelines remained much more general. These suggested that pupils should encounter a range of educational experiences including 'the aesthetic and creative, the ethical, the linguistic, the mathematical, the physical, the scientific, the social and political and the spiritual' (DES, 1977: 6). What was emerging within education was a broad consensus that the secondary curriculum should encourage young people to develop a sense of personal autonomy, enable them to take their place as citizens in a brave new world, empower them to stand up for liberty and to make a positive contribution to society. Schools in England and Wales continued to interpret the curriculum for their own context while ensuring a broad and balanced approach and the teachers were still very much at the heart of the process of curriculum development for their pupils.

In the 1980s, things began to change and under a Conservative government, a national curriculum was introduced in England and Wales for the first time in 1988. There was very little room for interpretation with this top-down approach to the school curriculum as Pring observed, 'The Secretary of State thus has greater powers under the 1988 Act for determining the general shape, the specific objectives and the programmes of study of the curriculum than any other previous Secretary of State or Minister of Education' (1989: 67). Others have questioned whether 'democratically elected ministers have the right to introduce whatever aims and curricula gain parliamentary approval' (White, 2004: 21). There were three core subjects: English, Mathematics and Science (four in Wales with Welsh being the fourth). Also included in the National Curriculum were the so-called foundation subjects: History, Geography, Art, Music, Technology, PE, Modern Foreign Language. Religious Education which was already required by law was not a part of the National Curriculum but it was included in the basic curriculum. The knowledge, skills and processes for each subject were established and assessments set up with targets for teachers to ensure that their pupils were achieving in each subject area. Later, in response to Lord Dearing (SCAA, 1993) the National Curriculum was slimmed down. The core remained but there was more flexibility for teachers to determine what pupils should learn in the rest of the curriculum. Reforms in 1998 under the Labour government established increased control over the core subjects, the emphasis being on literacy and numeracy but the content and targets for other subjects were relaxed. Indeed, some subjects became marginalised as a result. (If you are interested in a more detailed analysis of the development of the National Curriculum look at Ross 2000, Chapter 5.) The curriculum was now being determined by central government but of course, governments change and schools have to respond to new directives brought in by a new Secretary of State for Education.

In 2008, a new secondary curriculum was introduced in England, under the Labour government. This signalled a fairly radical shift away from the traditional subject structures that had dominated the National Curriculum at Key Stage 3 and a move towards a curriculum that was structured much more around skills and processes. The focus was on *how* the curriculum was taught rather than *what* should be taught and it was argued that teachers would be able to develop the content of the curriculum in a way that would be much more relevant to the needs of the pupils drawing on key themes such as: enterprise, community participation, technology and the media. The emphasis was on 'personal, learning and thinking skills' and pupils were to become 'independent enquirers, creative thinkers, reflective learners, team workers, self-managers and effective participators' (QCA, 2007). Teachers were to plan and structure the learning around these skills and they were given considerable freedom in terms of deciding the topics and content for Key Stage 3. This new secondary curriculum called for teachers to work across subject boundaries in order to build a more relevant and flexible approach to the Key Stage 3 curriculum.

Only two years later, this time under a coalition government, the Secretary of State for Education, Michael Gove, spoke of the need 'to ensure that all children have the opportunity to acquire a core of essential knowledge in the key subject disciplines' (DfE, 2011a). There will therefore be a new national curriculum that will 'have a greater focus on subject content, outlining the essential knowledge and understanding that pupils should be expected to have' (DfE, 2011b). Once again, teachers are being expected to change direction and take on board new guidelines for the curriculum. In contrast to the new secondary curriculum introduced under a Labour government, the emphasis in the new national curriculum is to be much more focused on *what* to teach rather than *how* to teach it.

In this chapter, we have only been able scratch the surface of the history of the curriculum, but even this brief overview raises interesting questions about who is in control of the curriculum in schools. With the move towards a 'top-down' approach to curriculum, the question arises as to whether it can be introduced effectively without the co-operation of the teachers (Kelly, 2009). But our focus here is, of course, on those starting out on their career in teaching and the knowledge, understanding and skills they will require in order to navigate their way through the different, and sometimes conflicting directives on the school curriculum. It has been said that 'curriculum development is teacher development' (Blenkin et al., 1992: 154) and this is the reason for investigating the nature and aims of the school curriculum in this chapter.

What are the goals or purposes of the school curriculum?

At the start of what is regarded as a classic text in terms of a manual for curriculum development, Tyler (1949) asked four questions that set the agenda for those involved in curriculum development and the first step is to look at the purpose or goal of schooling:

- What educational purposes should the school seek to attain?
- What educational experiences can be provided that are likely to attain these purposes?
- How can these educational experiences be effectively organised?
- How can we determine whether these purposes are being attained? (Tyler, 1949: 1).

We hear strong views expressed on what the goals or purposes of the school curriculum should be. On the one hand you might believe that the school curriculum should focus on the needs of the individual and provide opportunity for the pupil to 'be the best that they can be' as you may have heard the head teacher say. You might argue that every young person has an entitlement to a broad curriculum that opens new doors for them to go beyond the boundaries defined by home background so that they can fulfil their individual potential. You might hold this liberal view of education and say that education is a good thing in its own right and not a means to an end. On the other hand, you might argue that the curriculum must take account of the bigger picture and of society as a whole. You might want to say that the school curriculum should prepare young people for the world of work and that all educational provision must take account of the need for the economic growth and development of the country. You might call this an instrumentalist view as education becomes a means to an end. Others might say that the curriculum in schools should be about both of these things and so want to ask – 'why is it so often insisted that education aims should be either 'liberal' or 'instrumental' – why can't they be both, at once affording intrinsic satisfactions and yet serving useful social purposes?' (Bantock, 1980: 132). It is believed by some that it is up to the school to decide its educational goals and in his manual for curriculum design Tyler (1949), assumes that individual schools will agree their own purposes. With the recent move in England towards so-called 'free schools' that are independent from the local authority control there will be much more freedom for schools to decide their own goals or purposes and they will have greater control over their curriculum. In the light of this, the teachers in such schools will need to be equipped to meet the challenge of curriculum development.

Point for reflection

- Looking back to your own schooling do you think that the curriculum was based on a liberal view of education or was it more instrumentalist in its approach?

Case study 7.1 Secondary school teacher voices

The voices of these secondary school teachers are from a small-scale research project carried out in 2009–2010.

'I think it is about making what they study in class relevant to them ... try to remember what it was like in school – you know you go to maths and you learn about what three Xs are or whatever then you come to RE and learn lots of things ... that you are probably never going to need .. lots of facts ... but it is not really relevant

(Continued)

(Continued)

to the children and if they want to go and study something like that they can go and study it at A level or degree level. So ... make it much more relevant to them and help them to cope with real life really!' (School A)

'What I really think is that in this present climate ... in the world ... what we don't need is simply to impart knowledge to children the time for that is well past ... we can't give children what they need to know in 20 years' time or even 5 years' time. So what we really need and in terms of our subject and in terms of many subjects ... what we really need is a new, a re-working of the of the old traditional liberal education with a humanistic focus ... we have got to make a fairly swift shift to a much more moral based curriculum.' (School V)

'It is sort of about skills that are needed for the world beyond school, a fast changing world ... It is about collaborating, the fact that industry has been saying ever since I began teaching really we don't teach them to become articulate collaborators. We teach them to work on their own when they need to learn to work with other people.' (School M)

S.C. Mercier, (2010) 'The impact of the new secondary curriculum and the implications for ITE'. Paper presented at the BERA Conference, Warwick.

These observations from teachers would appear to reflect the view that, on the one hand, we need one curriculum for the schools where the goal is to equip young people going on to further study with the academic knowledge and skills they need and, on the other, we need a different curriculum for those pupils that are going to go directly into the workplace when they leave the classroom. This has been an area of considerable political debate in the past and it remains so today but we are not going to enter this discussion here. Instead we are going to turn our attention to two broad models of the curriculum which might help throw some light on the issue.

Two models of the curriculum

Once we have agreed the goals or purposes of schooling, Tyler's questions (1949) prompt us to move on to select and organise the learning experiences that will best achieve these goals. Exactly how to select and organise the curriculum is a matter of 'perennial' debate (Carr, 2007) and as we can see from the contrasting directives in recent government reviews, schools have had to work with very different models of the curriculum. But it might be helpful at this point to turn to curriculum theory rather than to government policy to look at different models of the curriculum. In Bernstein's (1971) theoretical analysis of the curriculum there are two models. On the one hand, there is a 'collection' type of curriculum, with clear boundaries between subjects and where the teacher holds control of the knowledge and the process of transmission. On the other, there is an 'integrated' model of the curriculum which is planned around concepts, skills and processes rather than subjects and where the learner is more in control of their learning.

Let us look at one model at a time. The collection model is based on the view that distinct and clearly identifiable realms of knowledge can be shown to exist. For example in the classic discussion on the curriculum in Hirst and Peters (1970: 63) there are eight realms of knowledge and these are mathematics, physical sciences, human sciences, history, religion, literature and the arts, philosophy, moral knowledge. The logical conclusion from this starting point is that a school curriculum should be structured around these 'modes of experience' to allow for 'systematic attention to be given to the progressive mastery of closely interrelated concepts, patterns of reasoning and qualities of mind' (Hirst and Peters, 1970: 70). This so-called 'collection' model where knowledge content is collected or packaged into discrete subjects is also associated with what Bernstein calls 'strong classification'. In other words, these collections of knowledge are clearly fenced off from one another and also from everyday knowledge gained outside the classroom. The collection model of the curriculum is usually characterised by strong 'framing' which means that clear structures are put in place, governing the stages in the transmission of knowledge. This controlled process of transmission determines the relationship between the teacher and learner as 'strong frames reduce the power of the pupil over what, when and how he receives knowledge and increases the teacher's power in the pedagogical relationship' (1971: 206). Therefore, the teaching is usually traditional or didactic.

Some find the arguments for a curriculum based on these distinct realms of knowledge persuasive (Marsh, 1997: 27). Others are less convinced (Kelly, 2009: 39) and question the motives of those supporting this model of the curriculum. It has been argued that those who maintain a curriculum based on realms of knowledge are motivated by the need to protect the status of their subject (Beane, 1997: 42) and the academic base from which the subject takes its credentials. This model of the curriculum fits with the view that schooling is a way to ensure that the realms of knowledge as well as the culture and values from which they emerge are transmitted to the next generation. Of course, you might want to ask whose culture is being passed on and who is it that decides which subjects are included. It has been suggested that the subject-based curriculum is narrow and offers a very 'Euro-centric view of knowledge organisation' Beane (1992: 46). The question arises as to whether the subject structures represent an elitist approach to knowledge and you might ask whether some of the learners would feel unconnected, disaffected or even unable to access the curriculum because it is an alien culture or just not seen as relevant.

Case study 7.2 Teachers' voices

These teachers' voices are taken from a small-scale enquiry carried out in schools between 2009–11. They indicate that some teachers are uncomfortable with the idea of a return to a curriculum that is subject-content driven and didactic in its approach to learning:

'I know it suits some people very well to teach like that. But it doesn't suit the children really..... and then they wonder why they are in special measures for behaviour.' (School H)

'If we are just giving a load of facts ... that is going to impact on behaviour and that is going to impact on the kids being able to pass exams and everything because we have got to put it to them in an accessible way.' (School P)

'We struggle to get students to just value learning for learning's sake ... You know I have been teaching for 20 years and I think it is something that is getting stronger and how do you deal with that?' (School B)

S.C. Mercier, (2011) 'Teacher perspectives on curriculum change'. Paper presented at the BERA Conference, London.

Other issues have been raised in the past in response to a curriculum based on collections of knowledge, for example there is the question of whether dividing the curriculum into subjects means that we present artificial divisions between the different bodies of knowledge. Some critics of the collection model question whether the 'subjects somehow fail to reflect the actual psychological learning processes of the child' (Carr, 2007: 11) and others suggest that there is good evidence that the brain itself seeks to integrate knowledge rather than compartmentalise it (Beane, 1997: 33) and so, in fact, a more integrated curriculum would suit the learner. As Hargreaves has pointed out, if the curriculum 'is taught with a sharp separation between each discipline, then it is left to the pupils to face the major task of integrating the different disciplinary perspectives into a coherent whole' (1982: 132).

In his analysis of the curriculum, Bernstein contrasts the 'collection model' described above with the 'integrated model' of the curriculum. This model is based on 'a fundamental belief that knowledge is provisional, speculative and thus indeterminate' (Dalton, 1988: 189). In this model, the dividing lines between the subjects are blurred and 'we have a shift from content closure to content openness and from strong to markedly reduced classification' (Bernstein, 1971: 216). In other words there is no one maintaining boundaries between the subjects and there is continuity between knowledge learnt in school and knowledge gained in the world of everyday life. With the integrated curriculum there is also 'a shift in the balance of power in the pedagogical relationship between teacher and taught' (1971: 217) and the teaching style is less didactic. Also, with this integrated model there is a much more relaxed approach to the framing so that the learner has much greater autonomy over their own learning. The focus is on how we learn rather than what is known and so there is greater emphasis on the attitudes, attributes and skills of the learner than on the subject content and state of knowledge to be attained.

The origins of this integrated approach have been traced back to Dewey (Carr, 2007: 8). Dewey regarded the idea of the division between discrete areas of knowledge as artificial and believed that to start from the idea of there being discrete subjects and then to try to interest the pupil in them, was absurd. Dewey's starting point is the learner. It is the pupil who constructs knowledge, actively exploring, experimenting and enquiring. The subject or content of the curriculum is what is useful to the child and education is essentially about transformation and growth. With this approach, the teacher does not limit or have control over what the pupils learn. Teacher and pupil learn together and construct knowledge together. There are no boundaries between what is learnt in the classroom and what is learnt outside the school. This model of the curriculum calls for a very different approach to teaching and learning. There are different versions of curriculum integration and you could distinguish between what has been called a 'multidisciplinary' approach and an 'integrated curriculum'. We do not have time to look at these here but, to find out more, read Beane (1997).

In secondary classrooms today, we can see evidence of different curriculum models at work and in schools where teachers embraced the new secondary curriculum introduced under Labour, cross-curricular subjects and themes such as identity and cultural diversity, healthy lifestyles, and enterprise (QCA, 2007) have been introduced. Subjects such as Citizenship have also been approached in a cross-curricular or integrated way (QCA, 1998). The fact is that very few schools follow a fully integrated approach to the curriculum and as White has suggested, these initiatives only pay lip service to the idea of connected learning and 'unless the impulse towards connectedness is sparked off within the subjects themselves, external solutions like this will not work' (White, 2004: 183). White contends that teachers really need to be involved at a deep level from within their subjects in order to bring an informed and rigorous approach to an integrated curriculum. Indeed, it has been observed that the truly integrated approach to the curriculum comes at a price and 'the cost falls on the teachers, who need to be flexible and open-minded' (Hargreaves, 1982: 166). One of the main findings of the Humanities Curriculum Project which promoted an integrated approach to the curriculum was that in order for this model to be successful, teachers had to work 'self-critically' (Stenhouse et al., 1980: 255) and become 'researchers' in their own classrooms. Others have remarked on 'the tensions and contradictions' experienced by teachers involved in cross curricular initiatives (Flores, 2005) and it has been shown that beginner teachers find working with an interdisciplinary approach very challenging (Richards and Shea, 2006). Paechter observes that secondary 'school structures ... do not fit well with cross-subject initiatives' (2000: 71) and shows how the integrated curriculum disturbs both the subject departments and the roles of those within them. Secondary teachers often feel that their sense of identity and belonging is related to the subject department (Kirk and MacDonald, 2001). As an integrated curriculum calls for a democratic approach to knowledge and learning, both the teaching and the structures have to change and this level of disturbance within a school is challenging.

Case study 7.3 Teachers' voices

These teachers described how they were expected to move to an integrated curriculum and the changes involved in terms of roles and school structures:

'As part of Humanities – we were given new roles in school to develop it and we were one of the first to roll it out last September ... so RE is part of Humanities ... with Geography and History. We worked on it last year – we spent some INSET time on it ... so you know there was a clear structure throughout the school as to what we were going to do ... we have got a VLE so we have more communication within the departments, we have discussion forums so that we all know what each other are doing ... I suppose in a way it has been very good because it has been quite competitive within our school we have all been wanting to give of our best.' (School C)

'We were sort of told that we would run a pilot ... in Year 7, whereby History, Geography and RE were going to become integrated and not taught as distinct hour-long subjects but taught together the whole day. And that was sort of the break-through ... collapsing the schemes of work as they were and re-writing them on sort of a skills-based curriculum.' (School H)

'We were asked where we wanted to go with it and we went off into faculties to discuss first of all. In Humanities we did want to work together, we did not want to stay separate so we worked in Faculties pretty much, developing where we wanted to go. I have taken a lead with (a colleague) in Humanities ... we have sort of built on that as a team effort really. Just speaking from my Faculty at the moment, we have regular meetings every week to evaluate where we are going, what has worked, what has been good, what do we need to look at next week. Staff have voluntarily joined in with that and made it work which I think is a major thing really.' (School P)

'Somebody stood up and said look this is how it is all working together ... and instead of little blocks now we are looking at nice flowing little ribbons ... other than that there hasn't been any kind of ... I think they are working towards this idea that we should be much more cross curricular with these kind of learning zone things ... but it is certainly in its early stages.' (School B)

S.C. Mercier (2011) 'Teacher perspectives on curriculum change'. Paper presented at the BERA Conference, London.

Conclusion

Having examined the two models of the curriculum identified by Bernstein you might want to ask whether we have to decide on one model or another. Is there another way forward? Can we work with both approaches? Do we need teachers to be persuaded that one approach is the right one? Morrison asks whether 'it is perhaps misplaced to seek a single theory of the curriculum' and do we have to define what is curriculum or should we 'embrace the complicated?' (Morrison, 2004: 489). On the other hand, it has been argued that you need decide on one curriculum model and run with that. Dalton captures the tension between these different models in the words of this teacher: 'I do not think you can ride two horses – the content and the process horse – you have to back one or the other' (Dalton, 1988: 96). In contrast to this, more recent research in schools where the curriculum is changing suggests that teachers are able to work with contrasting models of the curriculum at the same time and can 'survive in a pluralistic educational world in which they are exposed to divergent views' (Levin and Nevo, 2009). Many teachers today are involved in teaching within an integrated model for one context and a separate subject approach for another. For example schools may have an integrated humanities approach in Years 7 and 8 while maintaining separate subjects in the lead up to examination choices in Year 9. It will be very interesting to see how the new curriculum review will impact on schools working with these different models of the curriculum and you will be able to research this in your school experience.

In this chapter we looked briefly at different definitions of the curriculum and have drawn out some key issues that emerge from the story of how the curriculum has developed in secondary schools. We have explored two contrasting models of the curriculum and examined some of the theory behind them. We have also listened to the voices of teachers caught up in the process of curriculum change. In the course of the chapter, it should have become clear to the beginner teacher that they need to reflect on their own role in the development of the curriculum and gain an understanding of the curriculum models that are at work in their placement schools in order to be able to contribute the curriculum development in their school in the future.

Reflective questions

1. To what extent does the story of the curriculum indicate a trend towards more central or government control over what is taught in schools? Do you think this is going to change or reverse direction in the future?
2. What are the main differences in terms of the role of the teacher within the collection model of the curriculum and within the integrated model of the curriculum? Which role do you think is closest to your idea of the teacher?

Recommended further reading

Beane, J.A. (1997) *Curriculum Integration: Designing the Core of Democratic Education*. New York: Teachers College Press.

This text challenges the teacher to reflect on the opportunities offered by an integrated curriculum.

Kelly, A.V. (2009) *The Curriculum: Theory and Practice*, 6th edn. London: Sage.
This is a classic text on the curriculum which raises the important issues.

Ross, A. (2000) *Curriculum, Construction and Critique*. London: Falmer Press.
This is a good textbook on the curriculum and an interesting read if you want to get an overview of the way the curriculum has been developed.

White, J. (2004) *Rethinking the School Curriculum: Values, Aims and Purposes.* London: Routledge.
This textbook encourages the teacher to ask questions about the kind of curriculum we want for young people.

References

Bantock, G.H. (1980) *Dilemmas of the Curriculum.* Oxford: Martin Robertson.

Beane, J.A. (1992) 'Creating an integrative curriculum: making the connections', *NASSP Bulletin*, 5, 46–54.

Beane, J.A. (1997) *Curriculum Integration: Designing the Core of Democratic Education.* New York: Teachers College Press.

Bernstein, B. (1971) *Class, Codes and Control*. London: Routledge & Kegan Paul.

Blenkin, G.M, Edwards, G. and Kelly, A.V. (1992) *Change and the Curriculum.* London: Paul Chapman Publishing Ltd.

Carr, D. (2007) 'Towards an educationally meaningful curriculum: epistemic holism and knowledge integration revisited', *British Journal of Educational Studies*, 55 (1): 3–20.

Clark, J. (2005) 'Curriculum studies in initial teacher education: the importance of holism and project 2061', *The Curriculum Journal*, 16 (4): 509–21.

Dalton, T.H. (1988) *The Challenge of Curriculum Innovation: A Study of Ideology and Practice*. London: Falmer Press.

Department for Education and Science (1944) *Education Reform Act.* London: HMSO.

Department for Education and Science (1977) *Curriculum 11–16.* London: HMSO.

Department for Education (DfE) (2011a) 'Review of the National Curriculum in England: remit'. Available online at http://www.education.gov.uk/nationalcurriculum

Department for Education (DfE) (2011b) 'Review of the National Curriculum in England: core script and briefing'. Available online at http://www.education.gov.uk/nationalcurriculum

Flores, M.A. (2005) 'Teachers' views on recent curriculum changes: tensions and challenges', *The Curriculum Journal*, 16 (3): 401–13.

Gordon, P. and Lawton, D. (1978) *Curriculum Change in the Nineteenth and Twentieth Centuries*. London: Hodder and Stoughton.

Hargreaves, D.H. (1982) *The Challenge for the Comprehensive School: Culture, Curriculum and Community*. London: Routledge and Kegan Paul.

Hirst, P.H. and Peters, R.S. (1970) *The Logic of Education*. Routledge & Kegan Paul.

Illich, I.D. (1973) *Deschooling Society*. Harmondsworth: Penguin.

Kelly, A.V. (2009) *The Curriculum: Theory and Practice*. London: Sage.

Kirk, D. and MacDonald, D. (2001) 'Teacher voice and ownership of curriculum change', *Journal of Curriculum Studies*, 33 (5): 351–67.

Levin, T. and Nevo, Y. (2009) 'Exploring teachers' views on learning and teaching in the context of a trans-disciplinary curriculum', *Journal of Curriculum Studies*, 41 (4): 439–65.

Marsh, C. (1997) *Planning, Management and Ideology: Key Concepts for Understanding Curriculum*. London: The Falmer Press.

Morrison, R.B. (2004) 'The poverty of curriculum theory: a critique of Wraga and Hlebowitsh', *Journal Curriculum Studies*, 36 (4): 487–94.

Paechter, C. (2000) *Changing School Subjects: Power, Gender and Curriculum*. Buckingham: Open University Press.

Pring, R. (1989) *The New Curriculum*. London: Cassell Educational Ltd.

QCA (1998) *The Education for Citizenship and the Teaching of Democracy in Schools* (The Crick Report). London: Qualifications and Curriculum Authority.

QCA (2007) *The New Secondary Curriculum*. London: Qualifications and Curriculum Authority.

Richards, J.C. and Shea, K.T. (2006) 'Moving from separate subject to interdisciplinary teaching: the complexity of change in pre-service teacher K-1 early field experience', *The Qualitative Report*, 11 (1): 1–19.

Ross, A. (2000) *Curriculum, Construction and Critique*. London: Falmer Press.

Schools Curriculum and Assessment Authority (1993) *The Dearing Report*. London: SCAA Publications.

Scottish Education Department (SED) (1977) *The Structure of the Curriculum in the Third and Fourth Years of the Secondary School* (The Munn Report). Edinburgh: HMSO.

Stenhouse, L. (ed.) (1980) *Curriculum Research and Development in Action*. London: Heinemann Educational Books.

Tyler, R.W. (1949) *Basic Principles of Curriculum and Instruction USA*. Chicago: The University of Chicago Press.
White, J. (ed.) (2004) *Re-thinking the School Curriculum: Values, Aims and Purposes.* London: Routledge-Falmer.

CHAPTER 8

WHAT IS LEARNING THEORY? HOW CAN IT HELP ME?

Tony Ewens

By the end of this chapter you should have:

- an overview of theories about the nature and processes of learning;
- an insight into the structure of your subject and ways in which learners develop mastery of it;
- an appreciation of how learning theories can help teachers to plan, conduct and evaluate their work;
- an ability to use learning theories when investigating your subject and its pedagogy.

This book sees teachers as researchers, constantly reviewing pupils' performance and their own practice in order to extend pupils' learning and their own professional competence. This vision cannot be realised without some grasp of key theories of learning, especially those drawn from philosophy and psychology; this chapter aims to give you an introduction to some key theories of learning which you will find relevant to your teaching and pupils' learning.

The relationship between learning theory and subject teaching is complex. For example, in some lessons you may want pupils to gain and retain important information, and in others to acquire and practise certain skills. Sometimes you help them to formulate attitudes; at other times you emphasise the understanding of a key concept. The nature of knowledge, in any subject, is complex, so you need a sophisticated approach when using theories of learning to enhance your teaching.

What is meant by 'learning'?

A typical psychological definition of learning identifies, 'relatively permanent changes in behaviour or in potential for behaviour that result from experience' (Lefrançois, 1999: 41). This assumes a broad view of 'behaviour', including observable phenomena and changes in inner thought patterns. Assessment of learning consequently requires measurement of both observable and unseen changes in behaviour. For example, an ability to spell words, define mathematical terms or describe scientific experiments can readily be tested, because they can be observed. However, more subtle questioning is needed to investigate pupils' comprehension of passages of literature, their processes of reasoning in solving mathematical problems or their insight into interpretations of data in scientific experiments, since these entail changes in unseen thought patterns.

These examples portray different levels of learning. Bloom (1956) proposed a six-level taxonomy, beginning with a basic demonstration of knowledge and rising through comprehension, application, analysis and synthesis to the most complex level evaluation. Others have broadened the scope, to include intrapersonal and interpersonal factors as elements of learning (e.g. Gagné and Driscoll, 1988). In short, the notion of learning is difficult to pin down.

What is meant by 'knowledge'?

Knowledge, like learning, defies simple definition. Lehrer's remark, 'All agree that knowledge is valuable, but agreement about knowledge tends to end there' (Lehrer, 2000: 1) is an apt comment on epistemology, the branch of philosophy that studies knowledge. Two main strands in epistemology are rationalism, which views knowledge as produced by rational reflection on received wisdom, and empiricism, which sees it as the fruit of sensory perception, and therefore related to first-hand experience. These strands can be identified in a long-running debate about the purposes of education. Is education the accumulation of knowledge conveyed through a process of cultural transmission, or the development of skills to facilitate discovery or creation of knowledge?

Documentation for compulsory subjects at Key Stages 3 and 4 reveals that both sides of this debate are represented. For each subject there is a description of what pupils should know and be able to do, reflecting the 'body of knowledge' view and also the skills-based approach. Additionally, National Curriculum documents identify what pupils should understand and what attitudes they should develop. Much of the groundwork for the National Curriculum centred on analysing subjects in terms of knowledge, skills, concepts and attitudes (DES, 1989), drawing upon the work of Ryle (1949).

Ryle's distinction (Ryle, 1949) between 'knowing that' and 'knowing how' continues to influence curriculum design. Knowledge can be superficial or deep, and a key debate is about how to design the curriculum so that pupils are introduced to progressively deeper levels of knowledge and understanding. Some of the issues are illustrated in the following statements, which exhibit varied nuances of meaning:

'I know that Henry VIII had six wives.'

'I know how to climb a rope.'

'I know Tudor history.'

'I know trigonometry', and

'I know that that is a great piece of art.'

The first statement refers to a discrete piece of information, the second to a discrete skill. The third and fourth relate to broader areas of knowledge, implying an ability to deploy a range of knowledge and skills. The interplay of skills and information enables the learner to grasp the central concepts – or 'big ideas' – associated with the subject.

The final example involves a degree of subjective judgement. You and I may both say that that is a great piece of art, but for very different reasons. You may say it because respected art critics rate it highly and I because I like it a lot. The fifth statement reveals the difficulties in agreeing what counts as knowledge. For instance, is it enough to say that I really like a painting in order to say that it is a great work?

How do knowledge and learning interrelate?

In the five examples above, the first four can be accounted for within Bloom's six-level taxonomy (1956). The first and second statements represent what Bloom called basic demonstrations of knowledge and can easily be assessed.

The third statement, 'I know Tudor history' is more than a claim to know a great deal about the Tudors. It implies that: you can process your knowledge to demonstrate how discrete bits of information fit together to make a coherent whole; you can analyse texts from the period and synthesise their content with other material, and you can evaluate other people's judgements about episodes in Tudor history in a way that makes sense to others who 'know Tudor history'. In short, Bloom's approach to learning can help teachers to classify different types of knowledge so as to identify learning as superficial or deep.

Applying this approach to the fourth statement, 'I know trigonometry', shows the same process applied to another subject. 'Knowing trigonometry' includes basic demonstration of facts, for example that a tangent is defined as 'opposite over adjacent'. It demands competence in certain skills, for example using a clinometer to take an angle reading, and the application of knowledge, such as calculating the height of a structure. Two pupils may do this and achieve the correct answer. But one may reveal a deeper insight into trigonometry by showing an understanding that the process is an application of Pythagoras' theorem, while the other demonstrates no more than an ability to follow instructions. This is significant, and cannot be identified simply by seeing which pupils got the right answer.

Hierarchies of learning, such as Bloom's taxonomy, can assist teachers in unravelling the complexity of their subjects. Ryle likened this approach to the concept of mapmaking (Ryle, 1949: 9f.). An appreciation of the various elements – information, skills and concepts – which constitute the subject offers teachers a basis for deciding in what order to present material to pupils. It also enables teachers to design assessments that go beyond tests of factual information, to identify different levels of understanding.

The fifth statement presented above goes beyond the scope of Bloom's account of learning, because it entails subjective judgement on the part of the speaker. This is a crucial issue for aesthetic subjects such as art, literature, music, dance and drama. It is easy to be sceptical about the claim, 'this is a great piece of art'. How could you assess its accuracy? This discussion demonstrates the interrelated difficulties about the definition of learning and knowledge, the issue being what can be allowed to count as learning, or to count as knowledge.

Seeking clarification

In the examples above, the final statement could not be accounted for in terms of Bloom's taxonomy of learning. Yet, it fits Lefrançois' definition of learning with which this chapter began: 'relatively permanent changes in behaviour or in potential for behaviour that result from experience'. My claim that that is a great piece of art affects my thinking and my actions; for example, I may attend an exhibition where it is to be on display, or look for other examples of the same artist's work. In terms of theories of learning, 'knowing that that is a great work of art' is consequently valid. But in terms of theories of knowledge its validity is problematic, since it goes beyond demonstrable fact. Empiricists might therefore suggest excluding this sort of material from education, or at least from formal assessment. But that contradicts the practices of many disciplines in English education. For artists, musicians, dancers, gymnasts, poets and educators in literature, religion and morality, statements based on judgements, beliefs and opinions for which a reasoned argument can be made, are both valid and assessable. Examiners do indeed assess the artistic merits of gymnastic routines, musical performances or pieces of sculpture. To confine assessment to what is empirically testable would strip those subjects of some of their central features.

The key consideration is the phrase, 'for which a reasoned argument can be made'. The 'reasoned argument' used to establish the validity of knowledge that cannot be empirically tested relates to the notion that each subject has its own matters and processes, accepted by the community of those involved in the subject as experts. So, for example, the scientific community determines through ongoing debate what makes sense in science, and parallel processes take place in the other disciplines. That is why 'artistic merit' can make perfect sense in an arts subject, whereas a scientist would find the concept inadmissible.

It follows that, in any subject, the learner ought to be inducted into the discipline as practised by its community of experts. For example, in history, pupils should make discoveries using primary data, but should also learn about what historians have already established. Science, likewise, should be a balance between first-hand experimental work and learning about earlier scientific discoveries. Similar conclusions can be drawn for other subjects. In each case, the implication is that pupils need to acquire factual information and also develop skills with which to process it.

Creating a clearer picture through professional reflection and enquiry

Points for reflection

The following suggest starting points for investigations you might undertake to extend your thinking:

- First, in deciding what constitutes a good education in your subject, you might consider the main areas of knowledge, skills and concepts that you believe pupils of your subject should master during secondary education. It can be interesting to compare your list with other teachers to investigate the extent of agreement. Pupils' views of the purpose of your subject in the curriculum may help you to determine what you consider the main aim of your subject as part of a broad, balanced education.
- Second, you might examine statutory documentation and examination syllabuses for your subject looking for evidence of the information, skills, concepts and attitudes prescribed there and reflect on the extent to which your vision for your subject is matched in the requirements. Comparisons with other countries' curricula can also help you to reflect on your beliefs about your subject.
- Third, you could reflect on the extent to which Bloom's six-level taxonomy of learning can assist you in identifying progression in your subject, from the learning of straightforward facts and skills, through comprehension and application of knowledge to analysis, synthesis and evaluation. This might lead you to investigate what opportunities your plans offer pupils to acquire information, learn and practise skills, demonstrate comprehension and application of their knowledge, and address harder aspects such as analysis, synthesis and evaluation. Another point to consider is whether your plans for assessment allow you to identify pupils who are working at deeper levels of learning.

The processes of learning

Psychology offers a range of theories to explain how learning occurs. Two main approaches are behaviourism and constructivism. For full accounts of these, Child's book (Child, 2007) is a standard text, regularly updated. The following synopses are accompanied by suggestions that you can use to investigate your own practice.

Behaviourism

Psychologists' emphasis on changes in behaviour as a definition of learning led them to examine actual behaviours to understand how learning takes place. Behaviourists draw upon the approaches of physical science and view learning as a product of interactions between learners and their environment. Pavlov's experiment with dogs, dating from the 1890s, is an early example. By sounding a bell when dogs were fed, he conditioned them to associate the sound of the bell with the proximity of their meals. Subsequently, the bell was enough to instigate salivation. Key ideas here are stimulus and response, with a consequential reward providing reinforcement.

Skinner (see Benjamin, 2007) showed that rats could learn to use a lever to trigger the release of a food reward. Again, stimulus, response and consequence led to changed behaviour, since the rats repeatedly pressed the lever in the expectation of receiving more rewards. The notion of conditioning, of which this is an example, is a fundamental concept in psychology.

Notice the importance in both Pavlov's and Skinner's work of repetitive work by the 'learners' as a means of reinforcing the learning.

Behaviourist theories have influenced schooling significantly, in behaviour management as well as in the teaching of subjects. The sequence of stimulus, response and consequence underpins much class management. Teachers call for quiet, then reward compliance or punish non-compliance. Repetition, represented by consistency in using disciplinary codes, is an important component of teachers' professional practice.

In subject teaching, Skinner's theories have influenced so-called 'traditional' approaches, where the teacher controls the material to be learnt and the pace of learning. Rote learning, whether memorising information or repeatedly practising tasks and skills, are obvious examples. Repeated drills such as sequenced skills in sports or playing scales on musical instruments can help pupils to master the exercises so that they can replicate them fluently. Likewise, fingertip knowledge of multiplication tables and a facility to repeat phrases in a foreign language can be valuable components in learning those subjects.

Case study 8.1 Rote learning in different subjects

Laurie (art and design), David (geography) and Lina (chemistry) are PGCE secondary student teachers on placement at the same school. During a discussion on teaching approaches, they began to explore the learning theories underpinning their teaching methods. On the issue of rote learning, in art and design Laurie

(Continued)

(Continued)

stated that she felt strongly at the start of her course that that this was not appropriate in art and design, (it went against the spirit of the subject as being creative) yet at times she realised it had its place (for example when explaining a technique like printmaking). David believed that in geography rote learning was necessary for an introduction to a theme, but at a certain point, he wanted his pupils to move beyond this to research different opinions and evidence available, especially on controversial issues like global warming. Lina believed that it is sometimes a challenge to go beyond rote learning in chemistry; she wanted her pupils to be able to enjoy the practical nature of experiments, without always telling them the results before the experiments had been completed, therefore almost negating the point of pupils doing the practical work.

Rote learning is sometimes frowned upon for casting pupils in a passive role or giving them fragments of knowledge without understanding. Yet it is an economical way of imparting information and skills, the first levels of Bloom's taxonomy. Mastery of these basics can accelerate the subsequent learning of more advanced knowledge.

Two caveats apply. The first relates to motivation (Child, 2007: Section 3, Chapter 8). Pedagogy based on behaviourist theories often depends on extrinsic motivation, since the 'consequences' stage of the process is often connected with rewards unrelated to the subject matter. For example, teachers may use praise or house points in response to correct answers or good conduct. While younger pupils enjoy receiving rewards, there is a risk that pupils come to see the goal of learning as reward, rather than achievement. Moreover, by Years 9 and 10, receiving praise and rewards from teachers may be regarded as 'uncool', so that pupils actively avoid such situations. Successful teaching is more likely to be sustained if intrinsic motivation can be incorporated into teachers' routines, so that pupils gain satisfaction from completing tasks and making progress.

The second caveat relates to relevance. Pupils are more likely to engage productively in rote tasks if they can appreciate why they are doing them. Knowing the names and dates of English monarchs, or being able to catch and throw a ball equally well with both hands may seem pointless, but they acquire purpose if applied in realistic settings. By linking their knowledge to relevant contexts, pupils can gain and demonstrate comprehension and application, thus revealing higher-order learning in Bloom's terms.

Reflecting on your subject and behaviourism

In reflecting on the value of behaviourist approaches to learning for the pedagogy of your subject you could, for example, consider whether particular areas of factual knowledge or subject-specific skills lend themselves to rote learning in your subject. To investigate further, you could identify a couple of examples to explore, and plan activities to teach these examples as economically as possible. You would need to consider particularly how to motivate the pupils, thinking about intrinsic and extrinsic motivation. In deciding how to assess the learning, an important consideration is whether rote learning supports both the short-term and long-term retention of the information or skill.

Constructivism

Whereas behaviourists considered only observable changes in behaviour, constructivists focused on the learner's cognitive development, studying their thinking, reasoning and understanding in an effort to describe how learning takes place, and to deduce how teachers might support and enhance the process.

Constructivism and stage theories: Piaget and Kohlberg

Piaget investigated the perceptions of children from 3 to 12. He developed a stage theory, concluding that children's thinking goes through a sequence of qualitatively differing steps (Child, 2007: Section 2, Chapter 4). Rather than seeing children as mini-adults, Piaget contended that educators should focus on the predominant characteristics of the learner's thinking at any stage. Particularly interesting to secondary teachers is his distinction between a stage of 'concrete operations', typically between 7 and 11 years of age, when logical thinking depends on specific examples, such as the manipulation of structured apparatus in mathematics, and the next stage, 'formal operations', when abstract thinking has become possible. This theory suggests that, for pupils unable to grasp a specific concept, teachers should provide concrete examples to work through, with the intention that they will subsequently be able to deduce the abstract principle from the specific instances. This approach may be particularly valuable in subjects such as mathematics and science, in which progression most depends on sequential learning.

A practical drawback when applying Piaget's stage theory is that teachers may limit their expectations of learners by seeing them as 'not yet ready' to move on. If you plan to re-visit an earlier stage of thinking, you should see it as a way of reinforcing and consolidating knowledge, rather than an exercise in providing easy tasks for lower-achieving pupils.

Kohlberg built upon Piaget's work to identify a stage theory related to moral reasoning (Murray, 2007), and this can help teachers when considering behaviour management. Kohlberg concluded that individuals proceed through the stage of *heteronomy* (literally, 'other people's laws') to *autonomy*, when they can assume responsibility for moral judgements. An issue is whether passing through a stage of imposed disciplinary codes (*heteronomy*) is an essential prerequisite to reaching maturity in moral reasoning (Roberts, 2007). For secondary teachers, Kohlberg's work might provide support for an adult-directed framework of rules governing conduct, together with an expectation that adolescents will test and question the school's behaviour policy as they internalise and adapt moral principles in moving towards *autonomy*.

Constructivism and pedagogy: Bruner and Ausubel

Case study 8.2 Can discovery be 'facilitated'?

In continuing the discussions on their different subjects, Laurie, Lina and David explored the idea of allowing pupils to learn by discovering for themselves. They agreed that the concept of 'discovery' for pupils in their learning was important and they wanted pupils to experience what Laurie described as 'that penny dropping moment when you see pupils have really understood something you've been talking to them about, or even better, they have come up with a solution to a problem in their work which is better than anything you could have suggested for them'. The puzzle for all of them was, how to plan for this to happen, how to create the circumstances or right environment. Can something be over-planned to the extent there is no room for 'discovery' on the part of the pupil, because all possibilities have already been explored by the teacher?

Like Piaget, Bruner views children as active processors of information and ideas, constructing their own understandings rather than simply being instructed by teachers. Constructivist pedagogical theory (Powell and Kalina, 2009) proposes that pupils should not receive material in its final form, but should process it for themselves, perceiving connections with previous knowledge.

Because of this, Bruner is sometimes described as the main proponent of 'discovery learning', and some educators, especially in primary schools, have, in the past, organised their teaching on the misconception that he advocated uninhibited freedom to make discoveries as the hallmark of good education. In fact, Bruner emphasised the teacher's role in facilitating learning, selecting materials, experiences and guidance to enable learners to work within a defined area of knowledge, making it their own. His approach requires teachers to have an accurate knowledge of what pupils already know, understand and can do. Further, it implies that they will differentiate tasks in order to relate new activities to pupils' existing competences.

Two aspects of Bruner's thinking relevant to secondary education are the notion of a 'spiral curriculum' and an emphasis on conceptual understanding. Building upon Piaget's stage theory, Bruner advised re-visiting topics with an increasing emphasis on moving towards abstract levels; it is this process that he called the 'spiral curriculum'. An examination of a subject syllabus through consecutive key stages will show how this element of Bruner's work has influenced teaching. The implications for teachers' organisation of curriculum and classroom are clear, since groups of pupils may need to work simultaneously on the same topic, but at different levels. Some may need structured, practical activities while others can work at a more theoretical level.

Bruner viewed a subject's key concepts as the pillars supporting a superstructure of information and skills. Examples include cause and effect in history, a fair test in science, melody and timbre in music, addition and subtraction in mathematics, and faith and worship in religion. Such concepts, or 'fundamentals', he considered of crucial significance in learning for four main reasons (Bruner, 1960). First, by acting as organising foci they make a subject comprehensible. Second, they offer a way of representing detailed material in a structured and memorable way. Third, they promote transfer of training, so that if new material can be perceived as a fresh example of a concept previously understood, the learner is enabled readily to comprehend it. Finally, basing curriculum and teaching on a framework of concepts narrows the gap between elementary and advanced knowledge.

Placing concepts at the heart of pedagogical aims and practice complements Bruner's notion of the spiral curriculum. For example, small children may manipulate groups of objects to exemplify the process of adding two quantities together. Later, they may learn pairs of numbers that add up to ten, and next explore algorithms enabling them to add numbers up to hundreds, then thousands. Later still, come exercises involving fractions, negative numbers and algebraic symbols. Each is an instance of the concept of addition in mathematics, but at very different levels. Comparable examples may be identified in all subjects.

The challenge of using a subject's key concepts as a basis for planning is a valuable discipline. It ensures that the sheer quantity of information and skills that teachers must cover in any topic will be organised according to a medium- to long-term objective – that the pupils will gain a deeper understanding of a concept. This helps to promote sequenced learning, rather than simply the accumulation of disconnected facts (Gordon, 2008).

Ausubel and Robinson (1969), while agreeing with Bruner that new learning should be related to pupils' existing knowledge, found Bruner's insistence that pupils should process new material for themselves a recipe for inefficiency in teaching. Ausubel and Robinson advocated a greater degree of direct instruction. However, they emphasised the importance of teachers' subject knowledge and their ability to select appropriate material and relevant learning outcomes.

The focus of the constructivist element in Ausubel and Robinson's approach is on learners' ability to create links between the new material and what they already know. Their thinking avoids a criticism sometimes directed at constructivists, that they require pupils to rediscover knowledge that has been known for generations ('reinventing the wheel'). However, their proposals may not allow sufficiently for differentiation of teaching to meet the range of learning needs in a class.

Social constructivism – Vygotsky

Central to Vygotsky's psychology (e.g. Vygotsky, 1978) is 'cultural mediation', based on his observations that children are inducted into the thoughts, values and habits of their culture through a process of social interactions. These happen through contact with parents, other significant adults and wider social groups.

The importance of interaction between learners and more knowledgeable individuals is reflected in Vygotsky's 'Zone of Proximal Development' (ZPD). This concept relates to the difference between what learners know or can do independently, and what they can achieve with support from a more knowledgeable person, such as a teacher (Mcleod, 2007). In the early stages of learning, the teacher should provide significant amounts of help and encouragement, which can gradually be reduced. This approach, known as 'scaffolding', may include various teaching activities, such as clarifying objectives, breaking tasks into more manageable components, monitoring progress, correcting errors and explaining difficulties.

Vygotsky's ZPD theory informs classroom practice in several ways. First, it requires teachers to pinpoint the learner's starting point, so accurate initial assessment is vital. Second, teachers must be able to plan appropriate next steps for their pupils. Third, they must design suitable interventions to provide support and finally they engage in continuous assessment, to judge when to reduce support and identify when desired outcomes have been achieved.

It is implicit in this scheme that teachers should differentiate the amount of scaffolding they offer to groups and individuals in the class. That may be more important than differentiating the content of the lesson. This aspect of Vygotsky's work may be his enduring legacy to education. It has long been known that the level of support that pupils receive in their social settings has a significant bearing on their educational outcomes. Economic advantage is one factor; others include parental aspiration and guidance and community influences. Faced with two pupils of similar educational potential but different social circumstances, teachers may need to provide radically different degrees of scaffolding if both pupils are to achieve their potential. The emphasis in teachers' professional standards on having high expectations of all pupils is framed with such scenarios in mind. Teachers have no excuse for lowering expectations because of a pupil's social disadvantage.

Whereas Piaget's theories of development might suggest that teachers should wait for learners to reach an appropriate stage of development before introducing new work, Vygotsky's insistence on the influence of the social context upon learning supports a policy of active intervention by teachers to move pupils on in their learning.

Reflecting on your subject and constructivism

Reflection on the potential contribution of constructivist thinking to the teaching of your subject offers great scope for research-based professional practice, and might typically feature some of the following areas of enquiry.

Piaget's findings that a stage of concrete operations is a necessary prelude to being able to manage formal operations might lead you to identify a concept in the Key Stage 3 curriculum which some pupils typically find difficult. Your investigation might consist of designing practical activities which exemplify the principle, using them with pupils who initially struggle with the abstract idea and observing whether they begin to grasp the underlying concept.

Murray's (2007) or Roberts' (2007) texts relating to Kohlberg's theories about moral reasoning could support a study of pupils' responses to behaviour management strategies in your school, for example by investigating how exchanges between staff and pupils mirror Kohlberg's suggestions about stages of heteronomy and autonomy.

Reflecting on Bruner's contention that understanding a subject's key concepts is crucial to efficient learning, you might draw up a list of major concepts in your subject, then scrutinise documentation for your subject to trace how pupils can be helped to develop their conceptual understanding as they move through Key Stages 3 and 4 and beyond. One implication of Bruner's work is that it encourages teachers to think about long-term planning, rather than adopting a lesson-by-lesson approach. You might therefore review a sequence of lessons that you are planning, to judge how effective they are likely to be in helping pupils' conceptual understanding.

Finally, focusing on Vygotsky's notion of 'scaffolding' learning, you could usefully study a few pupils whom you are trying to move on in their learning. Once secure in your initial assessment of their previous attainment, you might experiment to find the most effective types of scaffolding for each pupil. Vygotsky's approach also suggests that you should consider whether lesson objectives are realistic and clear to pupils. Could tasks helpfully be broken into smaller stages? Can you help the pupil to link the new work to previous learning? Do difficulties with writing/spelling/grammar obstruct progress in other aspects of the task? You may find it instructive to ask pupils to suggest ways in which they think you might be able to help them – a useful insight into their own thinking and self-assessment.

Conclusion

The range of theories discussed in this chapter demonstrates that the study of learning is not an exact science. It is, however, an important aspect of your professional toolkit, since it focuses attention on the question of how learners can be helped effectively and efficiently to develop mastery of your subject. As such, it has much to offer to the design and conduct of professional enquiry among teachers who see themselves also as researchers.

Reflective questions

1. What are the theories of learning associated with your subject?
2. How would you describe significant learning in your subject?
3. How is it possible to develop pupils' sense of intrinsic motivation in your subject?
4. What are the 'key concepts' or 'pillars' of your subject?

Recommended further reading

Benjamin, L.T. (2007) *A Brief History of Modern Psychology*. Oxford: Wiley-Blackwell.
A very readable overview of how psychology and psychological theories have developed.

Child, D. (ed.) (2007) *Psychology and the Teacher*, 8th edn. London: Continuum.
A standard text that provides an overview of psychological issues and theories for the teacher.

Raiker, A. (2007) 'Cognitive development', in P. Zwozdiak-Myers (ed.), *Childhood and Youth Studies*. Exeter: Learning Matters.
A useful contextualised account of young people's development.

References

Ausubel, D.P. and Robinson, F.G. (1969) *School Learning: An Introduction to Educational Psychology*. New York: Holt, Rinchart and Winston.

Benjamin, L.T. (2007) *A Brief History of Modern Psychology.* Oxford: Wiley-Blackwell.

Bloom, B. (1956) *Taxonomy of Educational Objectives: The Classification of Educational Goals, Handbook 1, Cognitive Domain*. New York: David McKay.

Bruner, J.S. (1960) *The Process of Education*. Cambridge, MA: Harvard University Press.

Child, D. (ed.) (2007) *Psychology and the Teacher*, 8th edn. London: Continuum.

Department for Education and Schools (DES) (1989) *The National Curriculum for England and Wales*. London: The Stationery Office.

Gagné, R.M. and Driscoll, M.P. (1988) *Essentials of Learning for Instruction*. Englewood Cliffs, NJ: Prentice Hall.

Gordon, M. (2008) 'Between constructivism and connectedness', *Journal of Teacher Education*, 59 (4): 322–31.

Lefrançois, G.R. (1999) *Psychology for Teaching*, 10th edn. Belmont, CA: Wadsworth.

Lehrer, K. (2000) *Theory of Knowledge.* Boulder, CO: Westview Press.

Mcleod, S.A. (2007) 'Simply psychology'. Available online at http://www.simplypsychology.ord/vygotsky.html (last accessed 30 January 2010).

Murray, M.E. (2007) 'Moral development and moral education – an overview'. University of Illinois. Available online at http://www.library.spscc.ctc.edu/electronicreserve/swanson/MoralDevelopmentandMoralEducation.pdf (last accessed 27 January 2010).

Powell, K.C. and Kalina, C.J. (2009) 'Cognitive and social constructivism: developing tools for an effective classroom', *Education*, 130.

Roberts, I. (2007) 'Adolescence', in P. Zwozdiak-Myers *Childhood and Youth Studies*, Exeter: Learning Matters.

Ryle, G. (1949) *The Concept of Mind.* London: Hutchinson.

Vygotsky, L. (1978) *Mind in Society: The Development of Higher Psychological Processes*. Cambridge, MA: Harvard University Press.

CHAPTER 9

HOW SHOULD I ENGAGE WITH CLASSROOM ASSESSMENT?

Camilla Cole

By the end of this chapter you should be able to:

- reflect critically on the policy and practice of assessment;
- understand the nature and purpose of assessment;
- recognise the advantages and disadvantages of classroom assessment.

The importance of assessment is emphasised in the *Teachers' Standards* (DfE, 2011) with teachers being required to 'make active and productive use of assessment' (DfE, 2011: 6). Further statements regarding assessment can be found in the other standards which indicate the importance of assessment in the everyday practice of teachers' work in the classroom. As a student teacher, you may think you have a very clear understanding of what assessment is, what it is for and how it is to be used in the classroom as a result of your experiences of being a pupil. The aim of this chapter is to clarify what we mean when we talk about assessment inside the classroom and to create a critical understanding of why it may be important to pupil learning. Throughout this chapter experiences of previous student teachers will be highlighted. It is hoped that these illustrations will help to exemplify some of the practical issues regarding assessment in the classroom.

What is assessment?

A general definition for assessment can be expressed as a process by which it can be determined whether a person has developed their knowledge, understanding or skills. As Gipps (1999) helpfully puts it, assessment 'incorporates a wide range of methods for evaluating pupil performance and attainment, including formal testing and examinations, practical and oral assessment, and classroom-based assessment carried out by teachers' (p. 356). It is this general understanding of the term that will be used in this chapter.

As we embark on this journey into understanding assessment, a good starting point is to consider why teachers believe the assessment of pupils to be important. As you read this, you will undoubtedly be forming your own opinions. Reasons why teachers assess pupils could be because:

- they want to see how pupils are progressing;
- the data gathered in schools through pupil assessment can contribute to the calculation of league tables or other public indications of how the school is doing;
- of the need to have evidence to support teacher comments and findings when talking or reporting to parents and carers;
- teachers want to check pupil learning and understanding before moving onto the next learning and teaching phase;
- it may influence future planning.

All of these are valuable and worthwhile reasons for assessing pupils but are there any other reasons that are not about an external need or a teacher's need for assessment? Are there reasons that are more about the needs of the pupil?

Many of us will have been in the situation during our own childhood school experiences when examination or test results were shared. Pupils in competition with each other compare their grade with their best friend's in order to fathom how well they have done or are doing. While the teacher may not have intended a form of normative assessment (the comparison of pupils with other pupils), learners often compare themselves by asking what mark their friends received. The indicator of their success is perhaps a grade or a percentage mark but there may be little understanding of what that actually means in terms of what they have done well and in which areas they have progressed. As a result, there may be an over emphasis on marks and grades rather than useful advice regarding pupils' next steps in learning. As such, pupils can be de-motivated if their marks or grades are lower than expected without fully understanding why this may be and this can, in turn, affect self-esteem (Black and Wiliam, 1998: 6).

Assessment, therefore, is not only about what can be gleaned for the benefit of the teacher and outside agencies in terms of what a pupil has learnt, but about what a pupil understands about their *own* learning journey, enthusing them about where they are up to on that path and what their next steps are in order to make progress. The benefit of the assessment process can be relocated with the learner rather than only the realm of the teacher. The information gained from classroom assessment processes can support the learner in understanding their own progression rather than only creating data for use by the teacher and/or school. Such engagement with the assessment process can have a significant impact on self-esteem and motivation.

Point for reflection

- Consider how assessment was managed for you as a learner in school. How might this affect how you understand and undertake assessment in the classroom now as a teacher?

Assessment of learning

Assessment for the benefit of the teacher in order to judge how well a pupil is performing is known as an assessment *of* learning. This type of assessment is a snap-shot picture of pupil learning that usually takes place at the end of a unit of work, at the end of an academic year, or at the end of their school career through external examinations such as GCSEs and A Levels in England. This 'end of ...' assessment is generally known as *summative* assessment – a summing up of learning that has taken place. If assessment *of* learning happens at the end of a period of learning there may be no opportunity for a pupil to develop their understanding of where they were successful and where they were not. Once the assessment process is over, it is already time to move on and start the next learning phase. So while summative assessment is an important tool in how education systems work it is not necessarily a method of assessment that works for the benefit of the learner and their understanding about their own progression. It is worth noting here that summative assessment can also be used formatively. We will consider this a little later in the chapter.

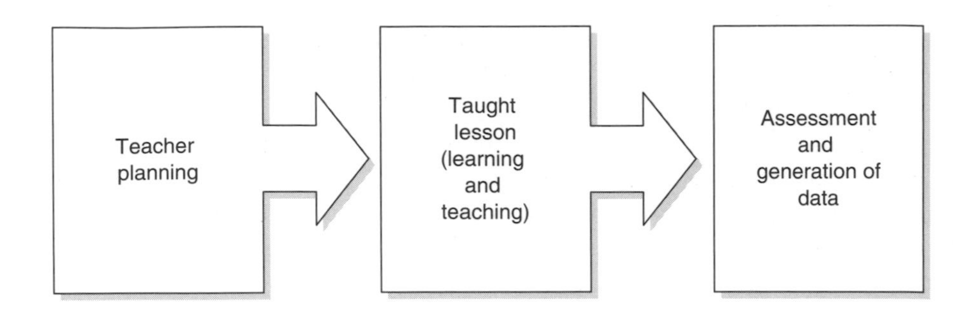

Figure 9.1 Summative assessment

Assessment of learning or summative assessment can be described as in Figure 9.1.

A teacher will plan for classroom learning (for example, a series of lessons on a particular topic area), pupils will engage with the learning in the lesson and at the end of the series of lessons there will be an end of topic test. Once the test has been marked and the results shared with the pupils, the process starts again with teacher planning. While this could be seen as a cyclical learning and teaching process returning to teacher planning, the emphasis is on checking learning has taken place, and not on pupil engagement and understanding of the outcomes of the assessment process.

Assessment for learning

As assessment of learning or summative assessment has a focus on checking learning has taken place, whereas assessment *for* learning is clearly pupil centred. Assessment for the pupils' benefit was identified by the Assessment Reform Group (2002) as 'the process of seeking and interpreting evidence for the use by learners and their teachers to decide where the learners are in their learning, where they need to go and how best to get there.' This type of assessment practice does not happen at the end of anything; it is not grafted onto the end of a scheme of work to summarise learning to date but is a regular event in classroom practice as part of the learning and teaching process. Assessment *for* learning (also known as *formative* assessment) also becomes part of the planning process for the teacher to address pupil needs that they recognise as a result of the assessment process, creating opportunities for pupils to understand their own learning journey and take ownership of it. Therefore, the focus of assessment *for* learning is the learning partnership between teacher and pupil. There is no hidden agenda in such a partnership as a pupil does not have to guess how to improve, or try and interpret what a grade or percentage mark means. Clarity and transparency become the focus in assessment *for* learning providing purposeful marking, clear feedback and opportunities for self- and peer assessment, so enabling pupils to have a clear understanding about where to go next in their learning journey.

From this perspective, assessment is no longer the scary and solitary experience of the individual at a desk with a blank piece of paper in a summative style, but an ongoing process or journey through learning experiences. Assessment becomes a routine part of classroom practice, an integral part of learning and teaching in the classroom (Butt, 2010: 1) which places the pupil at the centre of the learning and teaching process (Butt, 2010: 121). With such an emphasis on pupil ownership of learning and assessment, pupils are empowered and motivated to continue to strive to progress as they understand what the processes of assessment are. In turn, this has a significant effect on pupil self-esteem and motivation (Black and Wiliam, 1998: 5; Stiggins, 2006:5; Cowan, 2009: 73) and means they are less likely to become disaffected with learning as they can recognise their own progress. This is something the student teachers in case study 9.1 recognised in their work.

Case study 9.1 Student teacher voices

A group of student teachers who were part way through their second placement were asked to consider how assessment practices might affect pupil engagement and motivation. Their reflections focused on the importance of implementing a variety of assessment strategies in the classroom as assessment became a more embedded feature of the lessons.

> '...it is important that a variety of methods of assessment are used so that pupils do not switch off because they do not do well in one aspect [of learning]'

> '... it is important that we provide for our pupils excitement and passion for the subjects that we teach in order to do this effectively, assessment strategies must be varied and stimulating ...'

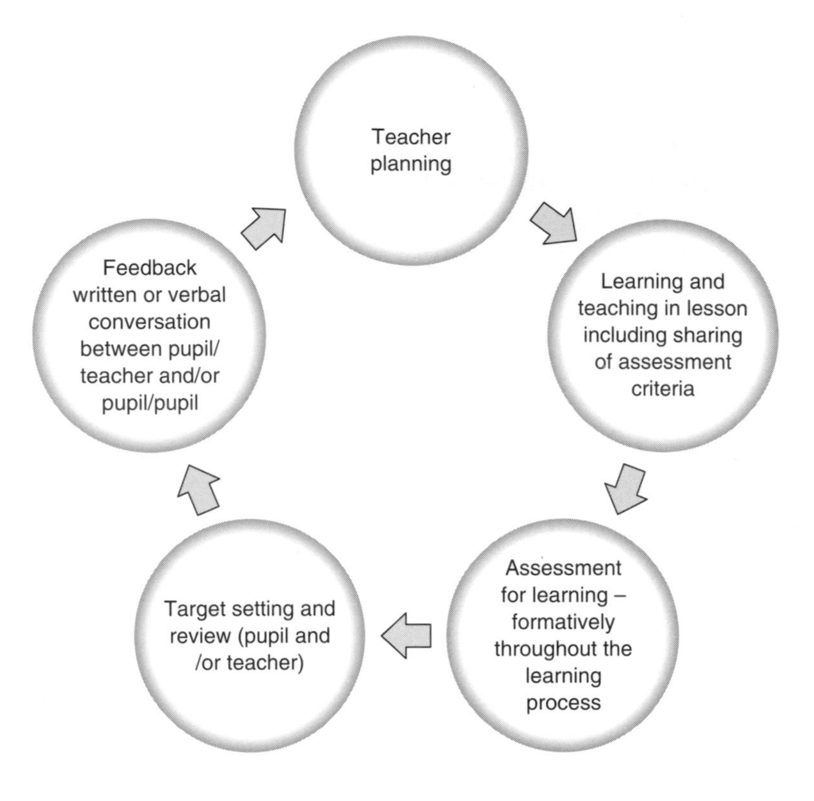

Figure 9.2 Formative assessment

Assessment for learning then is a continuing cyclical process engaging pupil and teacher in a learning conversation that affects pupil ownership of learning as well as teacher planning. This is represented in Figure 9.2 in contrast to the process shown in Figure 9.1.

Assessment *for* learning is based on an extensive survey of research literature by Paul Black and Dylan Wiliam. *Inside the Black Box* (1998) outlined the ways in which assessment could be used as a learning tool to raise standards through a learning partnership between pupil and teacher. A key feature of such formative assessment is that it 'helps the (so-called) low attainers more than the rest, and so reduces the spread of attainment whilst also raising it overall' (1998: 4). Therefore, a class teacher can utilise assessment for learning strategies as part of their differentiation strategy in conjunction with pupil learning and development. Black and Wiliam (1998: 4–5) suggested five key ways to enhance learning through assessment.

1. Enhanced feedback that clearly indicates what a pupil has done well and what needs to be developed further.
2. Pupils' active engagement in learning and assessment.
3. Results of assessment need to impact on learning and teaching through teacher planning and not just be stored as a measure.
4. Assessment can have a significant effect on motivation and self-esteem and account needs to be taken of such considerations.
5. Self-assessment is an important part of pupil understanding of assessment processes.

Enhancing pupil learning through assessment practices

Follow up research *Working Inside the Black Box* (Black et al., 2002) indicated that assessment for learning could enhance pupil learning through four key findings. The first is questioning. Consideration needs to be given as to whether the question being asked in the classroom is worth asking in the first instance and how far the question contributes to moving learning on. Therefore, framing the question is an important first step, followed by an increase in waiting time before expecting pupil response. Giving pupils time to consider their answers increases their involvement in the question and can encourage a more developed response. However, the weight of silence for the student teacher can result in the temptation to answer their own question or rush pupil thinking. The challenge is to create engaging, well-formed questions that create opportunities for learning, while at the same time allowing deep pupil engagement with them.

The second key finding was the use of purposeful feedback through marking. While it may not be advisable to challenge the school marking policy as a student teacher, Black et al. suggest that giving comment-only feedback engages pupils more 'productively in improving their work' (2002: 8) rather than giving a grade or mark which can distract from comments for development. Comments therefore should 'identify what has been done well and what still needs improvement, and should give guidance on how to make that improvement' (Black et al., 2002: 9). Such comments need to be carefully crafted so that they can be read by pupils in the way they were intended by the teacher. Stern and Backhouse's work highlights some issues of pupil interpretation of written comments. They give the example of the use of the word 'interesting' in written feedback. This was seen by pupils in a variety of ways; as neutral (neither good nor bad), as either genuine interest by the teacher or as sarcastic.

> Hence a teacher might say 'interesting, why do you think that?' to a child who says that two plus two equals five. Yet it can also be written with some sarcastic intent, and it can be read this way, too. (2010: 7)

Stern and Backhouse explain that pupils want to be valued and want their work to be valued. Learners want to be proud of their work and therefore teachers' comments can have a significant impact on how they feel about themselves which in turn can have a profound effect on their motivation (2010: 6).

Other findings from the work of Stern and Backhouse on 'The Spirit of Assessment' offer useful guidance to teachers regarding feedback to pupils:

- Teachers hold a position of power over pupils and therefore should exhibit magnanimity in written feedback by 'demonstrating patience, and writing in a way that avoids trying to belittle the pupil/student or "showing off" how much the teacher/tutor knows'.
- Pupils are keen for teachers to see beyond mistakes and highlight what is good as well as what can be improved upon.
- Pupils are looking for more than just ticks or 'good' in their feedback – but extended comments of more than a couple of sentences can be too overwhelming for pupils to respond to. A teacher needs to write useful, focused comment that pupils can do something with.

The third method to develop pupil learning is through peer and self-assessment. In order for pupils to progress in their understanding of what they are doing well and what they can do to improve, there must be transparency of assessment criteria, and pupils must become familiar with its application. Through peer and self-assessment strategies, pupils understand the assessment criteria *before* the task is undertaken. Pupils can then give and receive feedback in a purposeful exchange of ideas, making informed judgements about their own and their peers' work through the 'active management of their own learning' (Bryant and Carless, 2010: 5). Again, this has its challenges. Not all pupils will want to hear what another pupil has to say about their work and so self- and peer assessment strategies require dedicated time and commitment in order for them to be effective and make a productive contribution to assessment for learning.

Case study 9.2 Student teacher voices

The challenges of peer assessment become clear in this reflection by a student teacher using the strategy for the first time with a class. While the student teacher had encouraged pupils to become familiar with assessment criteria in order to understand their own and others' progress, she did not consider wider issues, such as social inclusion, when encouraging pupils to comment on each other's work.

> '... having such ownership of their work is not as important (at the moment) as having friends.'

Finally, Black et al. (2002) highlight the importance of the formative use of summative assessment. As noted earlier, one of the drawbacks of summative assessment is that once it has happened at the end of a scheme of work or academic year it is often the end of the matter. A mark or grade is given and that is the main outcome of the summative assessment task. However, preparation for such tests through self- and peer assessment can be useful tools in encouraging pupil engagement with, and application of, marking criteria in order to help them to understand how their work may be improved before and after the summative event.

In summary then, assessment for learning enables learners to take an active role in the 'management of their own learning' (Bryant and Carless, 2010: 5) but it also changes the nature of learning and teaching in the classroom. By understanding learning, teaching and assessment together as a holistic approach to classroom practice (Haigh and Dixon, 2007: 369), teachers and learners are able to recognise their own responsibilities within the learning partnership. Through this learning partnership, a genuine dialogic relationship (Stern and Backhouse, 2010) is hoped to encourage 'deep development with subject knowledge and skills.' (Ecclestone, 2007: 331).

Points for reflection

- How might a teacher develop a genuine dialogic relationship with a learner?
- What would this look like in practice in the classroom as well as within written feedback?

Later we shall consider what all this means in terms of planning for assessment but it is important to pause and reflect on issues regarding the implementation of assessment in general and assessment for learning specifically.

Challenges to assessment for learning

Assessment *for* learning (hereafter AfL) brought a whole new purpose to classroom assessment which was pupil centred and focused on enhancing learning. The term assessment *for* learning has been in the education arena since the early 1990s and as such has had opportunity to become a regular feature of practice in classrooms. However, some of the challenges of AfL identified in the literature are: whether practice is effective and whether it encourages instrumentalism; the difficulties of providing the time required to implement AfL effectively and issues of AfL and teacher accountability. These challenges will be considered in turn.

With regard to effective practice, it is pertinent to refer to Ofsted who are responsible for the inspection and regulation of schools. In 2008, Ofsted highlighted that, despite teachers knowing what assessment for learning was and the implementation of some of the key principles of AfL through identification of learning objectives, questioning and feedback to pupils, there was evidence to suggest that it was sometimes undertaken 'without enough precision and skill. As a result, pupils did not understand enough about what they needed to do to improve and how they would achieve their targets' (Ofsted, 2008: 5). The reason given for this was because where assessment for learning was not effective 'teachers failed to understand sufficiently how the approaches were meant to improve pupils' achievement' (Ofsted, 2008: 6). Practice appeared to be most effective in schools where the senior management team had a commitment to AfL, because without sustained support and training from senior leaders, AfL was often not embedded or developed (Ofsted, 2008: 5). This issue of implementing the 'letter' of AfL principles rather than the 'spirit' of AfL was highlighted by Hume and Coll (2009). Their work supported previous research findings (Marshall and Drummond, 2006; Ecclestone, 2007) that showed teachers were implementing the strategies of AfL (such as sharing lesson objectives and assessment criteria) but without enabling learners to engage more deeply with them through self- and peer assessment and reflection on next steps in learning. Such a process did not bring about the desired effects of AfL on pupil self-esteem or autonomy. Rather it developed pupil reliance on teacher-led target setting.

Another criticism regarding AfL as a practice to develop pupil confidence, autonomy and ownership of learning is that of encouraging instrumentalism. Torrance

(2007) suggests that by structuring learning and teaching so that pupils understand and apply assessment criteria effectively to their own and others' work (self- and peer assessment), a new mode of assessment is created.

> But transparency of objectives coupled with extensive use of coaching and practice to help learners meet them is in danger of removing the challenge of learning and reducing the quality and validity of outcomes achieved. This might be characterised as a move from assessment of learning, through the currently popular idea of assessment for learning, to assessment as learning, where assessment procedures and practices come completely to dominate the learning experience, and 'criteria compliance' comes to replace 'learning'. (Torrance, 2007: 282)

According to Torrance, assessment can become learning in itself and as such prepares learners for success in summative assessment. He continues by proposing that rather than supporting pupil ownership of their learning journey such processes encourage greater dependence on their teachers who provide the focused feedback on how to improve.

Case study 9.3 Student teacher voices

One student teacher reflected on their experience of asking pupils to set their own targets in relation to a recent self-assessed piece of work,

> I feel the lack of confidence pupils have about their own opinion is something of great concern.

In asking pupils to set their own targets the student teacher was encouraging pupil ownership and autonomy in their learning. However, rather than supporting self-esteem, it undermined it, creating a stressful experience for the pupils and leaving them unable to create meaningful targets for their progression. This perhaps illustrates the difference between teacher commitment to and engagement with AfL principles and pupils' full understanding of the processes and outcomes. The pupils needed further support and guidance after the self-assessment process in order to create meaningful targets for their own progression. Assessment for learning then is not just about a teacher's determination for pupils to become more autonomous but about a shared understanding of what assessment means and how it can affect next steps in learning.

Another challenge is the issue of time in the squeezed curriculum for the implementation of assessment for learning. As noted earlier, such skills as self- and peer assessment take time for pupils to develop in order to assess their work effectively and then frame and communicate their target setting. Although data from the Department for Education (DFE, 2010) suggests a small decrease in the class sizes in secondary schools, there is still a concern about the number of pupils one teacher may teach during the course of an average week. In some curriculum areas, teachers in England may teach Key Stage 3 pupils (age 11–14) once a week or even once a fortnight. In such cases, the sheer number of pupils to be assessed, monitored and tracked across a year is significant. Ofsted (2003) has previously suggested that the problem of 'manageablility' of assessment could be tackled by staggering or sample marking, suggesting that teachers may only mark in depth *selected* items of work, or that they may only mark three classes' work a week, or they may mark five or six pupils' work from each class they teach each week. Such sampling and staggering may give an overview of what learning is taking place in the classroom in general without the volume of marking that may arise in particular curriculum areas. The difficulty with this is precisely what Ofsted claim as an issue in the same report – namely creating limited guidance for improvement for pupils even though Ofsted's own evidence showed that pupils value discussion with their teachers in helping them identify next steps in their achievement (Ofsted, 2003: 4). Timetabled time and pupil-teacher ratios could be considered challenges in recognising, and then meeting, the needs of pupils through assessment for learning principles. However, time taken in implementing AfL strategies (questioning, clear feedback, self- and peer assessment and formative use of summative tests) could reduce the time needed for revision before key summative assessments and as such, may be a good investment rather than another draw on limited curriculum time.

A final challenge to be noted here (though probably not the only remaining one) is that of the accountability of the teacher. Within current education systems, assessment undertaken by the teacher is required. Brooks (2002: 113) asserts the importance of maintaining records of pupil assessment and achievement is important as a means to 'report the information to interested parties: learners themselves, other teachers, the next school, parents and so on.' However, this is not without its challenges. If pupils can demonstrate progress in their learning at any point, there are difficulties with recording this information accurately. For instance, if a teacher uses questioning as a method to develop pupil learning (Black et al., 2002) or overhears a learning conversation within a group work activity – what are the processes of recording oral contributions of individuals within the flow of the lesson? (See case study 9.4 below.) The challenge for the teacher is to remember the depth of response from pupils and update records later. However, can this always be accurate and is it valued as much as more formal assessment data derived from the marking of class and homework books? Butt (2010: 129–30) suggests that emphasis is perhaps still placed on high-stakes testing creating data for external use to demonstrate a school's ability to add value to pupil learning during their school experience through the use of optional tests from QCDA such as Standard Assessment Tests (SATs) for 14 year olds in England. While no longer statutory, Butt suggests that senior managers and teachers see such summative assessment as a more convenient and accurate process of charting pupil progress and that parents trust such data more than that derived from formative methods of assessment.

Case study 9.4 Student teacher voices

The challenges of recording formative assessment in the classroom are many and varied as it is not always a marked piece of written work that is being assessed. Formative assessment can include a range of opportunities for pupils to express their understanding, thinking and progression in their learning, for example, verbally raising and answering questions, contribution to small-group work and oral presentations to name but a few. This student teacher is aware that assessment can take place at any point of the learning process. During a small group discussion, she assesses a pupil's contribution but recognises the difficulty of then what to do with the observation.

> The assessment of such fleeting but worthwhile moments within a discussion is very difficult to convey to one who is not present or to write in a report.

This student teacher recognises that although what has been observed is valuable, it does not fit neatly into her record book. As teachers, we need to consider how we record the outcomes of a variety of assessment strategies rather than relying on only written assessment activities.

In this section of the chapter we have highlighted some of the perceived challenges of implementing assessment for learning as a strategy to enhance pupil achievement and attainment. The literature suggests that there is a fine line between effective implementation of assessment for learning strategies and 'training' of pupils in instrumental approaches of assessment for success, without a real focus on learning and developing subject knowledge and skills. The challenges for the teacher then are to plan effectively for assessment without losing sight of the importance of encouraging a genuine interest in learning as well as valuing the pupils by supporting the development of their confidence and self-esteem through their learning.

Purpose

- Why is assessment taking place?
- Will it be formative or summative?
- How will it affect learning?

Frequency

- If assessment is part of learning and teaching then it will happen often so that the information gained from the process creates a continuous picture of progress for both learner and teacher.

Transparency

- What are the criteria for the assessment and when will they be shared with pupils?
- What are your expectations for the assessment in terms of outcome? How will you share these with pupils? Is there an opportunity to model expectations or use previous pupils' work to clarify expectations?

Progressive

- In order for assessment to be meaningful and for pupils to take ownership of their learning, time needs to be built in for them to engage with the outcomes. For example, if the teacher has focused on meaningful feedback in a written form, opportunity for pupils to consider that feedback and act upon it becomes an important part of the process of assessment *for* learning. The danger is that if time is not built in for pupils to understand and plot their next steps in their learning (perhaps by target setting) then we are going through the motions of assessment for learning rather than effectively implementing the strategy (Hume and Coll, 2009: 284).

Developmental

- Assessment must be part of an ongoing and cyclical process. Therefore assessment needs to build upon previous learning and assessment 'outcomes' such as target setting, written feedback from teachers or verbal considerations through peer assessment.
- If each assessment process builds on the previous one, then there will be a continuous development of understanding of how learning has taken place and the best next steps to take.
- In order for this to happen, the teacher needs to have an accurate understanding of where each pupil is up to, where their next challenges lie and how they might meet them. Planning for assessment for all becomes a differentiated process appropriate to the needs and stages of pupil learning.
- In building on previous learning, teaching and assessment, the process begins again.

Figure 9.3 Planning for assessment

Points for reflection

- From your recent experiences and observations in schools, would you say that methods of assessment were effective in supporting pupil learning?
- What is your evidence?

Planning for assessment

If we take a holistic approach to learning, teaching and assessment, then planning for assessment is an integral part of the planning process. Consideration needs to be given to the purpose of the assessment taking place in the lesson as well as what is to be done with the information that arises from it. While the box below indicates considerations for planning for assessment (it is not exhaustive but offers some thoughts as a starting point) it is important that clear opportunities for learning to take place before assessment is a necessary part of the planning process.

Conclusion

This chapter has highlighted the origins and development of assessment for learning as key practice in the classroom for pupil development and progression. While assessment for learning is the accepted language of assessment, the chapter has illustrated some of the challenges such as, whether assessment for learning practice is effective, the difficulties of providing the time required to implement assessment for learning effectively and issues of accountability.

Reflective questions

1. Can you identify the differences between preparing pupils to be effective exam takers and assessment for learning for progression? What impact will this have on your preparation and planning?
2. As a teacher, how will you enable pupils to approach assessment as a positive marker of their progress rather than a stressful, silent and singular activity?

(Continued)

(Continued)

3 What do you need to consider when preparing pupils to engage in peer assessment activities?
4 When giving written feedback to pupils what will your 'golden rules' be?

Recommended further reading

Black, P. and Wiliam, D. (1998) *Inside the Black Box*. London: GL Assessment.

Black, P. and Wiliam, D. (2012) 'Assessment for learning in the classroom' in J. Gardner (ed.), *Assessment and Learning*, 2nd edition. London: Sage.

These two publications set the context of assessment for learning highlighting the research and thinking behind the strategy. They are a good place to start in understanding the theory behind the practice.

Butt, G. (2010) *Making Assessment Matter*. London: Continuum.

Butt deals with the practicalities of assessment for learning with helpful guidance regarding application and review of assessment processes.

Marshall, B. and Drummond, M. (2006) 'How teachers engage with assessment for learning: lessons from the classroom', *Research Papers in Education*, 21 (2): 133–49.

Helpful reflections on the practice of assessment for learning from Marshall and Drummond.

Torrance, H. (2007) 'Assessment *as* learning? How the use of explicit learning objectives, assessment criteria and feedback in post-secondary education and training can come to dominate learning', *Assessment in Education*, 14 (3): 281–94.

Torrance offers important critique of assessment for learning and reminds us that we need to engage critically with every new strategy.

References

Assessment Reform Group (2002) *Assessment for Learning 10 Principles: Research Based Principles to Guide Classroom Practice.* London: ARG/Nuffield Foundation.

Black, P. and Wiliam, D. (1998) *Inside the Black Box*. London: GL Assessment.

Black, P., Harrison, C., Lee, C., Marshall and Wiliam, D. (2002) *Working Inside the Black Box*. London: GL Assessment.

Brooks, V. (2002) *Assessment in Secondary Schools: The New Teacher's Guide to Monitoring, Assessment, Recording, Reporting and Accountability*. Buckingham: Open University Press.

Bryant, D.A. and Carless, D.R. (2010) 'Peer assessment in a test dominated setting: empowering, boring or facilitating examination preparation?' *Educational Research for Policy and Practice*, 3: 3–15.

Butt, G. (2010) *Making Assessment Matter*. London: Continuum.

Cowan, E.M. (2009) 'Implementing formative assessment: student teachers' experiences on placement', *Teacher Development*, 13 (1):71–84.

Department for Education (2010) 'Schools, pupils and their characteristics'. Available online at http://www.education.gov.uk/cgi-bin/rsgateway/search.pl?keyw=024&q2=Search (last accessed 25 April 2011).

Department for Education (2011) 'Teachers' standards'. Available online at: https://www.education.gov.uk/publications/eOrderingDownload/teachers%20standards.pdf (last accessed 10 October 2011).

Ecclestone, K. (2007) 'Commitment, compliance and comfort zones: the effects of formative assessment on vocational education students careers', *Assessment in Education*, 14 (3): 315–33.

Gipps, C. (1999) 'Socio-cultural aspects of assessment', *Review of Research in Education*, 24, 355–92.

Haigh, M. and Dixon, H. (2007) '"Why am I doing these things?": engaging in classroom-based inquiry around formative assessment', *Journal of In-Service Education*, 33(3): 359–76.

Hume, A. and Coll, R.K. (2009) 'Assessment of learning, for learning, and as learning: New Zealand case studies', *Assessment in Education: Principles, Policy and Practice*, 16 (3) 269–90.

Marshall, B. and Drummond, M. (2006) 'How teachers engage with assessment for learning: lessons from the classroom', *Research Papers in Education*, 21 (2): 133–49.

Ofsted (2003) 'Good assessment in secondary schools'. Available online at http://www.ofsted.gov.uk/Ofsted-home/Forms-and-guidance/Browse-all-by/Other/General/Good-assessment-in-secondary-schools/%28language%29/eng-GB (last accessed 23 April 2011).

Ofsted (2008) 'Assessment for learning: the impact of national strategy support'. Available at online at http://www.ofsted.gov.uk/Ofsted-home/Publications-and-research/Browse-all-by/Documents-by-type/Thematic-reports/Assessment-for-learning-the-impact-of-National-Strategy-support (last accessed 23 April 2011).

Stern, J. and Backhouse, A. (2010) 'The spirit of assessment'. Paper presented at the Association of University Lecturers of Religious Education Conference, July 2010.

Stiggins, R. (2006) 'Assessment for learning: a key to motivation and achievement', *Edge: The Latest Information for the Education Practitioner*, 2 (2): 3–19.

Torrance, H. (2007) 'Assessment as learning? How the use of explicit learning objectives, assessment criteria and feedback in post-secondary education and training can come to dominate learning', *Assessment in Education*, 14 (3): 281–94.

CHAPTER 10

WHAT IS DIVERSITY AND HOW CAN I RESPOND TO IT?

Joy Schmack

By the end of this chapter you should be able to consider critically:

- what diversity means within a school context;
- how you can support access and achievement for all pupils;
- how you can prepare pupils for life in a diverse world.

This chapter explores what is meant by diversity in the school context and explores its relationship with pupil achievement and preparation for living in a diverse world. It considers the statutory requirements that schools should meet and also strategies that can be used within curriculum planning and delivery for teachers of all subjects.

The area of diversity can appear so broad that it can be hard to know where to start. This chapter encourages you to understand how every teacher needs to be concerned about promoting diversity not only within their own teaching but within their relationships with pupils, parents and carers. You will be encouraged to recognise that no-one has all the answers but that there are many different strategies that can be adapted to use both in and out of the classroom.

What do we mean by diversity in the school context?

Synonyms for diversity include 'assortment', 'range' and 'mixture.' But what then does the word imply within a school context? 'We effectively promote diversity' is a claim often made in schools' brochures and mission statements but again what does this actually mean in practice and how do you set about achieving it?

Diversity is an issue for all schools and for each teacher because it is about facilitating different strategies and opportunities for the achievement and participation of all pupils. In order to work towards this goal, schools particularly need to ensure that access and potential is achieved by all groups within a school and is not limited by prejudice or discrimination. Schools also need to ensure that they engender respect for the worth and dignity of each individual. Each of these is distinctive in its processes and practices although fundamental to both is a respect for the individual and esteem for their culture and values.

When we are beginning to develop our understanding of diversity we should begin with our own experiences. As Martyn Lawson and Martin Watts argue in Chapter 5, every teacher brings with them their own values and cultural norms into the classroom and this affects their conscious and subconscious behaviour and attitudes.

Points for reflection

Perhaps you can start by thinking about your own school experiences.

- What practices did you see that engendered respect for individuals and ensured access by all groups? You might want to consider in your reflections:
  - How school celebrations were made inclusive.
  - How relationships within the school community showed a respect for the individual.
  - Were there any individuals or 'groups' which didn't participate in school activities? What strategies were used to encourage them?
  - How did resources used in lessons reflect a diverse world?

School legislation and policies

The 2012 Ofsted guidance on inspection (Ofsted, 2012) clearly acknowledges the importance of effective strategies for responding to diversity within the inspection process. It states that 'School inspection acts in the interests of children, young people, their parents and employers. It encourages high-quality provision that meets diverse needs and fosters equality' (p.11).

Education is always subject to changing priorities and changing legislation but as the list of legislation and guidance below shows, a concern with diversity is not new nor is it a passing phase. Each of the documents in this list has implications for diversity and education.

- Race Relations (Amendment) Act (2000)
- Special Educational Needs and Disability Act 2001
- Children Act 2004
- Disability Discrimination Act 2005
- Education Act 2005
- Racial and Religious Hatred Act 2006
- Equality Act 2006
- Equality Act 2010
- Ofsted Inspection Framework 2012

Although each of the acts and guidance documents referred to in this list reflects a specific aspect of diversity, they all share a common recognition – the importance of the individual not just in terms of their rights and dignity but the importance of them being free from harassment.

How a school interprets the acts and guidance should be explicit in a range of policies which are often found in staff handbooks and guidance to parents and carers. Ideally these should have arisen from consultation with the whole school community including senior management, teaching and non-teaching staff, governors and, most importantly, pupils. It is through this process that a whole school community develops clear common aims. However, as is always true, the test of any effective policy is not how it appears on paper but its effect on the practice and values of the whole school community.

Enabling access and potential for all

Although each of the acts referred to in the last section focuses on distinctive areas, they all consistently advocate the school's duty to enable access and achievement of potential of all groups with no limitations by prejudice or discrimination. Enabling access and realising potential may be interconnected aims but they require different considerations and practices.

It would be rare to find instances in school where direct discrimination has prevented a pupil accessing part of school life. A hypothetical example would be if it were advertised that only pupils from one particular ethnic group were allowed to be in the school production of 'Pride and Prejudice'. However, barriers to access often occur through indirect discrimination which, although equally as harmful, may be less obvious to detect. Indirect discrimination occurs when a school or teacher places an unnecessary condition or requirement that prevents certain members of the community from participating. An example of this would be if school entrance exams were only held on a Saturday thus preventing Jewish and Seventh Day Adventist candidates from sitting them. Many perceived acts of indirect discrimination have been taken to the law courts. One example is the case of *Mandla* v. *Lee* (1983). In this case, although the school in question was not explicitly refusing to admit Sikh pupils, it was considered that their 'no turban' rule would prevent some members of the Sikh community from being able to enter the school.

Indirect discrimination can occur through many aspects of school life such as the resources you use, the activities you ask pupils to engage with and the organisation of extra-curricular activities. Whilst recognising you can't get it right in every occasion you need to constantly reflect whether you have caused barriers for some pupils that could easily be eradicated.

Points for reflection

Consider each of the situations below. What issues regarding access might they pose for certain groups of pupils and what strategies could you use to make them more inclusive?

- Pupils are told to draw a picture of the house they live in.
- Only those pupils who pay to go on the French field trip can take a second modern language.
- Parents' consultations are held on Fridays at 4pm.
- Female pupils are not allowed to wear trousers.

Each of these situations might raise multiple issues. However, among the issues for diversity and inclusion they raise are the following: What about pupils who live in caravans, flats or residential care homes? Are you restricting the study of two modern languages to pupils from certain socio-economic groups? What about religions for whom Friday afternoon or evening has religious significance? Or what about communities in which many parents work evening shifts? What about communities in which girls need to keep their legs covered?

Fundamental to pupil's achievement is their access and participation in all aspects of school life. Gillborn and Mirza (2000) conducted substantial research on attainment inequalities in England and Wales in the period 1988 to 1997. Their results illustrated the significant impact that race and class plays not only on attainment but interaction with whole school life.

To ascertain if there are particular barriers for certain groups, data from schools should be constantly analysed to ensure there is fair access. The school's structures for the collection, analysis and implication of findings of such data will be of interest during any school inspections. The Ofsted inspection guidance from 2012 states that when evaluating the achievement of pupils, inspectors will consider:

- how well they make progress relative to their starting points;
- how well gaps are narrowing between the performance of different groups of pupils in the school and compared to all pupils nationally (Paragraph 38, Ofsted Guidance, 2012).

As the national data in the case study below shows, there can be considerable differences in attainment of different groups.

Case study 10.1 GCSE results by ethnicity and free school meals

Table 10.1 Percentage of 5 or more A–C grades at GCSE in 2009

	Percentage of 5 or more A–C grades at GCSE in 2009				
Ethnic Group	Boys in receipt of free school meals	Girls in receipt of free school meals	Boys not in receipt of free school meals	Girls not in receipt of free school meals	Overall percentage for ethnic group
White British	39.1	47.7	66	73.8	69.8
Irish	43.6	51.1	70.8	76.4	73.5
Traveller of Irish Origin	23.1	21.7	23.4	28.8	26.4
Gypsy/Roma	9.9	19.1	15.4	26.7	20.9
Indian	64	74.9	78.8	85.9	82.3
Pakistani	55.7	65.6	61.4	72.2	66.6
Bangladeshi	60.4	70.9	65.3	73.5	69.5
Black Caribbean	44.9	62.3	55.8	69.7	62.9
Black African	56	63	65.3	74.1	69.8
Chinese	83	93.1	84.8	91.4	88
Total for all pupils	44.5	53.6	65.9	73.0	69.8

(Continued)

(Continued)

What does the national data of GCSE passes in 2009 in Table 10.1 tell you about:

- Pupils who are receive free school meals?
- The difference between attainment of Irish pupils and Irish heritage/traveller pupils?
- The difference in attainment between white British boys and girls?

What strategies have you seen in your own school observations to try and counter underperformance by different groups of pupils?

Although national data help to inform us of any pervading trends, it must always be remembered that each school is individual and will have its own specific data. It is also important to look at other data that could have an impact on achievement such as exclusions, attendance, participation in extra-curricular activities, parental engagement and option choices.

How can schools prepare pupils for a diverse world?

It is a responsibility of all schools and teachers to prepare pupils for the diverse world they live in. This can be perceived as a particular challenge in a mono-cultural school but as Chris Gaine argues this is often where it is most needed. In a series of books *No Problem Here* (1987), *Still No Problem Here* (1995) and, more recently, *We're all White, Thanks* (2005) he sets out to explode the myth that schools in areas with little direct contact with people from ethnic minorities shouldn't be concerned about diversity.

The impact of the media means that irrespective of where pupils live they are aware of a range of different life-styles and cultures from their own. However, that awareness does not automatically mean they will hold positive attitudes. Knowles and Ridley (2006) identify how it is important for teachers to plan strategies for pupils to develop positive attitudes if they are going to embrace differences from their own life-style and cultures. This is a complex task for schools which often find themselves challenging many pre-formed attitudes of children shaped by media, family and peers. It also requires clarity of intended outcomes by staff. As Knowles and Ridley (2006) argue there needs to be precision concerning the positive attitudes we are trying to engender. Is it, for example, tolerance, respect, sympathy, empathy, understanding, appreciation, knowledge, critical analysis, or something else? Consider what the implications are of each of these attitudes. Toleration, for example, is not wholly positive. When we tolerate something it usually means we put up with it.

The history of multicultural education in England reflects this need for clarity of intentions. During the 1980s and 1990s there were many attempts to create positive pupil attitudes to diversity through multicultural celebrations at schools through experiencing different cultural practices in music, art and cooking. However, as Kincheloe and Steinberg (1997) identify, there are many types of multiculturalism. Some were tokenistic and reflected the superiority of the dominant culture. Others, whilst emphasising pluralism, did this through illustrations of exoticism. There has been frequent criticism that such practices can be counter-productive, reinforcing negative attitudes as pupils perceived the traditions as strange or exotic with little emphasis on shared values between cultures.

Whole school projects and interventions

Effective practice in schools requires consensus of whole staff policy and practice. There are many examples of whole school initiatives aimed to develop pupils' awareness and participation in the diverse world. Two particularly popular examples which we will explore are whole school diversity days and school twinning programmes.

Whole school diversity days often include a range of workshops which pupils experience throughout the day. There are two distinct models. The first model focuses on skills required for participation in a diverse world. Workshops may include strategies to counter stereotypes and racism and to develop skills of media analysis. The long-term aim would be that pupils would be able to transfer their analytical skills to all areas of the curriculum. Although one-off days can be a positive introduction to diversity, Maylor and Read (2007) warn that such initiatives have to be developed long term and consistently throughout the school if they are to have any effect.

The second type of day is organised to give pupils new cultural experiences. Examples may include Indian dancing, Mehndi painting, African drumming, and Chinese cooking. Such days can often be entertaining and enjoyable in the short term but their effectiveness over the long term needs to be considered. Troyna and Williams (1986) warn of the dangers of such tokenism in reinforcing stereotypes. They refer to such events as the 'three Ss' (saris, samosas and steel bands) and urge education to challenge racism in the curriculum, both formally and informally.

Case study 10.2 Pupil voices

Below are some views of pupils who recently experienced a diversity day. Consider the impact made on the pupils' attitudes towards diverse cultures. In what ways are the effects positive and in what ways might they be problematic?

> 'I really liked the Chinese food workshop. My friend is Chinese and I am going to ask if I can go to her house for tea.'

> 'I really liked getting dressed up for the dancing. It was really funny to see the boys trying to dance with those big hats on.'

The second popular whole school initiative aiming to broaden pupils' perspectives is school twinning. Activities might include correspondence with pen-pals and often include some form of fund raising for whichever of the schools was considered the most financially impoverished. Recently, there have been successful examples of schools twinning within England or even within the same local authority. The Schools Linking Network supports schools and other organisations across England to explore identity, diversity, equality and community, using four key questions of shared human experience: Who am I? Who are we? Where do we live? How do we all live together? The focus on shared human experiences and values in their work exemplifies the plea by Trevor Phillips that a constant barrier to community cohesion in Britain has been the emphasis on difference. In a speech given at the Commission for Racial Equality he argued we have 'focused far too much on the "multi" and not enough on the common culture. We have allowed tolerance of diversity to harden into the effective isolation of communities, in which some people think special separate values ought to apply' (Phillips, 2005: 4).

A key benefit of twinning is the opportunity to build relationships between pupils in different types of schools. The importance of 'intimate acquaintances' to break down stereotypes was recognised by Lippmann as early as 1922 and has been frequently recognised as a means of enhancing positive relationships and tackling prejudice. The DCSF Guidance on Community Cohesion (2007) identifies four sequential stages in creating 'meaningful' contact of different groups to break down stereotypes:

1 for conversations to go beyond surface friendliness;
2 for people to exchange personal information or talk about each other's differences and identities;

3 where people share a common goal or an interest;
4 where contacts are sustained long-term (one-off chance meetings are unlikely to make a difference).

Chapter 11 by Carolyn Reade and Carrie Mercier considers issues related to community cohesion in more depth.

How much difference can I make?

Preparing pupils to live in a diverse world should be the concern of each and every teacher as it is about each and every pupil. Often the difficulty is knowing where to start. It is not surprising that teachers have been found to be more comfortable talking about the environment than different cultures and ethnic groups (Ireland et al., 2006). Many would agree that the best place is to start with yourself and your own experiences. It is a professional expectation that you will be aware of the range and impact of issues associated with diversities within the catchment areas for your school. First-hand experiences can be gained by regularly walking around the local area of the school or reading the local newspaper.

Points for reflection

Before reading the next section, which explores a range of practical things that you can do in your classroom, you might want to take a moment to consider how your teaching would reflect the following local incidents:

- the English Defence League are planning to hold a march through the main high street at the weekend;
- the local library is due to be closed;
- the local Chinese restaurant has been vandalised and graffiti sprayed on the windows.

Every teacher in every classroom can make a difference in developing pupils' positive attitudes to diversity – but as, we have already stated, knowing where to start is important. We will now explore a range of strategies that not only supports a positive attitude to diversity but also the spiritual, moral, social and cultural development of pupils.

Strategy 1 – modelling expectations: fundamentally it is incumbent upon all professionals working in the classroom to explicitly model positive attitudes to all aspects of diversity.

Strategy 2 – research: no teacher, however long they have been in the profession, can feel they are an expert in diversity. When we talk about diversity we are referring to individuals and each year there will be pupils with different needs. As the suggested reading at the end of the chapter shows, there is a wealth of information on the internet. A useful place to start is the Multiverse website which identifies support for teachers in six distinct areas: race and ethnicity; social class; religions; bilingual and multilingual learners; refugees and asylum seekers; travellers and gypsies. Remember though that resources on the internet will only give you general advice. Parents'/carers' evenings are an ideal time to seek out more relevant information. Don't feel that you are being inquisitive or that you are showing an unprofessional lack of knowledge. Do your research in the local community as well. Be aware of the community groups your pupils may attend and their activities and be ready to share in celebrations. For example, if you have Muslim pupils, some of them might attend the local Madrassah after-school. Ask if you would be allowed to attend one of the lessons there or one of their celebration days.

Points for reflection

A pupil comes to tell you they are celebrating Divali tomorrow. What might be an appropriate response?

- 'We will be studying India soon. Will you tell the class about it?'
- 'That's interesting.'
- 'Should we call tomorrow a no-homework night?'
- 'What! In the middle of a week before an important test?'

Let's look at each of the responses and their implications.

- We will be studying India soon. Will you tell the class about it?

Primarily it would be useful to know if it is the Sikh or Hindu Divali being referred to as they both celebrate the festival but for different reasons and in different ways. This is where the research and local knowledge of Strategy 2 is important. This response is making an assumption that the pupil has knowledge of a very large and diverse country. Indeed the pupil may never have even visited India. Some pupils feel confident in sharing aspects of their lives with others but this should not be assumed and it can sometimes be counter-productive to make the child stand out. The teacher, instead, could ask for contributions from the pupil on shared human experience such as 'families' or 'times of celebrations' which are applicable to all pupils.

- That's interesting.

Although this may appear to value the pupil's experience, the pupil will tell by your body and vocal tone if you really think that! What further follow-up question could be asked? Remember you do not need to show you are an expert in everything. By asking the pupil further questions you show that you are interested.

- Should we call tomorrow a no-homework night?

This would be a kind gesture as it would not be the common practice to expect a pupil to do homework on Christmas Day!

- What! In the middle of a week before an important test?

Most of the festivals move in the calendar year and so the religious community have no choice as to when festivals are held. You can find out the festival dates for all religious festival from the Shap Calendar listed in the further reading. This is essential for your planning of extra-curricular activities and assessments.

Strategy 3 – diagnostic assessment: how can we prepare pupils for a diverse world if we don't know their existing conceptions and misconceptions? This knowledge is pivotal as Schneider (2005) argues, through an analogy to car mechanics, 'Saying we want to change a stereotype is like saying you want to fix a car but you don't know what the matter of it is now' (p. 209). Brown (1998) in her work on unlearning discrimination in the early years highlights the importance of diagnostic assessment. She argues that it is vital to establish the individual stereotypes held in order to select the appropriate strategies to be used. She argues 'We can only know about the misinformation and misunderstandings that children have absorbed if we provide opportunities for them to say what they think about discriminatory issues' (p. 87). A stark reminder of this is reflected by Davies's (2004) findings that young people between 11 and 21 were seven times more likely to support the BNP than the rest of the population.

To support this process, opportunities should be planned to encourage pupils to express their own understandings or world view. Through this process, the teacher needs to be a 'traveller' rather than a 'miner' as pupils may well be reticent or lack confidence in their use of language when expressing their world views. They may become more reticent if their views are probed by the teacher.

Strategy 4 – beware of stereotypes: the Diversity and Citizenship Review led by Sir Keith Ajegbo (2007) argues that the formation of stereotypes affects individuals' esteem and, in consequence, has a negative impact on attainment. He argues that 'Stereotypes are an insult to an individual's identity and can lead to frustration and demoralisation. These are likely to have a considerable impact on the individual and the wider community, which in turn knocks on to achievement levels' (p.70).

Schneider (2005) however argues the positive power of education in countering stereotypes. He maintains that 'Even strong stereotypes can be overridden by even stronger information about individuals' (p. 171). The sensitivities that surround the challenging of misconceptions are obvious, but so is the life-long damage if they are not challenged. Brown (1998) writes 'If children's perceptions of people who are different from themselves are based on stereotypical thinking it is likely that they will retain this misinformation for the rest of their lives unless positive steps are taken to counter this learning' (p.23).

Once teachers have ascertained the prevalent stereotypes, then their choice of lessons, resources and extra-curricular activities can be organised to help counter them. However, teachers themselves also need to wary of inadvertently holding or promoting stereotypes. Think back to the section on whole-school strategies in this chapter and some of the potential risks in relation to these. This need to avoid inadvertent stereotypes is also why we need the research referred to in Strategy 2.

Strategy 5 – mind your language: often pupils lack confidence in the use of any language associated with race and diversity and are worried that their vocabulary might be considered politically incorrect or impolite. The importance of language as a tool of power and emancipation is fully explored by Gluck Wood (2007). She recognises that pupils are often aware of sensitivities but unaware of the specifics of what is considered acceptable or unacceptable and more importantly why. There is often a fine balance between sensitivity, political correctness and political correctness gone mad! Knowles and Ridley (2006) illustrate the importance of teachers using a language associated with issues of diversity that is considered, shared with pupils and consistently modelled with confidence.

The Ajegbo Report reaffirms the pivotal role that language plays when it states that.

> Pupils need to develop an understanding of how language constructs reality and the different perspectives they use to make sense of the world around them. It is crucial for education for diversity that pupils are given the skills to challenge their own assumptions and those of others. (Ajegbo, 2007: 46)

Strategy 6 – resources: resources used within the classroom play a significant role in pupils' attitudinal formation. Think about the textbook you use most in the classroom and consider if the images reflect diversity within society. Remember we can think about diversity in a range of ways including race, gender, ability, faith, ethnicity, social condition, cultural background, disability. Schneider (1992) refers to four ways in which resources may distort perceptions of groups.

1 Under-representation of the group.
2 Selective presentation, such as representation in only one specific context or situation.
3 Stereotypic presentation. This might relate to reinforcing gender expectations such as male doctors and female midwives.
4 Framing and priming. Framing is when the media present complex issues within a particular framework. For example support among non-Hispanics for bilingual education for Hispanics is lower if bilingual education is presented as a way of preserving culture rather than presented as a way for people to learn English.

Conclusion

Throughout this chapter we have explored the impact of diversity on pupil engagement, achievement and preparation for living in a global world. Central to these outcomes is our constant reflective practice to ensure that pedagogies, activities and resources do not provide barriers to engagement but indeed counter misconceptions and stereotypes. Finally we have shown that, irrespective of our experiences, there are many strategies we can adopt to promote positive attitudes to diversity.

Reflective questions

1 How would you respond to someone who says 'We don't need to worry about diversity at our school; it is monocultural?'
2 From your recent school experiences and observations what strategies were used to prepare pupils for living in a diverse world?
3 In your first term what three strategies would you use to prepare pupils for living in a diverse world?
4 What do you see is the relationship between diversity and community cohesion? How might that relationship look in practice in school?

Recommended further reading

Dadzie, S. (2000) *Toolkit for Tackling Racism in Schools*. Stoke on Trent: Trentham.
A useful introduction to exploring issues of race in the classroom.

Elton-Chalcraft, S. (2009) *It's Not Just About Black and White, Miss: Children's Awareness of Race*. Stoke on Trent: Trentham.
Elton-Chalcraft gives a broad picture of the impact of diversity.

Knowles, G. and Lander, V. (2011) *Diversity, Equality and Achievement in Education*. London: Sage.
Knowles and Lander consider real issues that affect teachers in the classroom, and examine a variety of influences affecting child development.

Shap Calenders. Available online at http://www.shapworkingparty.org.uk/calendar.html
Details concerning the key dates and practices of religious festivals.

Troyna, B. and Cashmore, E. (1990) *Introduction to Race Relations*. London: Taylor and Francis.
A straightforward introduction to this area which has become a standard text.

References

Ajegbo, K. (2007) 'Diversity and citizenship curriculum review'. Available online at www.education.gov.uk/publications/standard/publicationdetail/page1/DFES-00045-2007

Brown, B. (1998) *Unlearning Discrimination in the Early Years.* Stoke on Trent: Trentham Books.

Davies, L. (2004) *Education and Conflict: Complexity and Chaos.* London: Routledge.

Department of Children, Schools and Families (2007) *Guidance on the Duty to Promote Community Cohesion*. London: DCSF.

Gaine, C. (1987) *No Problem Here.* London: Hutchinson.

Gaine, C. (1995) *Still No Problem Here.* London: Hutchinson.

Gaine, C. (2005) *We're All White, Thanks*. Stoke on Trent: Trentham.

Gillborn, D. and Mirza, H.S. (2000) *Educational Inequality: Mapping 'Race', Class and Gender: A Synthesis of Research.* London: Ofsted.

Gluck Wood, A. (2007) *What Do We Tell The Children*? Stoke on Trent: Trentham.

Ireland, E., Kerr, D., Lopes, J. and Nelson, J. with Cleaver, E. (2006) *Active Citizenship and Young People: Opportunities, Experiences and Challenges in and Beyond School Citizenship Education Longitudinal Study: Fourth Annual Report*. London: DfES/RR 732.

Kincheloe, J. and Steinberg, S. (1997) *Changing Multiculturalism*. Thousand Oaks, CA: Sage.

Knowles, E. and Ridley, W. (2006) *Another Spanner in the Works.* Stoke on Trent: Trentham.

Lippmann, W. (1922) *Public Opinion*. New York: Harcourt Brace.

Maylor, U. and Read, B. with Mendick, H., Ross, A. and Rollock, N. (2007) *Diversity and Citizenship in the Curriculum Research*, Report No 819: London Metropolitan University.

Ofsted (2012) 'The framework for school inspection'. Available online at www.ofsted.gov.uk/resources/090019

Phillips, T. (2005) 'After 7/7: sleepwalking to segregation'. Speech given at the Commission for Racial Equality, 22 September 2005. London: CRE.

Schools Linking Network. Available online at www.schoolslinkingnetwork.org.uk

Schneider, D.J. (1992) 'Red apples, liberal college professors, and farmers who like Bach', *Psychological Inquiry*, 2, 190–3.

Schneider, D.J. (2005) *Psychology of Stereotyping*. New York: Guildford Press.

Troyna, B. and Williams, J. (1986) *Racism, Education, and the State*. London: Routledge.

Websites

Multiverse website http://webarchive.nationalarchives.gov.uk

CHAPTER 11

HOW DO WE PROMOTE THE SPIRITUAL, MORAL, SOCIAL AND CULTURAL DEVELOPMENT OF PUPILS AND HOW DOES THIS RELATE TO COMMUNITY COHESION?

Carrie Mercier and Carolyn Reade

By the end of this chapter you should be able to:

- consider an understanding of the 'spiritual, moral, social and cultural development of pupils' that works for you and your subject,
- reflect critically on the concept of the school as a community and evaluate the role of the school community in terms of its contribution to community cohesion;
- consider ways in which your subject area has a contribution to make in terms of the pupils' spiritual, moral, social and cultural development;
- evaluate initiatives in schools that are intended to encourage shared values and a sense of community.

In this chapter, you will be able to gain some understanding of the background to the requirement that schools provide for the spiritual, moral, social and cultural (SMSC) development of all pupils and begin to examine what this might mean. You will be able to engage with some of the relevant literature and reflect critically on different perspectives on SMSC development in schools. You will be encouraged to find an interpretation of the SMSC agenda that you can work with in your subject or curriculum area. This chapter will also explore the idea of the school as a community with shared values and common concerns. You will also be asked to reflect critically on the ways in which a school can claim to have a set of shared values as a community and ask what the role of the teacher is in this respect.

The 1944 Education Act stated that every local education authority should ensure that the schooling in their area contributes to 'the spiritual, moral, mental and physical development of the community'. At this time, the end of the Second World War was in sight and it was thought that one way to help secure peace in the future was to ensure that the values and moral commitments that had served to overthrow the Nazis would be passed on to the next generation. In a more recent and very different context, the 1988 Education Reform Act required all schools to provide a broad and balanced curriculum that 'promotes the spiritual, moral, cultural, mental and physical development of pupils at the school and of society'. There are two points of interest that we might glean from these connected statements. The first is the decision to use the word 'spiritual', rather than the term 'religious' – perhaps spiritual was chosen because it is a broad term that is much more inclusive than the term 'religious' which tends to divide people into different camps (Gilliat, 1996: 164). The word spiritual does still carry a lot of religious baggage for some teachers and we do need to examine the meaning of this word 'spiritual' in a way that is fit for purpose in a community of people of different faiths or of no faith. A second point to note from these two statements is that they both indicate that the responsibilities that come with this spiritual, moral, social and cultural agenda go beyond the school gates to include the wider community. In the light of this, we will look at how SMSC links with the community cohesion agenda and the concern for shared values.

First, what do we mean by 'spiritual' within the context of the school curriculum? Many will assume that the provision for the spiritual development of pupils simply refers to the requirements regarding religious education and collective worship in schools. Indeed, perhaps this is how it was perceived in 1944 when it was assumed that religious instruction and worship in schools would be rooted in the teachings of Christianity. However, the term spiritual development was retained later in the 1988 Act and so teachers had to think again about how to interpret this term in a new context as it emerged that Ofsted was to inspect provision for spiritual development.

In 1993 a discussion paper on 'Spiritual and Moral Development' was published by the National Curriculum Council. This document identified aspects of spiritual development that would help schools to define it in a broad and inclusive way:

- beliefs;
- a sense of awe, wonder and mystery;
- experiencing feelings of transcendence;
- search for meaning and purpose;
- self-knowledge;
- relationships;
- creativity;
- feelings and emotions.

The beginner teacher in the secondary school might look at this list and say this is nothing to do with me and my subject. But let us say a bit more about each of these in turn and so begin with 'belief'. We all have beliefs whether individual or shared beliefs, religious or non-religious beliefs. These beliefs are an important part of our sense of who we are. Pupils who are in the process of developing their own sense of identity need opportunity to reflect on their beliefs as well as learn about those of others. If we look at 'a sense of awe, wonder and mystery' then we need to ensure that there are opportunities for pupils to experience a sense of 'wow' in looking at the universe or the natural world or to be inspired by the example and achievement of others. One aspect of spirituality that many teachers have struggled with is that of 'feelings of transcendence'. This might be taken to mean a sense of the presence of God but it could be seen in a more general sense that there is something more to life than just the physical and material and the 'here and now'. Some teachers might be more comfortable encouraging a sense of an inner strength rather than a transcendent one that can be drawn on to empower us. Being human means we seek to connect up our experiences to make sense of them and seek some kind of wholeness and this is behind the idea of a 'search for meaning'. Many teachers would agree that a part of their role is to help pupils to think about what is important in life or to develop a sense of direction and purpose. 'Self-knowledge' is another aspect of spirituality that most teachers feel able to nurture so that pupils reflect on their strengths, acknowledge their needs, value their talents and develop a sense of self-worth. One of the criticisms of the NCC discussion paper was that the emphasis was on the individual rather than the community. The spiritual must be concerned with 'relationships' and this aspect of spirituality might include our relationship with the environment and the animal world as well as our relationship with our fellow human beings. Schools can give pupils a sense of belonging and provide opportunity for them to develop positive relationships. 'Creativity' represents an aspect of spirituality that can be explored across different subjects and a 'broad and balanced' (DES, 1988) curriculum should offer opportunities for pupils to use their imagination and to express themselves through art, drama, music and story. Lastly, 'feelings and emotions' are an essential part of being human and so there needs to be opportunity for pupils to rejoice in good times and express sadness in time of loss. Pupils need to be able to reflect on their sense of anger when there is injustice and think about how we learn through dealing with our emotions. All these aspects of spirituality are said to be 'fundamental in the human condition' (NCC, 1993) and if we want to create humans rather than 'monsters' (Ginott, 1972) then the school must be a place where there is time to reflect and 'the space to breathe, grow and dream' (Bowness and Carter, 1999).

A more recent attempt to help schools identify what might be meant by 'spiritual development' can be found in the guidance to inspectors for Ofsted (Ofsted, 2012) which includes in its definition pupils' 'willingness to reflect on their experiences'. Some have looked at these various attempts to define spiritual development and asked whether there is a need to label these things as spiritual at all (see Lambourn in Best, 1996: 150). But the term spiritual could be seen as an abbreviated way of referring to the non-material aspects of life. It has been argued that teachers in every subject must allow time for reflection or 'deep-pondering' (Hay and Nye, 2006: 107). In her book on children's spirituality Nye says that spiritual development is 'hard to pin down, to define ...What matters most is that you develop your own habits of recognizing when spirituality is, and isn't able to flourish in your local context' (Nye, 2009: 19).

Point for reflection

- Which aspects of spirituality can you see as relevant in your subject and what examples could you give from your area of the curriculum to provide opportunities for spiritual development?

Provision for the moral development of pupils

It could be argued that that some of these aspects of spiritual development are really about moral development. Research suggests that many believe that teaching is an essentially moral activity (Bullough, 2011); after all, in order to manage the learning environment, every teacher needs an agreed set of positive behaviours and routines for interaction. These can be said to have moral foundations. For example pupils need to show consideration for others in the class and learn to listen to their fellow learners and to see them as having equal rights and opportunities. Learning to take part in group work or discussion in class will require a degree of give and take and sense of fairness. The teacher in the gym, the playing field and in the science lab will say that moral values underpin their teaching on teamwork and their good practice in terms of health and safety.

The NCC discussion document (1993) argues that every teacher should be involved in helping pupils to develop a sense of what is right and wrong. It suggests that there are:

Values a school should include	**and**	**Values a school should reject**
Telling the truth		Bullying
Keeping promises		Cheating
Respecting the rights and properties of others		Deceit
Acting considerately towards others		Cruelty
Helping those less fortunate than ourselves		Irresponsibility
Taking personal responsibility for one's actions		Dishonesty
Self-discipline		

Perhaps you want to argue that the way to ensure the pupils' moral development is to have a list of agreed values like this. Indeed, there are those who believe that learning to become a moral being is achieved through establishing a consensus on what counts as right and what counts as wrong and agreeing a set of rules with sanctions for those that step out of line. Others, it is argued (Bowker, 1998) believe that moral development is achieved, not by hitting up against a set of rules and regulations, but by growing up as part of a community that encourages certain virtues and ways of being and it is by internalising these ways of being that we come to develop moral character. Recent guidance issued to inspectors from Ofsted (2012) suggests that moral development is about the pupils:

- ability to recognise the difference between right and wrong and their readiness to apply this understanding in their own lives;
- understanding of the consequences of their actions;
- interest in investigating, and offering reasoned views about, moral and ethical issues.

Two important aspects to moral development are identified here. First, there is the concern for moral behaviour and developing a sense of responsibility. Secondary school pupils are in the process of finding out 'what works socially and morally, what confers adult status and therefore feel the need to make social experiments – to try out courses of action so that they can learn from the feedback which they receive' (McPhail, 1970). The feedback from the teacher should therefore motivate the young person to act morally and to take responsibility for their actions. Most teachers would agree that this is an important part of their role in school. The other aspect of moral development might be called the intellectual side and it has long been recognised that 'the curriculum is pregnant with possibilities for moral instruction. Indeed, it might be argued that the successful teaching of history, literature and science necessitates the reflection on, discussion of and criticism of moral issues in an objective and impartial fashion' (Archambault, 1963).

Point for reflection

- What opportunities can you see within your area of the curriculum for encouraging the different aspects of moral development?

Provision for social development

Many teachers see that encouraging moral development is a part of their role in preparing young people for adult life. They seek to ensure that their pupils develop the skills that will help them to get on with others and enable them to make a positive contribution in the community. Some might see this in terms of moral development, others in terms of social development. This is another aspect of the curriculum that Ofsted inspects and in doing so looks for pupils that are able to show:

- use of a range of social skills in different contexts, including working and socialising with pupils from different religious, ethnic and socio-economic backgrounds;
- willingness to participate in a variety of social settings, co-operating well with others and being able to resolve conflicts effectively;
- interest in, and understanding of, the way communities and societies function at a variety of levels (Ofsted, 2012).

Some of these points will emerge later in the chapter where we explore the idea of community cohesion. But in the light of this Ofsted agenda, teachers need to ask what the implications are for the way we set up classrooms, how we organise group-work or establish the kind of environment we want for learning. Teachers will also need to plan for learning outside the classroom in order to provide opportunities for social development.

Cultural development

As we turn to the last aspect of the SMSC agenda we need to focus on provision for pupils' cultural development. But what is this exactly – is it just a matter of a visit to a local museum or theatre production? The concept of culture is a matter of debate in relation to education (Jackson, 1997: 82; Hulmes, 1989: 16). On the one hand, you might hold the view that culture is something that is static, traditional and unchanging, indeed, perhaps something that needs to be preserved. On the other hand, you might argue that culture is essentially something that is dynamic, always changing and being changed through time and through encounters with other cultures. Teachers are in a unique position in that they can see how young people are right at the meeting point of different cultures. They are learning to negotiate a path for themselves between the culture of their home and family, the culture of their peers, the popular culture of the day presented by the media, the culture of the school as well as make sense of the other cultures they may encounter. So it is not surprising to find that schools are deemed to have a significant role to play in terms of pupils' cultural development. Indeed, Ofsted is required to inspect provision for pupils' cultural development which might be shown by their:

- understanding and appreciation of the wide range of cultural influences that have shaped their own heritage;
- willingness to participate in, and respond to, for example, artistic, musical, sporting, mathematical, technological, scientific and cultural opportunities;
- interest in exploring, understanding of, and respect for cultural diversity and the extent to which they understand, respect and celebrate diversity, as shown by their attitudes towards different religious, ethnic and socio-economic groups in the local, national and global communities. (Ofsted, 2012)

Promoting community cohesion

How teachers promote pupils' social and cultural development overlaps with another initiative aimed at promoting the healthy development of society as a whole. In 2007 a duty was placed upon schools to promote community cohesion, with Ofsted required to report on how well schools were doing (Education and

Inspections Act, 2006). A change in government led to the Education Act 2011 which removed all requirements which were thought to be unnecessary. Interestingly, this Act did not remove schools' duty to promote community cohesion, although this was no longer required to be inspected by Ofsted. The Department for Education explained that the new Ofsted inspection process would still take into account how well a school promoted community cohesion in judgements about the SMSC development of pupils and about how well the school met the needs of all pupils (DfE, 2011). Teachers hold many different views about their duty to promote community cohesion (Rowe et al., 2011). Some feel that it is so important it should be legally required and monitored, otherwise it would simply fall through the net as other issues are prioritised in school. Others feel that good schools promote community cohesion in any case, not because this is required by any government directive, but because it is so integral to the aims and practices of good education itself. We shall now examine what is meant by community cohesion, some of the issues it raises for teachers and how it provides another dimension to your developing understanding of SMSC. Three pieces of research have been selected to help you to consider how different types of evidence can be used to help inform your understanding and practice.

A cohesive is a bond or 'glue' which sticks or holds things together and the idea that the UK's diverse communities needed to develop a social 'glue' to bind them together was described in 2000 in a report called *The Future of Multi-Ethnic Britain* (Parekh, 2000). The term 'community cohesion' rose to prominence the following year as the title of a report by Ted Cantle into the causes of disturbances between different ethnic groups in Burnley, Bradford and Oldham during the summer of 2001. He described the 'parallel lives' lived by members of different ethnic communities and made 67 recommendations aimed at improving relationships and promoting a harmonious society (Cantle, 2001). The attacks on the London underground by British Muslim citizens in July 2005 intensified a sense of social crisis about the perceived fragmentation of society. This was encapsulated in the controversial and contested 'sleepwalking our way to segregation' speech made by Trevor Phillips, Chair of the Commission for Racial Equality, who felt that the policies of multiculturalism had placed too much concentration on diversity and not enough emphasis on the common ground shared across all cultures (Phillips, 2005). This would become the hallmark of new social policies designed to promote community cohesion.

A definition of community cohesion

The Department for Children, Schools and Families (DCSF) provided a definition of community cohesion for schools which collected together several key themes under this umbrella:

> By community cohesion, we mean working towards a society in which there is a common vision and sense of belonging by all communities; a society in which the diversity of people's backgrounds and circumstances is appreciated and valued; a society in which similar life opportunities are available to all; and a society in which strong and positive relationships exist and continue to be developed in the workplace, in schools and in the wider community. (DCSF, 2007: 3)

Immediately you can see that community cohesion is a broad and multifaceted concept which requires a multi-pronged response from schools. The DCSF (2007: 7) identified three distinct areas that should become a focus for developing community cohesion under the following headings:

- Teaching, learning and the curriculum
- Equity and excellence
- Engagement and extended services

The content of your subject and the way you design your learning activities may naturally help to promote community cohesion, if all pupils are valued, mix together happily and are helped to engage with the community cohesion issues raised by your subject. Equity and excellence refers to the equal opportunities you provide for all of your students to succeed to their highest level and how you work to eliminate any variations in outcomes for different groups. Third, you could become involved with opportunities for pupils, their families and the wider local community to interact with people from different backgrounds, through participation in various activities and events.

Given the complexity of the definition there has been uncertainty about what was actually required from schools, as on the one hand it duplicated requirements which already existed, and on the other it appeared to require schools to take new responsibilities for social issues which were beyond their capacity to control. Schools already had the duty to eliminate unlawful racial discrimination and to promote equality of opportunity and good relations between people of different groups under the existing Race Relations Amendment Act 2000. The 2006 Equality Act paved the way for the 2010 Equality Act which drew together numerous anti-discrimination regulations into one single Act. This identified 'protected characteristics' in relation to age, disability, gender, gender reassignment, marriage and civil partnership, race, religion or belief, sexual orientation and pregnancy/maternity. However, the duty to promote community cohesion did not require schools to promote cohesion in relation to all diversities. Instead only three particular strands were identified:

- ethnicity
- faith
- socio-economic

The DCSF (2007: 5) explained that although the other diversities were interconnected with the aspiration to promote community cohesion, the main focus of the duty is 'cohesion across different cultures, ethnic, religious or nonreligious and socio-economic groups' because '[r]ace and faith are often seen as the most frequent friction points between communities, and the most visible sources of tension' (ibid.).

Diversity and community cohesion

This separation of community cohesion from other strands of diversity has led to concerns that it provides only limited opportunities for thinking about the matter in a holistic way (Gavrielides, 2010). After all, the ethnic, faith and socio-economic communities are diverse in themselves and every individual has multiple dimensions affecting their sense of identity. Some argue that the policy actually obscures our ability to engage with the real social issues which impact upon community cohesion, such as inequality and the causes of economic and social disadvantage, or the 'pathologising' of Muslim communities in the media and social policies (Miller, 2009). The definition itself cannot help but raise some controversial questions. What exactly would be the 'common vision' which schools would promote as the 'glue' to hold communities together? Some fear that community cohesion has taken a particular assimilationist and nationalistic turn, ignoring the essential complexities of the very issues which it aimed to resolve (McGhee, 2008; Modood, 2010). How are teachers to respond to the duty to promote a cohesive society, when there is no agreement in society at large over what exactly this should look like, or how it should be achieved? Akram and Richardson (2011) warn that it is miseducation, or even indoctrination, to say or imply there is consensus around certain issues when in fact there is not. You might feel that the values already promoted through SMSC are sufficient in their focus and inclusiveness to develop the desired attitudes to ensure community cohesion. However, even if people find agreement on personal and social values, the questions of which principles should govern how to accommodate plural and sometimes incompatible values in society, or how diversity itself should be valued in balance with a shared common identity, lead to strongly disputed answers. Attempts have been made to identify core British values to which all citizens should be expected to subscribe. These have variously been described in terms of fair play, creativity, tolerance, inventiveness, enterprise, or commitment to liberty and fairness (McGhee, 2008). These may be conceptualised as kinds of 'citizenship values' which are promoted by teachers alongside the values promoted through SMSC. Both kinds of values can be seen in the Department for Education's 2012 standards for teachers which lists the 'fundamental British values' of democracy, the rule of law, individual liberty, mutual respect, and tolerance of those with different faiths and beliefs (DfE, 2011).

Case study 11.1

D. Rowe, N. Horsley, T. Thorpe and T. Breslin (2011) 'Teaching learning and community cohesion: a study of primary and secondary schools' responses to a new statutory duty'. Research report, CfBT Education Trust.

This 2010 research report investigated how teachers had understood and implemented their duty to support community cohesion, using interviews and focus groups with teachers from 27 schools.

The report found that the duty had been greeted with ambivalence, although it was universally accepted that schools could contribute to community cohesion. The DCSF guidance was criticised for failing to address the range of complex issues faced by schools, such as how teachers should deal with objections from parents who did not want their children to mix or develop attitudes of respect. The Ofsted inspections between 2008 and 2011 led to improvements in practice, but raised serious questions about the nature of community cohesion 'evidence' and the links between cause and effect.

Point for reflection

- What, in your view, are the benefits and problems associated with your school's duty to promote community cohesion?

How do you develop a sense of belonging to a community? A community can be regarded as a group of people who share a common identity, or who live in geographical proximity, or who simply share interests and experiences in common. They share a common understanding or 'likemindedness' (Grimmitt, 2010: 28). In addition, a sense of belonging includes awareness of the expectations, responsibilities and norms of the social group and a level of trust and confidence in how you will be treated within it. DCSF guidance (2007) identifies four expanding dimensions of community:

1 the school community itself, i.e. its students, families, staff, governors, etc.;
2 the community within which the school is located and the people who live or work there;

3 the UK community;
4 the global community.

Point for reflection

- How might 1) your curriculum topics and 2) your teaching and learning approaches contribute to community cohesion across each of these four dimensions of community?

One useful perspective for developing your understanding of how relationships are developed within and between communities is the concept of 'bonding' and 'bridging' capital. Just as individuals hold financial capital, 'social capital' influences how well they are able to interact in society using social networks. Bonding social capital refers to the close relationships between similar individuals such as families and close friends and tend's to be inward looking, while bridging social capital refers to the outward-looking networks of relationships with associates, those outside their immediate circle and with those dissimilar to themselves. The activities and ethos of your school are essential for bonding your school community together. However, it is bridging social capital which is more conducive to community cohesion, as this enables people to engage in positive relationships which are diverse. Your school may need to help its students to develop bridging capital among its own students, if they tend to self-segregate, or show reluctance to build positive relationships outside their immediate networks.

Case study 11.2

DCSF, Communities and Local Government, Social Exclusion Task Force (2008) 'Aspiration and attainment amongst young people in deprived communities: analysis and discussion paper'. Cabinet Office Social Exclusion Task Force.

This research involved an analysis of existing statistical data and interviews with over 150 people and identified the socio-economic significance of a person's bonding and bridging capital.

The findings identified certain community characteristics which are associated with low aspirations. The report found that high levels of bonding social capital and low levels of bridging social capital restricted young people's horizons. Social interactions took place within a very limited geographical area and the absence of a broader and more diverse network of contacts meant that young people lacked access to other sources of inspiration and opportunities. Moreover, strong bonding networks may predispose individuals to avoid those experiences that might build other forms of social capital and potentially lead to change. The report indicates that improving bridging social capital would help to raise aspirations amongst young people in deprived communities.

Is contact alone sufficient to promote community cohesion?

The former community cohesion inspection criteria required inspectors to make judgements about how well the school knew its ethnic, faith and socio-economic context, its planned actions for promoting community cohesion within and beyond the school and how well it could demonstrate the impact of its actions (Ofsted, 2009). Many schools made efforts to bring together people who would not ordinarily mix on the principle that contact will bring about more positive attitudes and relationships. However, how do you ensure that these activities actually promote *meaningful* insights and relationships? Contact alone has been shown to be insufficient and may actually increase prejudice, especially if the different groups do not meet and work on an equal footing (Institute of Community Cohesion, 2010). Research from the Commission for Racial Equality (2007) indicated that the best results are achieved when interactions between different groups are by-products of people coming together for another purpose, beyond simply engaging in an inter-cultural contact in itself (ibid.). Eaude (2010) argues that shared action and endeavour is a stronger bonding and bridging agent than an appeal to shared values. There are educational projects and websites which can help you to develop your contacts to achieve this, for example the Schools Linking Network (http://www.schoolslinkingnetwork.org.uk/) or Global SchoolNet (http://www.globalschoolnet.org/). Initiatives in the areas of sport, arts, culture, festivals, volunteering or charities can hugely contribute to engaging meaningfully with different communities, as well as linking explicitly to the promotion of SMSC development. The Commission on Integration and Cohesion confirms that meaningful contact between people from different groups has been shown to break down stereotypes and prejudice. It identified the characteristics of meaningful contact as:

- conversations go beyond surface friendliness; in which people exchange personal information or talk about each other's differences and identities;
- people share a common goal or share an interest;
- and they are sustained long term (so one-off or chance meetings are unlikely to make much difference). (Commission on Integration and Cohesion, 2007 cited in DCSF, 2007: 10)

Case study 11.3

M. Parker-Jenkins and M. Glenn (2011) 'Levels of community cohesion: theorising the UK agenda and the implications for policy and practice in schools', *International Journal of Multicultural Education*, 13 (1): Available online at http://ijme-journal.org/index.php/ijme/article/viewArticle/323 (last accessed September 2011).

This report researched how faith-based schools contributed to sustaining a community's sense of identity and promoting community cohesion by investigating the experiences of five Muslim schools and four Jewish schools in 2007–8. The research involved classroom observation and semi-structured interviews with over 100 people. The report argues that a more useful and realistic term than 'community cohesion', is 'community engagement' because this is achievable immediately, unlike cohesion, which is more of an 'aspiration'. The report proposes a framework based on six measurable levels of engagement:

1. meaningful engagement (significant interaction);
2. sustained engagement (strong evidence of different forms such as knowledge of and interaction with other faiths/wider community on a regular basis);
3. temporary engagement (perhaps due to one teacher or member of the school community but not sustained because that person has left or the strategy is discontinued);
4. tokenistic engagement (a one-off event or trip, assembly meeting);
5. superficial engagement (a veneer but weak and of no consequence);
6. no engagement (ethnocentric, mono-cultural, Eurocentric in curriculum, school ethos).

The report argues that this approach would support Cantle's reflections five years after his original report that community cohesion developments should be modified with clear objectives, indicating what is critical to success and built around a set of core initiatives (Cantle, 2006: 13).

Point for reflection

- How might you develop your own skills in promoting meaningful bonding and bridging capital among your students?

In a long teaching career, you will find that many educational initiatives will come and go, but some questions about your role in promoting well-rounded individuals and healthy relationships in society, and about what you should actually do to achieve these, will always remain pertinent. A school community cannot help but pass on values through the way it behaves and what it deems to be important, whether or not it articulates these in deliberate SMSC or community cohesion policies. Many people would see the transmission of a society's values as an essential function of schooling and teachers are expected to display those attitudes and dispositions they wish to nurture in their students. This is an indispensable vehicle for promoting pupils' SMSC development. Some might worry that attempting to heal perceived fractures in society is overstepping the boundary of a school's core business. Others would argue that the essential purpose of education is not only to help create a vision of what it means to be human, but also a vision of how to live together harmoniously.

Reflective questions

1 Is it unnecessary to talk about the spiritual development of pupils – could it be argued the moral, social and cultural development of pupils already covers all that is claimed to be included in the spiritual dimension?

(Continued)

(Continued)

2 What are the connections between the SMSC agenda and the community cohesion agenda?
3 Is it appropriate for Ofsted to have community cohesion on their agenda?
4 To what extent should the issue of community cohesion be a concern for teachers in secondary schools?

Recommended further reading

Best, R. (1996) *Education, Spirituality and the Whole Child.* London: Cassell.
This is a good reader which brings together a range of perspectives on the subject.

Rowe, D., Horsley, N., Thorpe, T. and Breslin, T. (2011) *Teaching, Learning and Community Cohesion: A Study of Primary and Secondary schools' Responses to a New Statutory Duty: Guidance Report*. Reading: CfBT Education Trust.
This report will help you to reflect on how your school is promoting community cohesion.

References

Akram, J. and Richardson, R. (2011) 'It's not just any old discussion – being controversial, being sensitive, a pilot project', *Race Equality Teaching*, Summer 2011: 26–30.

Archambault, R.D. (1963) 'Criteria for success in moral instruction', *Harvard Educational Review*, 33 (4): 474–81.

Best, R. (1996) *Education, Spirituality and the Whole Child*. London: Cassell.

Bowker, J. (1998) 'Implicit morality: an empirical ethical perspective', *Implicit Religion*, 1: 69–75.

Bowness, C. and Carter, M. (1999) 'Bread not stones – nurturing spirituality', in A. Thatcher (ed.), *Spirituality and the Curriculum.* London: Cassell.

Bullough, R.V. (2011) 'Ethical and moral matters in teaching and teacher education', *Teaching and Teacher Education*, 27 (1): 21–8.

Cantle, T. (2001) *Community Cohesion: Report of the Independent Review Team*. London: HMSO.

Cantle, T. (2006) 'Parallel lives', *Index on Censorship*, 35 (2).

Commission for Racial Equality (2007) *Promoting Interaction Between People from Different Ethnic Backgrounds: A Research Project for the Commission for Racial Equality*. London: Commission for Racial Equality.

Department for Children, Schools and Families (DCSF) (2007) *Guidance on the Duty to Promote Community Cohesion*. London: DCSF Publications. Available online at http://www.education.gov.uk/publications/eOrderingDownload/DCSF-00598-2007.pdf (last accessed September 2011).

DCSF, Communities and Local Government, Social Exclusion Task Force (2008) 'Aspiration and attainment amongst young people in deprived communities: analysis and discussion paper'. Cabinet Office Social Exclusion Task Force. Available online at http://webarchive.nationalarchives.gov.uk/+/http://www.cabinetoffice.gov.uk/media/109339/aspirations_evidence_pack.pdf (last accessed: September 2011).

Department for Education (2011) 'Disclosures about children, young people and families: community cohesion'. Available online at http://www.education.gov.uk/aboutdfe/foi/disclosuresaboutchildrenyoungpeoplefamilies/a0077108/community-cohesion (last accessed: September 2011).

Department for Education (2012) 'Teachers' standards effective from 2012'. Available online at https://www.education.gov.uk/publications/eOrderingDownload/teachers%20standards.pdf (last accessed: December 2011).

Department for Education and Science (1944) *Education Act*. London: HMSO.

Department for Education and Science (1988) *Education Reform Act*. London: HMSO.

Eaude, T. (2010) 'Community cohesion – the real challenges', *Race Equality Teaching*, 28 (2): 31–36.

Department for Education (DfE) (2006) Education and Inspections Act. London: HMSO, Chapter 40.

Gavrielides, T. (2010) 'The new politics of community cohesion: making use of human rights policy and legislation', *Policy and Politics* 38 (3): 427–44.

Gilliat, P. (1996) 'Spiritual education and public policy 1944–1994', in R. Best (ed.), *Education, Spirituality and the Whole Child*. London: Cassell, p. 164.

Ginott, H. (1972) *Teacher and Child*. London: Macmillan.

Grimmitt, M. (ed.) (2010) *Religious Education and Social and Community Cohesion: An Exploration of Challenges and Opportunities*. Great Wakering: McCrimmons.

Hay, D. and Nye, R. (2006) *The Spirit of the Child* (revised edn). London: Jessica Kingsley Publications.

Hulmes, E. (1989) *Education and Cultural Diversity: The Effective Teacher Series*. London: Longman.

Institute of Community Cohesion (2010) 'Literature review of ICD – related concepts'. Available online at http://www.cohesioninstitute.org.uk/live/images/cme_resources/Public/documents/ICD%20toolkit/lit_review_ICD_concepts.pdf (last accessed September 2011).

Jackson, R. (1997) *Religious Education: An Interpretive Approach*. London: Hodder and Stoughton.

Lambourn, D. (1996) 'Spiritual minus personal-social = ?: a critical note on an empty category', in R. Best (ed.), *Education, Spirituality and the Whole Child*. London: Cassell.

McGhee, D. (2008) *The End of Multiculturalism? Terrorism, Integration and Human Rights*. Buckingham: Open University Press.

McPhail, P. (1970) 'The motivation of moral behaviour in moral education', *Moral Education*, 2 (2): 99–106.

Miller, J. (2009) 'Community cohesion and teachers' professional development', *Race Equality Teaching*, 28 (1): 30–36.

Modood, T. (2010) *Still Not Easy Being British: Struggles for a Multicultural Citizenship.* Stoke-on-Trent: Trentham Books.

National Curriculum Council (1993) *Discussion Paper on Spiritual and Moral Development*. York: NCC Publications.

Nye, R. (2009) *Children's Spirituality*. London: Church House Publishing.

Ofsted (2009) 'Inspecting maintained schools' duty to promote community cohesion: guidance for inspectors'. Crown copyright. Available online at: http://resources.cohesioninstitute.org.uk/Publications/Documents/Document/Default.aspx?recordId=7 (last accessed: September 2011).

Ofsted (2012) 'RE today', Ofsted Subsidiary Guidance issued to Inspectors. Available online at http://www.retoday.org.uk/media/display/Extracts_from_Subsidiary_Guidance_issued_to_inspectors_January_2012.doc (last accessed January 2012).

Parekh, B. (2000) *The Future of Multi-ethnic Britain*, London: Profile Books.

Parker-Jenkins, M. and Glenn, M. (2011) 'Levels of community cohesion: theorizing the UK agenda and the implications for policy and practice in schools', *International Journal of Multicultural Education*, 13 (1). Available online at http://ijme-journal.org/index.php/ijme/article/viewArticle/323%20accessed%20September%202011 (last accessed September 2011).

Phillips, T. (2005) 'After 7/7: sleepwalking to segregation'. Speech given by CRE Chair Trevor Phillips to the Manchester Council for Community Relations. Available online at http://www.humanities.manchester.ac.uk/socialchange/research/social-change/summer-workshops/documents/sleepwalking.pdf (last accessed September 2011).

Rowe, D., Horsley, N., Thorpe, T. and Breslin, T. (2011) *Teaching, Learning and Community Cohesion: A Study of Primary and Secondary Schools' Responses to a New Statutory Duty: Guidance Report*. Reading: CfBT Education Trust.

CHAPTER 12

HOW CAN I PREPARE FOR MY NQT YEAR?

Gail Fuller

By the end of this chapter you should be able to:

- critically examine the Teachers' Standards and the relationship between these Teachers' Standards and the reality of being a teacher and also reflect on whether there are areas of professional learning not included in the standards;
- critically reflect on your own journey in teaching so far and consider how your personal characteristics have affected your professional role as a teacher;
- reflect on your own views concerning the importance of relationships within school and explore the emotional investment in teaching in order to help you prepare for your NQT year.

During your training, you are expected to learn how to teach and to practise your skills in the classroom, with a view to becoming a newly qualified teacher (NQT). This chapter is concerned with issues you may face as a new teacher just starting your teaching career and will draw your attention to the relational and emotional aspects of teaching. There may be issues that surface during this first year which were not evident during your training, such as, developing your identity as a teacher and the emotional investment required in teaching.

Recent research suggests (Findlay, 2006; Bush and Middlewood, 2005) that your first year in teaching is significant and that induction is important for teacher retention and career progression, 'few experiences in life have such a tremendous impact on the life of a teacher as does the first year of teaching' (Findlay, 2006: 511). The induction phase, as well as being a steep learning curve and very demanding on emotions, is also recognised as being crucial for learning and professional growth. The early years of teaching can be both a period of 'finding your feet and fitting in' as well as an intense process of discovery.

As a new teacher, you will have to practise and refine the teaching skills you acquired during your training, effectively consolidating your training and meeting the Teachers' Standards (www.education.gov.uk) consistently over a sustained period. The Teachers' Standards contained in this document replace standards for Qualified Teacher Status (QTS) and the core professional standards that were published by the Training and Development Agency for Schools (TDA). In addition to this, you will have to develop new relationships with colleagues, pupils and parents, become familiar with school routines and practices, as well as perceive and respond to the 'unspoken rules' and expectations within your school. So, emotional, relational and cognitive factors are important in your PGCE and induction year (Keates, 2008; Rippon and Martin, 2006). In terms of recent research relating to beginner teachers, there has been growing attention to the place of the personal element in the process of becoming a teacher (Flores, 2004; McNally et al., 2008). All of these issues will influence the experience of your first year in teaching. We will consider each of these, drawing on the real experiences of NQTs of different ages, genders, subject areas and life experiences. These case study examples of early career teachers will be reflecting on their experiences at the end of their first year.

Points for reflection

- Is learning to teach merely a matter of following and meeting a set of formalised teaching standards or is there more to it than this?
- What do you think it means to become a teacher?

The Teachers' Standards

The Teachers' Standards can be viewed as an attempt to conceptualise the role of the teacher as a list of competences, which student teachers and NQTs must know, understand, and be able to put into action in order to successfully complete induction. They reflect the areas of professional practice and characteristics or attributes expected of you as an NQT as you begin to work more confidently and independently as a teacher. This might suggest that once you have met these Teachers' Standards, your professional identity is stable and that your professionalism can be measured against the absolute scale of the standards. Chapter 2 discusses these Teachers' Standards in more detail.

This model of induction, where the NQT is measured against the Teachers' Standards throughout the first year of teaching, is not without its critics. Whilst the 'standards model' of teacher identity has been viewed by some as a powerful tool in the development of teaching as a profession, you might find that this model does not fully encompass or capture your lived experience as a new teacher in your first post. Teaching is a complex professional role and therefore learning to teach is complex too. It involves the whole of the individual, including, beliefs, emotions, identity and personality, and is much more than an abstract set of skills to be employed.

Research suggests there are tensions between the formal process of induction and the informal learning that takes place outside the parameters of these structures, especially the learning that comes through relationships with pupils and colleagues (Tickle, 2000; McNally et al., 2008). Various studies suggest that the all-encompassing process involved in learning to teach is about 'becoming' a teacher. It is an organic process through which the newly qualified teacher has to re-invent themselves, gaining their identity through a range of emotional, relational and cognitive experiences. Beginning teachers, we are told, report an emotional-relational dimension, a sense of self and relationships with colleagues and pupils as being central concerns in their early teaching experiences, themes that are not visible in the standards (McNally et al., 2008; Flores, 2001). It is this informal but crucial learning for which there are no standards provided for guidance or measurement. This more three-dimensional model of early professional learning suggests that the experience of beginning teachers is largely dependent on engagement with pupils and colleagues, with high correlation between job satisfaction and working relationships with colleagues. These social interactions produce the crucial relationships for the new teachers' professional identity and role.

For many, the initial experiences as a teacher can have a sustained effect on the development of a professional identity. Your journey into becoming a teacher is one that is influenced by people, experiences and your understanding of them. Evidence from research suggests that 'beginning teaching is demanding for just about all beginners and is special for each beginner' (McNally et al., 2008: 295).

Points for reflection

- Consider your views of the Teachers' Standards. Are these just a list you need to tick or do you see them as foundational elements to being a teacher?
- Reflecting on your own experience, can you identify areas of learning not included in the standards?

Case study 12.1

This case study is taken from a small-scale unpublished research project by G. Fuller (2010).

These NQTs were asked: 'What is your view of the Teachers' Standards? How do the Teaching Standards fit in to your experience of teaching?'

> 'Standards cover the formality of being a teacher, you need to know them and be aware of them, measured against them, and they have a reality in the classroom but are also somewhat removed from what happens in the classroom.'
>
> 'Standards are in place to ensure standards in school but they're not the be all and end all of teaching – you can tick off a list but it's not why you do things, it's more than that.'
>
> 'You can't teach some things about teaching; it's experience that brings the knowledge of how to be a good teacher.'
>
> 'Some elements of the job can't be taught only experienced.'
>
> 'During ITT some standards didn't seem as important but this year's experience has brought understanding of issues like bullying and isolation, etc., they make more sense now.'

'There's no standard for the constant pressure and how to keep all the balls in the air.'

'A lot of learning this year was not covered by the standards, they're just the basics, and any good teacher sees them as that – far more to teaching than that.'

The new teachers in these case studies identified some of the necessary skills not covered by the standards, for example, the ability to pick up the learning again quickly after an interruption in a lesson, dealing with the unpredictability of the classroom, the need to be adaptable, the constant juggling of tasks and deadlines, skills in arbitration, spontaneity or thinking on your feet and coping with the sometimes overwhelming feeling of responsibility. These new teachers did not want to suggest the standards were not beneficial. They were able to see that they have their place, but, perhaps they are not broad enough to include all the informal learning that takes place in school for a new teacher.

The journey into becoming a teacher

Your development as a beginning and newly qualified teacher can be considered a journey that is influenced by the people you meet and experiences that you have, both good and bad. These, along with your personality and characteristics, will shape the kind of teacher you become. As a teacher, you will be influenced and changed by the experiences you go through, constantly changing and evolving, making decisions and choices based on beliefs and experiences and reflection on those experiences. In fact, your journey to becoming a teacher may already have been shaped in some way by events prior to your training. Childhood and adolescent experiences in school will have, subconsciously, influenced the way that you view the process of teaching, how pupils should be managed and how teachers are meant to behave (Smith, 2007). To add to this, we can include your own experiences on initial teacher training, both positive and negative, as well as issues in the media, which will inform the concept you hold of the role of the teacher and the nature of teaching. As you are progressing through training and thinking about your first post as a teacher in today's challenging school context, you will have undergone a shift in identity. As a result of interactions within the schools where you have taught and within those wider communities, further developments in your professional identity as a teacher are bound to occur throughout your career. Thus you will continue to grow and change throughout your professional life and induction is a very significant part of this longer journey.

Within the research literature, there has been much emphasis lately on the richness and complexity of becoming a teacher and the variety of idiosyncratic and contextual factors involved (Williams, 2003). This process of 'becoming' is often viewed as developing a professional identity which plays a pivotal role in teachers adhering to professional norms and their commitment to their work. 'Teachers' identities are central to the beliefs, values, and practices that guide their engagement, commitment, and actions in and out of the classroom' (Cohen et al., 2007:80). The concept of identity is a complex one and for the purposes of this chapter, it refers to the combination of the personal and professional aspects of teacher identity. The idea of teacher identity is not new and you can look some at different perspectives on teacher identity in Chapter 5 of this book. The research by Nias (1989) suggests there is a huge investment 'of the personal' in teaching for some teachers, and teaching 'partakes of and shapes the person'. Researchers such as Clandinin and Connelly (1987) have identified the personal dimension to professional knowledge suggesting that our professional learning to be a teacher will influence us as individuals and vice versa. This brings into focus the significance of the personal in teaching: for example, some teachers 'appeal' more to some pupils than others, and with some they just 'click' due to their personality as well as teaching style and this is revealed in the classroom. It seems obvious that the style of teaching you adopt will be influenced by your personality. For example, a teacher who has a good sense of humour will often use this in the classroom to diffuse any conflict and to manage the group. It is not really surprising that the personal dimension is significant as schools are social settings where people interact all the time and learn about each other day in day out and this changes the way we behave with each other. There is then a sense of the personal dimension in school; it is not just a professional setting.

Dimensions of teacher identity

An idea that recurs within the research literature is the view that identity is dynamic, and that a teacher's identity shifts over time under the influence of a range of factors both internal to the individual, such as emotion (Rodgers and Scott, 2008), and external to the individual, such as work and life experiences (Flores and Day, 2006;

Rodgers and Scott, 2008). Therefore, teacher identity is not something fixed or imposed but is shaped by experiences and also by the sense a teacher makes of those experiences. Sachs (2005) has the view that this sense of identity is a useful starting point as it not only highlights the importance of identity in the profession, but also points to the different dimensions of identity. These dimensions can be conceived as three overlapping areas or elements for attention: 'how to be', 'how to act' and 'how to understand'. Sachs suggests that the teacher's professional identity 'provides a framework for teachers to construct their own ideas of 'how to be', 'how to act' and 'how to understand' their work and their place in society' (Sachs, 2005: 15).

Points for reflection

- In your view, to what extent is the professional development of the teacher closely linked with the whole process of personal development and growth?
- Do you think that this might be especially true of those for whom teaching is their first career?

Recent research (Smith, 2007) indicates that development of the self and self-understanding would appear to be advantageous for the classroom teacher personally and professionally. It is also significant in terms of helping to improve relationships in school. It will certainly be helpful to reflect critically on your own journey in teaching, so that you can identify those views or beliefs that have changed as a result of your experiences so far. It is also worth considering the ways that your view of yourself as a teacher altered and how your personal characteristics have affected your professional role as a teacher. During your meetings with your induction tutor or subject mentor in school you may find it helpful to talk about your view of the role of a teacher and this may include some discussion on your preferred style of teaching. It is worth identifying which of your beliefs about teaching are helpful and worth keeping and which are unhelpful, those of which you need to let go. In this process of critical reflection, you will need to consider the personal attributes or characteristics you bring to the classroom and recognise those that you can build on and which are beneficial and those which might need some change or review.

Case study 12.2

This case study was taken from a small-scale unpublished research project by G. Fuller (2010).

These NQTs were asked 'If you think you are a teacher, what does this mean? Do you think becoming a teacher is different to learning another job?'

> 'You have an identity with colleagues – are you dependable, can you take on roles in the department – and an identity in the classroom – having excellent lesson to stretch the pupils, so I think professional identity is a mixture of lots of things you do in school.'
>
> 'What makes a person a person is experience, so I'll be a different teacher tomorrow, always developing and character evolving, you change and grow as you change as an individual.'
>
> 'This made me feel like I was now a teacher; it was my decisions in the classroom and the pupils responded to me not another teacher.'
>
> 'I feel I can give something back to my department ... I can contribute ... and that increased my self-confidence and I felt I had grown so much.'
>
> 'The unpredictability of students, the responsibility and the social/emotional environment make it very different to other work places.'
>
> 'I'm an insider and inputter now rather than an observer – it feels different to ITT'.

Your journey into becoming a teacher will be different from the journey of other new teachers as everyone brings their own ideas about teaching with them. These views are informed by previous teaching placements, individual experiences of being a student, as well as beliefs and expectations about the profession. It is highly likely your experience this first year will cause you to re-think some of your ideas about teaching, so your new experiences and knowledge will allow you to bring your beliefs and views about teaching up to date.

'Becoming' a teacher, in other words developing a professional identity, is no easy task and seems for many NQTs to involve personal characteristics and professional skills, which invariably affect each other. For example, if you have a teacher who is skilled in teaching methodology, a professional skill, but yet is not disciplined enough to arrive at school on time each morning due to an aspect of their personality this will have an impact on their role as a teacher. Both colleagues and pupils will have a view concerning the kind of teacher this is. It seems clear that teaching does involve the personal as well as the professional for most teachers and it could be argued that it is impossible to separate entirely the personal from the professional. Whatever job an individual has, something of their personality will come through. You bring yourself to every role you take on in life. The NQTs in the case study mentioned integrity and morality as being part of their personal investment in teaching, supporting the previous research carried out by Clandinin and Connelly (1987) and Nias (1989) highlighting the personal dimension to professional knowledge. You might want to look at this issue of the moral dimension of the role of the teacher in relation to issues in Chapter 11 on SMSC and community cohesion.

The NQTs in the case study seem to be upholding the view that a teacher's identity is dynamic, and shifts over time. During the interviews, several of these mentioned the influence of a range of factors both internal to the individual, for example, emotion and external, such as the pupils and life experiences, which had shaped and would continue to affect their identity as a teacher. This is not surprising as teaching can be seen as a two-way process where pupil and teacher continually influence each other and have an effect on each other.

Point for reflection

- To what extent is your sense of having a positive relationship with the pupils the key to unlocking your idea of being a good teacher?

The emotional investment

Recent developments in new teacher research acknowledge the importance of the emotional-relational aspects of becoming a teacher. The developing relationships with colleagues and pupils are seen as vital to the new teacher's sense of efficacy and acceptance in the workplace beyond the merely social. In some cases, the research is arguing that for new teachers 'they (i.e. relationships) almost define the job' at these early stages of professional development (McNally et al., 2008; Eraut et al., 2004). Emotional involvement is an essential part of the process of learning to teach as revealed through the language used by new teachers. For example we hear expressions of how they are feeling: 'I felt very nervous', 'I felt like I was in control', 'I like that class' and this aspect of becoming a teacher may be more significant than previously recognised.

On the one hand, induction can be seen as a matter of passive socialisation, the process whereby you as the new teacher become a participating member of the school work force, and the changes in you as an individual take place in and because of the work situation. On the other hand, induction can involve reflexive engagement, and in some cases a personal struggle, with the experience itself, so there is reciprocal interaction between you and the workplace. Induction in this sense is something you are 'involved in' as an active way rather than something that is 'done to you'. Every beginning teacher is unique and will experience the process differently; the journey from student to teacher will be subjectively understood according to your individual background, beliefs and values.

The importance of relationships

Becoming a teacher is closely intertwined with the developing relationships within school (McNally et al., 2008; Capel, 1998). These developing relationships create a sense of belonging and community which is essential if you are to remain in the school and in the teaching profession. The belief that others care about you and will support you in school is, for some, a critical factor in continuing as a teacher. Some research has suggested that a powerful network of personal and professional support is the most critical aspect of your induction. So, alongside providing professional support in teaching skills, the human needs of the beginning teacher must also be addressed. Indeed, Hewitt (2009) argues that the key to successful induction comes, first of all, from developing 'powerful, personal relationships' and then a focus on developing professional skills. Cognitive development theory also complements this idea. In order to grow and develop as a teacher, new teachers must socialise and interact personally and professionally, whilst physical and/or mental isolation can impede teacher development (Lundeen, 2004). Some new teachers view themselves as changing from 'outsiders' to 'insiders'. In other words they see themselves as accepted members of the group rather than someone who does not belong. This sense of belonging will be more important to some people than others.

In your early meetings with your induction tutor or subject mentor, you may find it useful to discuss your relationships within school, with pupils and colleagues; self-awareness about how you present yourself is important. It will become apparent which colleagues are 'good' at relationships with pupils and parents and you may want to ask them for guidance and advice. You can ask your induction tutor to recommend the colleagues whom you might find it helpful to talk to. In other words, it is important to reflect on the relationships you are developing as you become a teacher and you can gain valuable insights from others on this front.

Points for reflection

- Reflect on your own views about the importance of relationships within school.
  - Are you good at building and sustaining relationships?
  - What kinds of interactions might help you to do this?
  - Do you need to consider how others perceive you and would it help to develop more self-awareness?

Some of the readings listed at the end of this chapter might be helpful in terms of increasing your self-awareness and willingness to work on areas of personal growth and these in turn might enhance your classroom skills. Effectiveness as an individual is not based on any particular personality style; it is really about how well you know yourself and others. Each one of us is the central person in all our relationships so knowing ourselves leads to better relationships. It might be helpful to ask someone you trust to give you feedback on personal character traits or talk to your induction tutor or subject mentor about how you come across to others.

Case study 12.3

This case study is taken from a small scale unpublished research project by G. Fuller (2010).

These NQTs were asked 'What has helped you become a teacher? What is the most important aspect of teaching in your view?'

> 'Relationships with pupils are vital, you can't teach without it, planning and organisation can be overcome but the ability to develop relationships is essential.'

(Continued)

(Continued)

'Teaching takes an emotional hurdle, you have to feel something, interact with pupils, build up relationships and that's not always easy – you may have someone who doesn't want to speak to you and hates your subject and you've got to make it work and take the time.'

'I suppose it was realising that my relationships with the kids is the most important thing and their enjoyment of my subject.'

'It's an investment of time and energy to build relationships in school – pupils and staff – you have to make an effort to learn and take part, that gives you a sense of belonging when you do.'

These NQTs all spoke at length about the importance of relationships at school during their first year. They all said in very similar ways that relationships at school were the most important part of teaching. It adds weight to research by McNally et al. (2008) and Eraut et al. (2004) who argue that, for most new teachers, relationships define the job. Relationship building takes energy and emotional intelligence; making connections with pupils and colleagues is of great importance in teaching and learning. It seems that building personal relationships is the key to successful induction, followed by development of professional skills. The building of relationships creates a sense of belonging which is a human need and when we feel we belong and others care about us we thrive and grow, not only personally but also professionally, as we gain confidence and become more at ease in our surroundings.

This leaves us with the question 'what kind of teachers are those who cannot build relationships?' An initial response might be to say the teacher who finds it difficult to develop relationships with colleagues and pupils may be viewed as cold and clinical, perhaps distant. Perhaps it is important to bear in mind that this definition of relationship is not referring to just being liked by the pupil. It is impossible for every pupil to like you as a teacher and with some pupils there is a better rapport than with others, but rather this encompasses the feeling that there is a level of care and interest and knowledge of you as a person. This is a basic human need. We all want to be noticed and valued, even if the noticing is negative. It is possible to have relationships with pupils who constantly misbehave in the classroom. They may not like you, but they will hopefully understand at some point that you noticed because you cared and wanted them to do well.

Your training year and the first year in teaching can be very powerful in terms of learning who you are as a teacher and how you want to teach. Findlay (2006) suggests that your first year of teaching has a very significant effect on the personal and professional life of you as a teacher, even going as far as saying it 'imprints and embeds perceptions and behaviours' concerning your whole grasp of the role of the teacher. That is not to say that every beginning teacher will have a crisis or find the experience traumatic but it is for most a transformative experience due to the emotional labour involved. The transition from student to teacher is an emotional experience as can be seen in the way new teachers describe having 'butterflies', 'overwhelming panic' or going on 'a rollercoaster ride'. The language that new teachers use to describe their early experiences is often emotional. 'I found the first year a little overwhelming' and 'I had to fight my ground in September, but now I've made it' tell the story. Sometimes the first year can be, as suggested by Hodkinson and Hodkinson (2003), a personal struggle and McNally et al. (2008) view beginning teaching as a process of deep personal change out of which there is an emergence of a teacher identity. The induction process will therefore involve an emotional investment from you, where you have to process daily the formal and informal learning that takes place and adjust your view of yourself as the teacher as reflected to you by colleagues and pupils. For some teachers, teaching is a lifestyle choice and a personal choice, supporting the idea of the personal and the professional being involved in teaching.

We have looked at how teaching is a complex job that often involves skills developed through informal learning and personal growth for which there are no standards. There is a potential for the complexity of 'becoming a teacher' to be obscured by the standards and having successfully completed their teacher training year, many new teachers enter their first post believing the hardest work is over. This lack of awareness can lead to bewilderment and anxiety in the first year when expectations are not met and things don't go smoothly. Teaching involves emotional, relational and cognitive aspects and these factors need to be addressed during induction if it is to be successful.

In this chapter, we began by reflecting critically on the Teachers' Standards, so we might now return to the question of where they fit in to all of this. In September 1999, induction became a formal process and the introduction of the Induction Standards represented an attempt to address the problem of high numbers of NQTs leaving the profession as well as to raise the standards and improve the quality of teaching in schools (Findlay, 2006). These Standards were revised twice and eventually became the Core Standards in 2007 (TDA, 2007). All NQTs were assessed against these Core Teaching Standards. From September 2012, NQTs will be assessed against the Teachers' Standards during their induction year and these standards will apply to all teachers regardless of their career stage, from ITT through to retirement. However, the motives that lie behind the actions taken by you as a new teacher cannot be simply a matter of ticking off standards on a list during your induction year. Perhaps this is the 'X' factor in teaching. A good teacher meets all the standards but does so because they believe it is the right thing to do, therefore involving personal integrity, intrinsic motives and genuine commitment. Young people are very adept at recognising those teachers that are genuine in their interactions with them and this helps build the relationship between teacher and pupil and this in turn has a knock-on effect on pupil welfare and their learning experience.

The skills that you bring with you and the learning from other workplaces as well as your own personality will define the needs that you have as a new teacher and the journey and experiences along the way will be uniquely yours. We all make our own mistakes and need support and guidance tailored to us as individuals. Thus you need to invest in the relationships with colleagues and recognise that personal skills are important for a teacher and not just teaching skills. Positive social interactions are necessary to build relationships with colleagues. Schools are social and psychological settings, as well as physical settings and formal institutions.

In this chapter, we have explored four important aspects of the process of becoming a teacher in your NQT year. We have reflected on how teaching is about relationships with pupils and colleagues, which involves commitment and an emotional investment and note that some elements of the job cannot be taught, only experienced. We have looked at the development of a professional identity, which includes feeling that 'I am a teacher' and this may take a while to develop. We have noted that the teaching standards are only a narrow view of what you need as a teacher and often these do not represent the whole picture of learning to teach and real life in school. There is clearly more to teaching than following the standards. We have also talked about the process of induction, an individual experience as everyone has different needs that often only become apparent in the NQT year. Age and previous experience, and social skills can all affect beginning teachers' needs.

Reflective questions

1. To what extent is the journey to becoming a teacher a matter of personal growth as well as professional development?
2. It is the case that relationships with pupils and with other members of staff are the key to a successful NQT year – is this what the evidence suggests? How does this fit with using the teaching standards as the criteria for judging a successful NQT year?

Recommended further reading

Beauchamp, C. and Thomas, L. (2009) 'Understanding teacher identity: an overview of issues in the literature and implications for teacher education', *Cambridge Journal of Education*, 39 (2): 175–89.

This article focuses on the link between personal identity and professional identity, and discusses the idea that self-knowledge is the key to a teacher's successful practice.

Hodkinson, P. and Hodkinson, H. (2003) 'Individuals, communities of practice and the policy context: schoolteachers learning in their workplace', *Studies in Continuing Education*, 25 (1): 3–21.

Reading this article will help you explore the idea that dispositions, experiences, past and present, and interactions with others affects formal and informal learning in the workplace.

McNally, J., Blake, A., Corbin, B., Gray, P. (2008) 'Finding an identity and meeting a standard: connecting the conflicting in teacher induction', *Journal of Educational Policy*, 23 (3): 287–98.

McNally and co-authors discuss the importance of the emotional-relational aspects of becoming a teacher, suggesting developing relationships with colleagues and pupils are vital to your sense of efficacy and acceptance in the workplace.

http://helpguide.org/mental/eq5_raising_emotional_intelligence.htm

We need emotional intelligence to build positive relationships. Developing emotional intelligence comes through five key skills. Use this website as an introduction to these skills and read more about emotional intelligence, conflict resolution, and improving nonverbal communication.

References

Bush, T. and Middlewood, D. (2005) *Leading and Managing People in Education: Induction and Retention*. London: Sage.

Capel, S. (1998) 'The transition from student teacher to newly qualified teacher: some findings', *Professional Development in Education*, 24 (3):1.

Clandinin, D.J. and Connelly, F. (1987) 'Teachers' personal knowledge: what counts as personal in studies of the personal', *Journal of Curriculum Studies*, 19 (6): 487–500.

Cohen, L., Manion, L., and Morrison, K. (2007) *Research Methods in Education*, 6th edn. London: Routledge.

Eraut, M., Maillardet, F., Miller, C., Steadman, S., Ali, A., Blackman, C. and Furner, J. (2004) 'Learning in the professional workplace: relationships between learning factors and contextual factors'. Paper presented at the AERA Conference, San Diego.

Findlay, K. (2006) 'Context and learning factors in the development of teacher identity: a case study of newly qualified teachers during their induction year', *Journal of In-service Education*, 32 (4): 511–32.

Flores, M.A. (2001) 'Person and context in becoming a new teacher', *Journal of Education for Teaching*, 27 (2): 135–148.

Flores, M.A. (2004) 'The impact of school culture and leadership on new teachers' learning in the workplace', *International Journal of Leadership in Education*, 7 (4): 297–318.

Flores, M.A. and Day, C. (2006) 'Contexts which shape and reshape new teachers' identities: a multi-perspective study', *Teaching and Teacher Education*, 22 (2): 219–232.

Hewitt, P.W. (2009) 'Hold on to your new teachers', *Leadership*, 38 (5): 12–14.

Hodkinson, P. and Hodkinson, H. (2003) 'Individuals, communities of practice and the policy context: schoolteachers learning in their workplace', *Studies in Continuing Education*, 25 (1): 3–21.

Keates, C. (2008) 'NQTs get a helping hand', *Teaching Today*, 64.

Lundeen, C.A. (2004) 'Teacher development: the struggle of beginning teachers in creating moral (caring) classroom environments', *Early Child Development and Care*, 174 (6): 549–64.

McNally, J., Blake, A., Corbin, B., Gray, P. (2008) 'Finding an identity and meeting a standard: connecting the conflicting in teacher induction', *Journal of Educational Policy*, 23(3), 287–98.

Nias, J. (1989) *Primary Teachers Talking*, London: Routledge.

Rippon, M. and Martin, M. (2006) 'Call me teacher: the quest of new teachers', *Teachers and Teaching: Theory and Practice*, 12 (3): 305–24.

Rodgers, C. and Scott, K. (2008) 'The development of the personal self and professional identity in learning to teach', in M. Cochran-Smith, S. Feiman-Nemser, D.J. McIntyre, K.E. Demers (eds), *The Handbook of Research in Teacher Education*. London: Routledge, pp. 732–55.

Sachs, J. (2005) 'Teacher education and the development of professional identity: learning to be a teacher', in P. Denicolo and M. Kopf (eds), *Connecting Policy and Practice: Challenges for Teaching and Learning in Schools and Universities*. London: Routledge, pp. 5–21.

Smith, R.G. (2007) 'Developing professional identities and knowledge: becoming primary teachers', *Teachers and Teaching: Theory and Practice*, 13 (4): 377–97.

Training and Development Agency for Schools (TDA) (2007) *Professional Standards for Teachers: Core*. London: TDA.
Tickle, L. (2000) *Teacher Induction: The Way Ahead.* Buckingham: Open University Press.
Williams, A. (2003) 'Informal learning in the workplace: a case study of new teachers', *Educational Studies*, 29 (2/3): 207–19.

Websites

www.education.gov.uk
www.teachernet.gov.uk/professionaldevelopment/induction
www.tirp.org ESRC (2008) Teaching and learning research briefing

CHAPTER 13

WHAT CAN MASTER'S-LEVEL STUDY DO FOR ME?

Helen Scott

By the end of this chapter, you should be able to:

- understand different definitions of what constitutes Master's level;
- relate to the context in which Master's-level study has developed in relation to teacher training, teaching and classroom-based research for all teachers;
- understand what Master's-level study and research might mean for you, in terms of your professional development on your teaching course and in the future.

Before 2010, Master's-level study for teachers (trainee and experienced) was promoted and funded by the government as means of encouraging a particular kind of approach to the linking of theory and practice in initial teacher education, as a vehicle for experienced teachers' professional development, to enable individuals to improve their classroom practice and as a way of teachers implementing government education policies. Based on the experience of other European countries (e.g. Finland), the view that creating a 'Master's-level profession' would raise the status of teachers in society and therefore attract higher qualified applicants was promoted, as well as the notion that this in turn would lead to improved educational outcomes for pupils. Most primary and secondary PCGE courses include Master's-level modules and this chapter will consider some of the professional benefits and challenges of working at Master's level for student teachers.

A brief overview of the history of Master's-level study for teachers in England

I begin by outlining some background context to teachers undertaking Master's-level study. Practising teachers have for many years studied for Master's degrees part time alongside their jobs for professional development related to areas such as leadership and management, special educational needs or a particular subject specialism. Modes of study, assessment and content associated with different courses varies a good deal; some are largely theoretical, related to various issues in education, for example philosophy of education, or evaluating existing knowledge related to a broad educational area, such as assessment. Other courses involve practitioner or action research where teachers relate a broad theme introduced in university sessions to an area of their practice which they wish to investigate or improve and modules include learning and practising research and enquiry skills. Levels of participation have been small though; for example, in 2008–9 it was estimated that only around 7 per cent of qualified teachers were involved in some kind of Master's study (Ibbottson, 2008: 167).

Until fairly recently it was unusual for newly qualified teachers to undertake Master's-level study, as it was thought they had enough to cope with in their induction year. However, over the last ten years, the numbers of student teachers (you may be one of them) leaving their course with some Master's-level credits has increased; almost all one-year postgraduate courses in secondary and primary teacher training now offer the opportunity to gain credits which can be taken towards Master's degrees later on. Some teachers choose to continue with Master's-level study in their NQT year. This situation has arisen partly due to the alignment of postgraduate qualifications throughout Europe in the Bologna Agreement of 1999. Awards with 'postgraduate' in the title have to include some element of Master's-level study. There was also growing concern amongst teacher educators that one-year courses were becoming too competency based and less concerned with developing 'reflective practitioners' capable of becoming critical, independent teachers with a broad knowledge of issues in education. Carr (2003: 23) considers that competency models 'are predicated ... on the idea that professional expertise is reducible to a set of discrete experimentally testable behaviours'. This is not a view shared by most teacher educators and teachers, but for you as a student teacher perhaps it may feel as if you are doing a good deal of 'ticking off' the different elements within the current version of the Teachers' Standards.

Individuals' motivations for continuing academic study once they are qualified vary but can be summarised as to enhance career progression, to develop understanding and skills in particular areas, research practice, for personal satisfaction or a mixture of all of these. Teachers undertaking Master's-level study can be seen as indicative of the growth of the 'teacher researcher' which developed in the UK, the USA and Australia during the 1970s and 1980s (Noffke and Somekh, 2005) and the idea that those best placed to examine a profession (especially if for the purposes of improvement) are its own members. Interestingly, (as Carey Philpott also explores in Chapter 2) recent government thinking on how to improve various aspects of schooling also demonstrates a belief that the solutions to many challenges teachers face (especially how to raise pupils' attainment) lie within schools themselves (see for example 'The importance of teaching' (DfE, 2010) and 'The case for change' (DfE, 2010)).

Before 2010, the government funded universities in England who offered Master's-level awards for qualified teachers which enabled courses to be heavily subsidised or even offered free to encourage teachers to participate. One of the reasons for promoting Master's-level courses for teachers was that it was thought that those in possession of a postgraduate degree would be better teachers, producing higher achieving and attaining pupils. This concept was endorsed by the Labour government following the publication of the McKinsey & Company Report of 2007. This document attempted to identify the characteristics of the world's most successful education systems (for example, Finland and South Korea) and made clear links between the quality of teachers and their pupils' attainment. In December 2007. Ed Balls, then Secretary of State for Education, announced the Labour government's children's plan which declared for the first time the necessity of teaching to become a 'Master's-level' profession (DCSF, 2007).

In Finland, all initial teacher training is via a four-year programme which awards a Master's-level qualification on completion and this appears to make teaching a high-status profession which attracts the best graduates (Sahlberg, 2007). The more recent Coalition government's educational reforms also reflect a strong interest in the Finnish educational system (for example in 'The case for change' (2010)). Finnish trainee teachers' Master's-level qualifications 'are distinguished by their depth and scope' (Jussila and Saari, 2000; Westbury et al., 2005). The balance between the theoretical and practical in these programmes helps young teachers master various teaching methods as well as the science of effective teaching and learning' (Sahlberg, 2007: 9). Sahlberg states that 'high professional competency' beginning teachers develop as a result gives them motivation to undertake further development projects in their schools and beyond. So, in Finnish teacher education, it is thought that making strong links early between theory and practice, through Master's-level work, helps student teachers to become excellent teachers. We will return to the important issue of theory and practice later, but first let us examine other benefits of Master's level work.

Student teachers and definitions of Master's level

As a student teacher contemplating your significant workload, you may be thinking about what Master's-level study could do for you. Before answering this question, you might like to consider what exactly Master's-level study is , what it is like and what the tangible outcomes might be. You may think that Master's-level work is associated with writing at a particular academic level. Macmillen, Garcia and Bolin subscribe to this view, describing Whitney's notion of 'the essential connection between writing and the critical thinking necessary to be an informed professional. Whitney says "[write] my way into what I think ... (to) discern what the central point is"' (Whitney in Macmillen, Garcia and Bolin, 2010: 428). Macmillen et al. go on to describe further benefits of academic writing as a professional development tool, which includes connecting student teachers to their more experienced colleagues in a learning community, engendering a sense of achievement in producing a record and account of their learning and increasing confidence as they develop their professional identity (adapted from Macmillen et al., 2010: 428). Much Master's-level study in education involves writing, but *thinking* at Master's level is important, too, as writing, (as described above by Whitney) cannot be done without thinking and can indeed be a sort of thinking in itself.

All universities have Master's-level assessment criteria, which are varied but give us a place to start to describe qualities of higher-level thinking associated with Master's level. These often include statements such as 'critical thinking and evaluation', 'advanced problem-solving', 'highly specialised knowledge of the field informed by extensive engagement with literature', describing characteristics that a student operating at Master's level would demonstrate. The methods by which Master's-level work can be demonstrated vary. For example, in recent years, the idea that evidence of Master's-level enquiry might not be solely text-based, but also visual, in the form of sketchbooks, drawings, films, videos, or a mixture of these, in addition to text has been promoted (Holtham et al., 2008). Most interestingly perhaps, the government has used the term 'master teacher' (DfE, 2011); although this does not directly refer to teachers holding Master's-level qualifications. Many of the qualities of 'master teachers' outlined are very similar to those referred to above, for example: 'Deep and extensive knowledge of their specialism. ... their classes demonstrate a stimulating culture of scholarship ... they engage with professional networks beyond the school'. In other words, these statements raise the challenging question of whether it is possible to demonstrate Master's-level qualities in your classroom practice.

The experiences of student teachers working at Master's level

In this section, I will give a brief overview of some of the research that has been undertaken relating to trainee teachers working at Master's level, which remains a relatively under-researched area (Eady and Jackson, 2009, 2010; Dymoke and Cajkler 2010). However, there are some key issues which may relate to your experience.

Eady and Jackson (2009, 2010) found in their work 'that students do not immediately see the benefits of Master's-level study early on in their training, nor how it can link to either improvement or development in learning and teaching in their induction year and beyond' (Eady and Jackson, 2010: 3). However, their small-scale research with a group of teacher educators showed that they believed Master's-level work 'overcomes the technicist view of teaching being a matter of ticking the boxes of the standards' (Eady and Jackson, 2010: 5).

Other positive views reported were 'Master's encourages student teachers to influence and understand their own professional development ... there was a strong sense that it is about "linking academic study skills and classroom skills", and 'master's was seen as a process which helps student teachers develop an understanding about teaching and themselves as teachers' (Eady and Jackson, 2010: 6–7).

However less positively, a view was expressed that Master's-level study could feel detached from the 'messy reality of schools' (Eady and Jackson, 2010: 6). However, it may be important for you to know that the above comments came from teacher educators, not student teachers! What have student teachers said about Master's level study?

In Eady and Jackson's earlier and larger study of student teachers' views (2009: 4) some found Master's-level work very challenging to fit in with the rest of the demands of the course and that early enthusiasm for higher-level study was not usually felt by all students by the end of their PGCE course.

More positively, Dymoke and Cajkler (2010) stated student teachers engaged in Master's-level study were able to get a sense of why they had made certain decisions in their planning and teaching. They had been more reflective, more attuned to what was happening in their classrooms and they had developed a good understanding of the body of educational research which had helped them to understand their own and pupils' development. Students' Master's-level assignments were thought to have developed 'Master's-level thinking' which was also very helpful to their development as teachers.

Consider the case of Zara below.

Case study 13.1

Zara was a confident student teacher of art and design and was settling into her second placement at a large secondary school in the suburbs of a city. She was making good progress in different areas and enjoying teaching all her classes, apart from one, a Year 9 class. The class comprised 32 pupils of mixed gender and ability.

> I just couldn't get them to be quiet or do their work and the sheer number of them meant I couldn't get round them to explain things if they didn't understand my introduction to the lesson. I had observed my mentor with the class and she seemed fine with them and they with her. I spoke to her about things I could try but none of them worked. Things I tried with other classes to make them behave didn't work with this class. My mentor advised me to simplify the project, and stop them working in groups, because she thought pupils were finding it too hard but this just made it worse and I suppose I saw this as a 'dumbing down' to appease the pupils somehow; it didn't work in any case. After a few weeks I really dreaded the lessons with this class. I had to choose a topic for my second Master's level assignment on some aspect of classroom practice so out of desperation I decided to focus on how I could improve things with this class. Another teacher suggested I actively involve the pupils as participants which I wasn't keen on at first but actually this really helped.

Points for reflection

- What do you think are the key issues in Zara's situation?
- What is the place of Master's-level thinking here? How could it help?

Zara's case is very typical of a situation many student teachers find themselves in and her initial ideas for improving things might be familiar to you. She tended to focus on one aspect of the situation and hoped to find a simple solution. Having tried many different strategies, suggested by her colleagues, without much success, she decided to take a more complex approach to the issues by relating her experiences to her Master's-level assignment and in preparation for this, focused on three key areas:

1. **Background reading:** for example, related to behaviour management (the 'how to' type books, as well as research about pupils' motivation, the possible causes of their poor or disruptive behaviour and the possible relationship between content of lessons and pupils' behaviour).
2. **Critical reflection on her own actions:** for example, Zara tried to take a 'step-back' from her work with the class and asked herself some difficult questions about how and in what way, her own behaviour, actions and decisions 'at the moment' of different lessons had impacted on the pupils' behaviour. She used different models of reflection to help structure her thinking. For example she found Ghaye and Ghaye's (1998 in McAteer and Dewhurst, 2010) five-part typology of reflection (descriptive (personal and retrospective), perceptive (has an emotional aspect), receptive (relates personal views to others), interactive (links learning to future action) and critical (locates the individual teacher within a broader 'system')) very helpful.
3. **Planning how to involve the pupils in the research:** Zara did some background reading about how best to get pupils involved in the research project and what she hoped to gain from this. There were also ethical issues to consider (for example, gaining informed consent from pupils and trying to ensure they felt their ideas would be taken seriously) and other concerns such as pupils feeling they could be honest, yet constructive in responding to certain questions whilst Zara felt her relationship with the class overall was not very positive.

Zara's three-pronged approach describes an effort on her part to take a critical, reflective, enquiring stance towards a thorny problem in her classroom practice. In preparation for her assignment, she was taking an 'action research' approach; where a problem had arisen, she decided to try different things, evaluate them, and then try alternatives. In fact she was already working in a way similar to action research without calling it that, before she made the decision to formalise and structure the process, by relating it to a Master's-level assignment. Kemmis and McTaggart's definition of action research fits with Zara's thinking and practice; 'to do action research is to plan, act, observe and reflect more carefully, more systematically, and more rigorously than one usually does in everyday life' (Kemmis and McTaggart, 1992: 10).

In engaging with theory through others' research and thinking from a number of sources, she was able to gain a deeper understanding of certain issues, for example, the different factors that might cause pupils to behave inappropriately in the classroom, the effect certain approaches to presenting art and design content in her subject might have on pupils' understanding and engagement and how she might need to adjust her own responses to pupils' behaviour. Thinking about her practice in this way was not easy; this level of critical reflection required a commitment to feeling disrupted for a time and meant having to re-think previously deeply-held views about how things (and people) ought to function. Not everything she read about struck a chord or related directly to her context, but in extending her knowledge and understanding of others' views on experiences similar to her own and theories about pupils' behaviour, Zara was able to make more sense of her experience with this class. Her reading in preparation for working with the pupils as 'research participants' was particularly helpful in thinking about what kinds of questions she would like to ask them about their experience of being in her class. In fact, the pupils' responses were probably the most important element in helping Zara to think about the situation and what she could do next.

Case study continued ... what Zara did next

Zara produced a short questionnaire for pupils to complete at the end of the lesson. She asked questions such as:

Rate your behaviour during this lesson on a scale of 1–5 (1 being excellent, 5 being inappropriate/disruptive behaviour).

What do you find interesting or engaging in the lesson?

What do you find less interesting in the lesson?

Zara wrote in her assignment:

> *Most of pupils were very honest about their bad behaviour, even a little bit harsh on themselves; they obviously knew that their behaviour wasn't very good in the lesson. I was surprised to see what they said they found interesting – they said they liked doing practical work best in pairs or small groups because they could plan their work and benefit from each other's ideas. They found the project less interesting once I had simplified it and wrote that they had been bored at times.*

Zara was encouraged by a colleague, a more experienced teacher who had undertaken a Master's in education recently to ask the pupils one or two more 'risky questions'. Here are some of the responses pupils gave to the question 'If you had one piece of advice for your teacher, what would it be?':

> *'Sometimes the teacher interferes in the way our sculpture is going and that gets on our nerves a bit ... if we don't like her suggestions we sometimes play up and waste time ... she could let us have a bit more freedom I think.'*
>
> *'We can get a bit noisy and I think this really winds her up ... but she needs to notice the quiet pupils as well as the noisy ones'*
>
> *'Some pupils get a lot more help than others ... in our group we just get on with stuff and sort out any questions about the work between us ... maybe she could encourage other groups to work a bit like us?'*
>
> *'Don't give all the bad kids so much attention ... that is really annoying!'*
>
> *'We think that Miss takes a lot more notice of the girls than the boys.'*

Points for reflection

- What do you think are the key messages or issues for Zara to consider from her pupils' responses?

(Continued)

(Continued)

- What kinds of things could she try next?
- What kinds of approaches would you take in this situation in the light of the pupils' responses?

There isn't space here to describe the whole of Zara's situation and how she used her Master's-level assignment and the related activities she undertook to improve pupils' behaviour in her lessons. Suffice it to say, she demonstrated the Master's-level characteristics of critical evaluation, problem-solving, knowledge of her 'field' (her pupils and her subject), through linking her experience and background reading. There was no magic wand for Zara; but her binding together of the three different areas of focus helped her to understand what she needed to be more aware of and act accordingly. For example, she re-considered her decision to 'dumb-down' the content of the pupils' project and tried to communicate higher expectations to all. Although she did not necessarily agree with all the pupils' comments, she brought together a small group to discuss their views further and she took on board some of their suggestions and observations. She tried not to 'jump in' with suggestions for pupils' work, but rather asked them to explain their ideas to her and respond to her questions. In this way she could be sure they were working purposefully and everyone in the group was involved in the artwork. She asked her mentor to observe her focusing on her interactions with different pupils; this confirmed to some degree the pupils' comments that she sometimes ignored pupils behaving well. In short, she developed what Buitinck (2009) calls a 'practical theory'; for example, through taking her pupils' comments seriously, relating her reflections to literature on a number of issues and rethinking her own behaviour and reactions to what occurred in her classroom.

Theory and practice

Let us return to the issue of theory and practice which has already been raised in earlier sections of this chapter. For example, it was noted that the highly-regarded Master's degree Finnish beginning teachers gain, is characterised by students experiencing in-depth study in a variety of educational issues and a balance between theory and practice. The teacher educators that Eady and Jackson interviewed also considered that Master's-level work could help their student teachers bridge their theoretical and academic study with their classroom practice. Zara's situation outlined in case study 13.1 is an excellent example of a student teacher improving her relationship with a class she struggled with, through a systematic, intentional (and uncomfortable) process involving her pupils as her research participants, taking account of what she had read about on a number of issues. Zara did not start out conceptualising her grappling with the various issues she faced as action research; however it fits with Somekh's definition of action research as a process which 'directly addresses the problem of the division between theory and practice ... (it) integrates the development of practice with the construction of research knowledge in a cyclical process' (Somekh, 2005: 8). Let us now turn to what others have to say about theory and practice and student teachers.

Frances Gilbert, writing in the *Observer* (April 2011) about the government's proposals to move teacher training to schools and away from universities stressed that 'without a strong theoretical framework with which to understand how children learn, the trainee teacher is often left floundering and can jump to counter-productive conclusions'. Gilbert was making a strong argument for universities to provide the theoretical context for teaching practice, vital for student teachers to be properly prepared for their careers. The relationship of theory and practice has long been considered problematic in teacher education, for example, 'Critics of teacher preparation courses make the accusation that too many educators assume effective teaching to be primarily a matter of applying theoretical principles to practice (MacLure, 1993; Schon, 1983). These critics point to research indicating that everyday teaching involves more complex decision making than the one-way action of applying theory to practice' (Black and Halliwell, 2000: 104). Thomas also explains the problematic relationship between theory and practice, 'there has been a taken-for-granted assumption in education that pursuance of theory ultimately confers improvements on practice' (Thomas, 2007: 3). The movement between theory and practice is rarely in one direction. The experience of learning to be a teacher is not about being introduced to a theory in university one day and then 'doing' the theory the next. It is more likely that you may become aware of a theory, and then at a later point realise how it can help you partially understand a situation, which in turn may help you develop your ability to resolve an aspect of that situation. Equally, you may be thinking very deeply about an issue in your classroom practice and at a later point come across some research or writing which helps to confirm, explain or contradict the way you were thinking. This may give you a new perspective on an issue or you may consider your way of addressing the issue was better. Confusingly, your experience of the relationship between theory and practice may be a mixture of all of the above. Thomas warns that 'many of the questions we would like to ask are too complex for satisfactory answers, and it is here that theory is so tempting. We are tempted to oversimplify, generalise and theorise' (2007: 17). A theory may not give us all we need to deal with the specific nature of a problem we face; however, this does not mean that we should disregard all theories.

Hascher et al. (2004) examined a range of views amongst those writing about Swiss teacher education and the relationship between practice and theory which provide some useful food for thought. They found that amongst the literature in their country, there was a consensus that 'becoming a good teacher not only requires practice but professional learning environments which also foster advanced theoretical knowledge, for instance for reflection on the teaching process which is a necessary precondition for improving teaching and modifying epistemological beliefs' (Hascher et al., 2004: 624). In summary, their work with student teachers and their mentors found that both parties focused too much on the 'mechanics' of teaching and that mentors tended to judge highly competent those students who worked like them and that this was limiting the possible development of student teachers'

> it is not sufficient that student teachers imitate their mentors and acquire the methodological tools for teaching. What they also need is to develop professional attitudes which foster life-long learning. As long as mentors and student teachers focus exclusively on experience, essential learning aspects are lost ... and the gap between theory and practice persists or even deepens. (Hascher et al., 2004: 635)

Master's-level study is **one** way of considering the relationship between practice and theory which can assist your development whilst a student and beyond. It may be possible to make the links between theory and practice without Master's-level thinking and enquiry, but my experience is that the mindset required for Master's-level work will help set you up for not taking things for granted early on and in your future career. It will not be easy as grappling with complex ideas of others in the light of one's own day-to-day experience is not straightforward and is often troubling, as Zara's case illustrates.

Hobson et al., (2008) cite the work of Darling-Hammond (2000) to suggest that using 'inquiry-based methods, including those in which teachers' seek to identify problems of practice and understand them through action research coupled with reviews of others' research (are) methods which 'allow the application of theoretical principles to problems in specific contexts while appropriately complicating efforts to draw generalisations about practice' (Darling-Hammond, 2000: 171 in Hobson et al., 2008: 426–7) and that 'there is an argument ... that the conscious use, by student teachers, of conceptual tools (or "theory") in the practices of teaching (e.g.: planning and assessment) facilitates both the creation of appropriate in-class teaching methodologies for different settings and the informed management of their own learning and development' (Hobson et al., 2008: 425).

Conclusion

The position of Master's-level work in relation to student teachers and indeed all teachers is currently at an interesting point. Whilst the current government's notion that the solution to many of the challenges in schools relating to teacher performance and pupils' attainment, lies in the sharing and dissemination of teachers' expertise in and between different schools, it has also significantly reduced funding for those who wish to undertake Master's-level study. PGCE courses continue to either require or offer the opportunity for Master's-level study; many students find this work challenging but beneficial as a link between theory and practice in their development. However, the current government's reduction of teacher education in universities signals a particular position to theory (Adams, 2011). Adams quotes Northcott's view that 'the Government has decided to resolve the tension between theory and practice by simply cutting out theory altogether, to leave only practice' (Northcott, 2011: 9 in Adams, 2011: 157). Zara's Master's-level assignment provided a structure and means for her to improve a difficult situation with one of her classes, combining elements of practice and theory; either one on its own would not have helped her. Some consider that the embedding of Master's-level work in initial teacher education has prevented the process of learning to be a teacher from becoming solely competency based and technicist in nature. In Chapter 2, Carey Philpott concludes that the knowledge that will be of most value to you is that which results from you deliberately setting out to engage with a range of research and enquiry encompassing different perspectives and viewpoints. Lindsay Poyner and Jon Tibke similarly promote and explore the notion of 'informed enquiry'; that in many aspects of your classroom practice, you will benefit from intentionally reflecting on different incidents and relating your reflections to the work of others. 'Informed enquiry' is at the centre of Master's-level study undertaken by all teachers. If we accept that Master's-level work for student teachers can be beneficial for their development and that highly effective education systems claim their success is based on all teachers having Master's-level qualifications, then the question may become how you can continue to benefit from Master's-level study and thinking once you are no longer a student teacher. Does it make sense for newly qualified teachers to leave Master's-level study behind them? Zara and many others would want to continue with the kind of thinking and practice associated with their Master's-level inquiry in their early teaching careers and beyond.

Reflective questions

1. What are the greatest challenges for you in doing Master's-level work whilst a student teacher?
2. What do you feel you can gain in your development as a student teacher from doing Master's-level work?
3. Think about your experience of the relationship between theory and practice; consider examples where theory has helped you to understand practice or your practice has helped you to understand theory.
4. Thinking to the future, how do you think Master's-level study could contribute to your continuing professional development once you are qualified as a teacher?

Recommended further reading

Elton-Chalcraft, S., Hansen, A. and Twiselton, S. (eds) (2008) *Doing Classroom Research: A Step-by-Step Guide for Student Teachers.* Maidenhead: Open University Press.

This book has various chapters aimed at student teachers to help them research their work, considering various important issues.

Mills, G.E. (2011) *Action Research: A Guide for The Teacher Researcher*, 4th edn. Boston: Pearson.

This book provides excellent practical, step-by-step advice for teacher researchers and is recommended by students and teacher educators I have worked with.

Kincehloe, J. (2012) *Teachers as Researchers* (Classic Edition). Abingdon: Routledge.

This text encourages teachers not only to carry out research into their own practice to make it more effective, but also so that they can critically engage in wider debates in education. This is a new edition of a classic text, providing excellent historical perspectives on teachers researching their own practice.

References

Adams, G. (2011) 'The degradation of the arts in education', editorial, *International Journal of Art and Design Education*, 30 (1): 156–60.

Black, A.L and Halliwell, G. (2000) 'Accessing practical knowledge: how? why?' *Teaching and Teacher Education*, 16: 103–15.

Bologna Declaration (1999). Available online at http://ec.europa.eu/education/policies/educ/bologna/bologna.pdf (last accessed 2 February 2011).

Buitinck, J. (2009) 'What and how do student teachers learn during school-based teacher education?' *Teaching and Teacher Education*, 25: 118–27.

Carr, D. (2003) *Making Sense of Education: An Introduction to the Philosophy and Theory of Education and Teaching*. London: RoutledgeFalmer.

Darling-Hammond, L. (2000) 'How teacher education matters', *Journal of Teacher Education*, 51 (3): 166–73.

Department for Children, Schools and Families (DCSF) (2007) 'The children's plan: building brighter futures'. Available online at http://www.dcsf.gov.uk/publications/childrensplan/downloads/The_Childrens_Plan.pdf (last accessed 12 February 2011).

Department for Education (DfE) (2010) 'The importance of teaching – the schools White Paper'. Available online athttps://www.education.gov.uk/publications/eOrderingDownload/CM-7980.pdf (last accessed 2 July 2011).

Department for Education (DfE) (2010) 'The case for change'. Available online at https://www.education.gov.uk/publications/standard/publicationdetail/page1/DFE-00564-2010 (last accessed 2 February 2011).

Department for Education (DfE) (2011) 'Great teachers could become master teachers', press release. Available online at http://www.education.gov.uk/inthenews/inthenews/a00200711/great-teachers-could-become-master-teachers (last accessed 31 March 2012).

Dymoke, S. and Cajkler, W. (2010) 'Beginning teaching and learning at Master's level: student teachers' pedagogic and academic concerns'. Paper presented at the British Educational Research Association Annual Conference, University of Warwick 1–4 September 2010. Available online at EducatiOn-line (last accessed February 2011).

Eady, S. and Jackson, A. (2009) 'Perceptions of Master's level PGCE: a pilot investigation', University of Cumbria and the ESCalate Initial Teacher Education Subject Centre of the Higher Education Academy Final Report.

Eady, S. and Jackson, A. (2010) 'Teaching as a master's profession: the need for continued debate', Paper presented at the British Educational Research Association Annual Conference, University of Warwick 1–4 September 2010. Available online at EducatiOn-line (last accessed February 2011).

Ghaye, A. and Ghaye, K. (1998) *Teaching and Learning through Critical Reflective Practice*. London: David Fulton.

Gilbert, F. (2011) 'Our children will suffer if their teachers are trained on the job', *Observer* 17 April 2011.

Hascher, T., Cocard, Y. and Moser, P. (2004) 'Forget about theory-practice is all? Student teachers' learning in practicum', *Teachers and Teaching*, 10 (6): 623–37.

Hobson, A.J, Malderez, A., Tracey, L., Giannakaki, M., Pell, G. and Tomlinson, P.D. (2008) 'Student teachers' experience of initial teacher preparation in England: core themes and variation', *Research Papers in Education*, 23 (4): 407–33.

Holtham, C., Owens, A., Bogdanova, A. (2008) *M Level Inquiry Across Disciplinary Boundaries: Using Reflective Sketchbooks*. Paper presented at the British Educational Research Association Annual Conference, Heriot-Watt University, Edinburgh, 3–6 September. Available online at http://www.leeds.ac.uk/educol/documents/174420.pdf (accessed 15 December 2010).

Ibbottson, J. (2008) 'Turning the corner: towards a model of sustainable collaborative partnerships in Master's-level postgraduate professional development in England', *Journal of In-service Education*, 34 (2): 165–79.

Jussila, J. and Saari, S. (eds) (2000) 'Teacher education as a future-molding factor: international evaluation of teacher education in Finnish universities' (Helsinki, Higher Education Evaluation Council), *Journal of Education Policy*, 22 (2): 147–71.

Kemmis, S. and McTaggart, R. (1992) *The Action Research Planner*. Geelong: Deakin University Press.

McAteer, M. and Dewhurst, J. (2010) '"Just thinking about stuff"': reflective learning: Jane's story', *Reflective Practice*, 11 (1): 33–43.

McKinsey and Company (2007) 'How the world's best performing school systems come out on top'. Available online at http://www.mckinsey.com/App_Media/Reports/SSO/Worlds_School_Systems_Final.pdf (last accessed 20 June 2011).

MacLure, M. (1993) 'Arguing for yourself: identity as an organising principle in teachers' jobs and lives', *British Educational Research Journal*, 19: 311–22.

Macmillen, P. S. Garcia, J. and Bolin, D.A. (2010) 'Promoting professionalism in Master's level teachers through research based writing', *The Journal of Academic Librarianship*, 36 (5): 427–39.

Noffke, S. and Somekh, B. (2005) in B. Somekh and C. Lewin (eds), *Research Methods in the Social Sciences*. London: Sage.

Northcott, D. (2011) 'What do teachers want from education?', *SCETT*, 8–9). Rhodes, C., Neville, A. and Allan, J. (2005) 'How will this help me? Evaluating an accredited programme to enhance the early professional development of newly qualified teachers', *Journal of In-service Education*, 31 (2): 337–352.

Sahlberg, P. (2007) 'Education policies for raising student learning: the Finnish approach', *Journal of Education Policy*, 22 (2): 147–71.

Schon, D. (1983) *The Reflective Practitioner: How Professionals Think in Action*. New York: Basic Books.

Somekh, B. (2005) 'Research communities in the social sciences', in B. Somekh and C. Lewin (eds), *Research Methods in the Social Sciences.* London: Sage.

Thomas, G. (2007) *Education and Theory: Strangers in Paradigms*. Maidenhead: Open University Press.

Westbury, I., Hansen, S.-E., Kansanen, P. and Björkvist, O. (2005) 'Teacher education for research based practice in expanded roles: Finland's experience', *Scandinavian Journal of Educational Research*, 49 (5): 475–85.

CHAPTER 14

CONCLUSION – HOW DOES IT ALL FIT TOGETHER AND WHAT DO I NEED TO DO NOW?

Carey Philpott

By the end of this chapter you should have developed your understanding of:

- possible connections between different issues in education;
- some recurring themes in researching and reflecting on education;
- your future role in untying or retying these issues in your own practice.

Legend has it that Alexander the Great was faced with the challenge of untying a knot so complex that it was impossible to find the ends and to untangle the elaborate way in which the strands of the knot were interwoven. He solved the problem by taking out his sword and slicing the knot into pieces.

It is the nature of books like this one to try to slice the knot of secondary education and its related professional issues into discrete pieces. However, as will quickly have become apparent as you were reading the book, in the world of education everything is connected to everything else in a complex knot of influences and dependences. In a limited way, this has been acknowledged throughout the book as chapter authors have occasionally made references to what is discussed in other chapters. The purpose of this chapter is to return to some of those connections between professional issues in secondary teaching and explore them again. This chapter will also identify themes that recur throughout the book. In other words, the attempt here is to retie, at least partially and imperfectly, the knot of connections that the rest of the book has unavoidably sliced.

This book has a dual focus on learning throughout. It has focused on the ways in which you learn to be a teacher and it has focused on the ways that your pupils learn. This is the most fundamental of the connections that bind together the different parts of this book: what is true about how you learn to be a teacher is also true about how your pupils learn, and vice versa.

One of the central recurring themes of this book has been that learning (for you or for pupils) is not straightforward. It is a complex and multifaceted activity. Let's take some time to unpick that complexity. We could start to unpick in a variety of places. Because of the interconnected nature of issues, it is difficult to find an obvious beginning or end to the knot. However, let's start with the insight that when we learn we are not only learning one kind of thing.

In Chapter 2 Carey Philpott explores the ways in which what you need to learn in order to teach can be separated into three kinds of accomplishment: dispositions, knowledge and skills. He goes on to argue that because they are different types of accomplishment they are best learnt in different kinds of ways. In Chapter 12 Gail Fuller discusses the things you need to learn in order to make a success of your early teaching career. She goes beyond the accomplishments as they are conceptualised in the Teachers' Standards current at the time of writing and discusses how you need to learn (or develop) in relation to emotional and relational factors as well as dispositions, skills and knowledge. Once again, given the qualitatively different nature of these things, how you go about successfully learning or developing them will vary. This should obviously have an influence on how you *plan* to go about developing your abilities in any particular area. What types of experiences will you seek out in order to do this? If you want to develop a better knowledge of special needs legislation, you will clearly plan or seek out a different kind of experience than if you want to build better relationships with your colleagues.

This reflection on your professional learning links to some of Tony Ewen's discussions of learning theory in Chapter 8. Your theories of how learning takes place are going to be intimately connected with the ways in which you conceptualise what there is to be learnt. This is true both in relation to your own learning and the learning of your pupils. If you think of learning as primarily about duplicating certain prescribed behaviours or memorising and repeating in an unreconstructed way certain pieces of knowledge, then you are going to seek out for yourself or plan for your pupils certain types of learning experience. If you think of learning as being able to produce creative new solutions to problems or acquire certain values and dispositions, then you will seek out and plan other kinds of experiences. Of course, we can also reverse that relationship and say that the learning theory you hold, explicitly or implicitly, will influence, through the teaching and learning methods that you adopt, the types of things that you or your pupils are able to learn. In Chapter 11, Carolyn Read and Carrie Mercier forcefully articulate the risks of conceptualising the outcomes of education too narrowly.

This issue of the intimate connection between what we teach and how we teach it is also explored by Carrie Mercier in Chapter 7 in relation to curriculum design. As Mercier argues, when discussing the curriculum you can't separate what you plan to teach from the methods you plan to use to teach it. Once again, how you teach will affect what is learnt, so you need to take account of that in your curriculum planning and not just see curriculum planning as a process of selecting various subjects, topics or bodies of knowledge. This intimate connection between methods of teaching and learning and the types of knowledge and skills developed is also relevant to Camilla Cole's chapter on assessment (Chapter 9). There are at least two issues here. One is whether the assessment methods we use are able to 'capture' the learning we are hoping will take place. For example, you may easily be able to think of how to assess whether pupils have acquired certain pieces of factual knowledge but how do you assess whether they have developed creativity or a particular disposition? The second issue is, I think, arguably a more powerful one as it is connected to the nature of the learning that will take place as a result of the assessment methods that you adopt. In an assessment-driven system, which much of secondary education is, there is a pressure for learners to learn and teachers to teach what learners will be assessed on. So if you value creativity or a tolerant disposition but the assessment for your subject, course or topic can easily be passed without creativity or a tolerant disposition, then it is likely that creativity or a tolerant disposition will not be what is learnt. So not only does the type of teaching we do influence what is learnt but so does the type of assessment we do.

This question of what kinds of learning we prioritise could well be connected with what Patrick Smith and Kathryn Fox explore in Chapter 6, the extent to which your subject specialism influences your views of teaching and learning. Similarly in Chapter 5, Martyn Lawson and Martin Watts explore how the identity that you attribute to teachers and learners will influence how you conceptualise teaching and learning. However, I am not going to pursue these particular strands of the complex knot of interconnections at this stage as I want to return to them below in relation to another one of the interconnected knot of themes, identity.

So, to sum up at this stage, what there is to be learnt is related reciprocally to how we think we might go about learning it (and assessing it). But there are also other issues that affect what you learn. In Chapter 3, Helen Scott reflects on the ways in which what you learn from experience will depend on what you are looking for and how purposefully you are looking for it. In Chapter 4, Jon Tibke and Lindsay Poyner develop this idea by discussing the ways in which active reflection on what we observe may alter our first understanding. Similarly in Chapter 2, Carey Philpott argues that the beliefs, assumptions and prior knowledge that you bring to learning as part of a process of experiential learning will affect the sense you make of experience or, in other words, what it is that you learn. In one sense, this is the constructivism that Tony Ewens discusses in Chapter 8; what you learn depends on what you already know. However, it is important to recognise that this isn't only a cognitive issue, that is to say about the ways that the knowledge you have affects how you understand and build new knowledge. It isn't just an issue about knowledge, narrowly conceived. This is also an issue about beliefs, dispositions and identity. The sense you make of an experience, that is to say what you learn from it, will also be influenced by the disposition you have towards it. It will be influenced by the convictions or beliefs that you bring to it and it will be affected by your sense of your own identity. In fact, whether you are even prepared to engage with learning something at all will also be related to these things about you.

This brings us back to identity. Identity has been a growing theme in thinking about education for a number of years and it is a theme that is found in a number of chapters in this book. By identity I mean who we think we are. And what sense we make of ourselves in relation to those around us and the rest of the world. Many people would argue that we don't only have a single unitary identity that we carry with us into every situation but that we have multiple identities that we move between in different situations. So, for example when you are being a teacher, you may have a teacher identity that is different from the identity you have when being a mother or a scientist. In Chapter 5, Martyn Lawson and Martin Watts discuss the effects that your teacher identity might have on your professional practice and how you respond to changes in educational technology. Whether you conclude that you should embrace these changes, ignore them, or actively resist them will depend, to an extent, on the teacher identity that you have. If you choose to embrace them, the kind of use you put them to will also be influenced by what you think the identity of a teacher is.

In Chapter 7, Carrie Mercier also introduces the idea of teacher identity in relation to different models of curriculum design. She suggests that curricula that are not structured according to subjects but according to concepts or processes can challenge the identities of teachers both as subject specialists and as authoritative purveyors of knowledge. So our attitudes to curriculum design may also be influenced by our teacher identity and curriculum development may require a shift in teacher identity. This observation clearly links to Patrick Smith and Kathryn Fox's reflection on subject-specific issues in Chapter 6. Camilla Coles' chapter on assessment (Chapter 9) also has identity implications. Involving pupils more in peer and self-assessment and in a greater understanding of the assessment process has effects on the identity we might traditionally attribute to learners and may have corresponding effects on the identity we attribute to teachers. Similarly, in Chapter 12, Gail Fuller writes about the importance of being aware of the personal and relational aspects of being a teacher in order to be successful during your early career.

Helen Scott's reflections in Chapter 13 on the place of Master's-level study in the lives of beginning teachers also have a connection to identity. Do you think that Master's-level study is integral to the role of being a teacher? In my experience, a significant minority of initial teacher education students often feel that the demands of Master's-level study are not relevant to being a good classroom teacher. Some serving teachers believe this too. They do not see the ability to carry out Master's-level enquiry as being an integral part of a teacher's identity. Put another way, teachers and education researchers are seen as having different identities. If we wanted to, we could trace this identity thread of the complex knot back to the question of what we need to learn and how we need to learn it. Scott's reflections in Chapter 13 are linked to Philpott's in Chapter 2 on the importance of teachers (and teaching students) generating their own knowledge rather than expecting to be handed someone else's knowledge. Also that the knowledge they generate needs to be rigorously reflective and evidence-based and not just folk wisdom or 'tips for teachers' passed around the teaching community. This idea is itself linked to ideas about different types of knowledge, in particular the importance of personal practical knowledge generated by teachers referred to by both Philpott and Fuller. The positions argued by Philpott, Fuller and Scott would lead to the conclusion that carrying out enquiry in your classrooms that is consistent with Master's-level expectations is an integral part of your identity as a teacher.

However, rather than pursuing this particular connection further at this stage, I want to continue to follow the identity theme or thread in another direction. In Chapter 10, Joy Schmack writes of the importance of responding to diversity in the school and the classroom. One way of thinking about diversity is in terms of identities: identities of teachers and identities of pupils. I occasionally hear the conclusion from beginning teachers in relation to particular groups of pupils that 'the problem with these pupils is they just don't want to learn'. If you are one of the ITE students who is not keen to engage in Master's-level study because you think that Master's-level study is not relevant to the identity of a good classroom teacher, would it be fair for us to conclude that you 'just don't want to learn'?. Or would it be fairer for us to conclude that you *do* want to learn but that you don't believe some forms of knowledge or skill are relevant to your identity and to the identity-related narrative that you have of your current situation and future development?

If this is true of you, isn't it also true of your pupils? It would be wrong to characterise any particular social group as uniform, because they are not. However, if, for example, you found that some Traveller children in your classes were apparently disengaged, would you conclude that they didn't want to learn? Or is it that they do want to learn but that their sense of their identity and the narrative of their life doesn't sit comfortably with what you are trying to teach and how you are trying to teach it? Might it also be the case that their identity doesn't sit comfortably with the identity they attribute to you? Because, of course, we all attribute identities to others as well as constructing them for ourselves. This issue of identity is one of the places where the fundamental connection, referred to at the beginning of this chapter, between what we understand about our own learning and what we understand about pupils' learning, is worth paying particular attention to. We may often feel justified in rejecting learning opportunities on offer to us on the grounds that they are irrelevant to what we feel we need to know. We may even feel that the learning opportunity itself is at fault rather than us. Are we equally willing to accept that pupils are justified in rejecting as irrelevant learning opportunities that we provide them? Are we equally willing to think that, if they do, we are at fault rather than them? So, to sum up this connection again, the more we understand our own learning and how and why it takes place, the more we understand pupils' learning and how we might effectively foster it.

This chapter has been an attempt to reconnect some of the threads that were cut by the organisation of the rest of the book. Throughout this chapter I have explored some of the ways in which the sense you make of a situation depends on a variety of factors. These included the knowledge you bring to the situation, your beliefs and values, your own sense of identity and what you were looking for and how you were looking for it. This all adds up to a view that the sense we make of the world is personal to us. This insight also applies to the sense that I have tried to make in partially retying the Gordian knot. The connections that I have made are not all the connections that could be made. Even if I spent a lifetime making connections, they would still not be all the connections that could be made. This is because the connections you make between these issues will depend on who you are and where you are standing. You will make different connections and generate your own understanding. And that is exactly as it should be.

This brings us back to the third of the learning objectives given at the beginning of this chapter: what your future role is in untying or retying these issues in your own practice. All of the chapters in this book are written by people who are both practitioners in education and researchers. All of the chapters have tried to maintain a balance between focusing on the details of practice while showing the relevance and value of being an active researcher in relation to that practice. Let's explore two specific examples in relation to this general point.

In Chapter 9, Camilla Cole explores issues in assessment practice. She identifies that in recent years assessment for learning has been accepted as good practice in assessment. In departments and schools across the country, there have been AfL strategies and initiatives and many schools would believe that AfL is now well embedded in their practice. However, Cole's familiarity with recent research in the area allows her to see that there may be problems with current practice that could go unnoticed if you were not familiar with the research. It allows her to take an informed critical perspective in relation to current established practice and to think about ways that it might need to be developed further for the benefit of pupils and teachers. If you are a practitioner who does not maintain an active contact with research it is possible that you will not as easily spot the limitations of current practice. Even if you do spot limitations, without the various perspectives that come from maintaining contact with research, it may be more difficult to conceptualise what that problem is and, therefore, plan appropriate practical action.

In Chapter 10, Joy Schmack considers practical strategies in response to diversity. Some of the strategies she outlines have been very popular in schools. A common sense view would suggest that it is good practice to allow children to develop an understanding of other cultures by exploring aspects of those cultures' lives and beliefs that are different from our own (whoever 'our' refers to in any particular situation). However, Schmack's continuing active enquiry in this area and her familiarity with the literature allows her to see that a focus on difference can itself create problems. It can lead to reinforcement of the idea that diverse cultures may be strange or exotic or unlike 'us' Perhaps we need to plan activities that focus on the similarities rather than the differences. Perhaps these generalisations about cultures are themselves unhelpful because there is as much diversity within a culture as there is between cultures. So perhaps we need to focus on specific individuals rather than generalised cultures. This is why Schmack includes among her *practical* strategies 'research'. I have italicised 'practical' in the last sentence because it might be common to think of research and practice as contrasting activities, like theory and practice. The research Schmack advocates may be very small scale and localised focusing on the details of the lives of the pupils and communities where you are. Or it may be on a larger scale, familiarising yourself with the literature and data of the whole issue of diversity.

For example, without the table of GCSE data in Case study 10.1, you would probably know that being in an economic group that is in receipt of free school meals correlates with a negative effect on pupils' academic achievements. However, did you know that it has a negligible or non-existent effect on the achievements of Chinese heritage pupils? Does knowing this change the way you think about the effects of socio-economic status on pupils' achievements in your own classes? Similarly, without familiarity with the work of Schneider would you assume that a commitment to diversity means that you should prevent pupils in your classroom from expressing potentially offensive views about diverse groups or individuals? Familiarity with Schneider's work enables us to see that if we don't allow pupils to *say* what they think, we will not *know* what they think. If we don't know what they think (and why they think it) how can we plan to develop or enhance their understanding? So, in practice, perhaps we need to create a space where people feel free to articulate their views rather than trying to prevent them.

These are just two specific examples from the book. If space didn't preclude it, such examples could be drawn from all of the chapters. In general terms then, one of the key messages of this book is that you should not assume that the identity of a teacher does not include continuing active research into your practice. It is not enough to rely on acquiring the practices of the school or department that you are in or to expect to transfer ideas or strategies unreconstructed from one context to another. You need to be active in generating your own understanding and knowledge while making use of the ideas that you find around you. This research may be in the form of maintaining familiarity with the work of others or it may be in the form of actively enquiring into you own practice in order to improve it. Ideally it should be in the form of both. It is common for teachers to reflect on their practice and adapt it as a result of those reflections. However, this reflection is greatly enhanced and made more practically effective if it is informed by the perspectives or information that come from familiarity with the reflections and enquiries of others. In other words, in order to be most practically effective, teachers are researchers.

INDEX

A Lucky Duck Book
The Behaviour Management Toolkit
Avoiding Exclusion at School
Chris Parry-Mitchell

DAVE VIZARD
HOW TO MANAGE BEHAVIOUR IN FURTHER EDUCATION
AGE RANGE 16+
PHOTOCOPIABLE RESOURCES
2ND EDITION

A Lucky Duck Book
Second Edition
The ANGER Alphabet
Understanding Anger
An Emotional Development Programme for Young Children Aged 5 to 12
Tina Rae
A Lucky Duck Book
DEVELOPING EMOTIONAL LITERACY WITH TEENAGERS
Building Confidence, Self-Esteem and Self Awareness
TINA RAE
Bill Rogers
Third Edition
Classroom Behaviour
A Practical Guide to Effective Teaching, Behaviour Management and Colleague Support
978-1-4462-4913-0
978-1-4462-4915-4
978-0-85702-167-0

EXCITING TITLES ON BEHAVIOUR MANAGEMENT FROM SAGE